THREE INTELLECTUALS IN POLITICS

THREE INTELLECTUALS IN POLITICS

JAMES JOLL

HARPER COLOPHON BOOKS
HARPER & ROW, PUBLISHERS
NEW YORK

This book was originally published by Pantheon Books, a Division of Random House, Inc., New York, New York, and is here reprinted by arrangement.

First HARPER COLOPHON edition published 1965 by
Harper & Row, Publishers, Incorporated
New York

Library of Congress Catalog Card Number: 61-10030

To John Golding

ACKNOWLEDGMENTS

I should like to thank the people who have helped me with information and advice while writing this book, and, in particular, Mme Jeanne Léon Blum, M Robert Blum, M Oreste Rosenfeld and M Henri Fluchère; Dr E. Rosenbaum; Mr Denis Mack Smith; Sir Maurice Bowra; Mr Max Hayward; and Mr F. W. Deakin. I am also deeply grateful to the President and the History Department of Stanford University, California, for an appointment which enabled me to work in the Hoover Institute, and to the Warden and Fellows of St Antony's College, Oxford, for making it possible for me to go to Stanford. I am also indebted for much help to the staff of the Hoover Library, Stanford, and of the Wiener Library and The Royal Institute of International Affairs, London.

Part of the essay on Léon Blum has appeared in *Encounter*, and I am grateful to the Editors for permission to reprint it.

CONTENTS

INTRODUCTION

THE THREE MEN who are the subjects of these essays were
born within ten years of each other; and, at first sight, this
might seem all they have in common. Yet there are certain
links and similarities which perhaps justify their appearance
together in one volume. Léon Blum, Walther Rathenau and
Filippo Tommaso Marinetti were all men who had made
careers in other fields before they entered political life.
They were all men who were aware that the development of
machines and of mechanised industry had created a new age;
and they were all concerned to come to terms with it. Moreover,
they all belonged to a European intellectual and artistic world
that was truly international, and, although they never met,
they had friends and acquaintances in common. They were all
men of ideas who were, in one way or another, compelled to go
into politics because of the intellectual position they had
reached. All three experienced the difficulties and frustrations
which confront the man of theory in the world of practice; and
all of them suffered as a result of becoming politicians.
Entry into politics led to Rathenau's death; it endangered
Blum's life and made nonsense of Marinetti's.

Léon Blum once wrote of 'that pernicious influence, which by
imperceptible deviations distorts and perverts all actions'.[1]
Nobody is more exposed to this influence than the idealistic
politician, faced with a world where none of his intellectual
concepts apply precisely, and where the hesitations or reservations demanded by his intellectual honesty are swept aside by
his colleagues in the interest of practical necessity, or denounced
by his critics as cowardice or weakness. Blum and Rathenau
were men of sensibility, for whom the compromises, half-truths
and personal sacrifices of political life were extremely painful;
and, while nobody would claim that sensibility was a notable
trait in Marinetti's character, his natural rebelliousness and his
hatred of pomposity made him out of place and even ridiculous

in the organised political party and the authoritarian state he had helped in a small way to found. The careers of all three men raise the question of how far a man of intelligence or imagination, sensibility or originality, independence or scrupulousness can in fact stand up to the strain of the ruthless machine-politics of the twentieth century, and whether the intellectual in politics is not always going to be doomed to failure because of the nature of his own virtues.

Paradoxically, of these three men it was the one whose political importance was least and whose vocation to enter politics the most misplaced, who became involved in active politics soonest. Marinetti believed that his aesthetic revolution could only come about if linked to a political revolution in Italy, and his artistic activities, from the foundation of the Futurist movement in 1909, when Marinetti was 33, always had their political side. Rathenau, on the other hand, in spite of being a successful industrialist and financier, persisted in regarding his true vocation as that of a writer and philosopher, and only entered politics with extreme reluctance after the First World War, when he was in his early fifties. Rathenau, as far as his experience and qualifications were concerned, might have had a successful career as a politician if he had not refused to give up the idea that his true life's work was philosophy. Marinetti, by letting his activities as an artistic impresario, propagandist and pamphleteer become involved with political groups which had no interest in his aesthetic theories, soon lost all importance both as an artist and as a politician. Both men, by misunderstanding their true vocation, excluded themselves from the sphere of action where they might have achieved most. The case of Blum is more complex, because he was the only one of the three to have a long and, in many ways, successful political career. But he too did not enter active politics till after the First World War, when he was 47, and it was owing to a series of personal and political accidents that he did so at all. What is impressive about him, however, is the consistency with which the ideas, and the moral and intellectual standards, which he had developed during his career as a critic and man of letters, were applied to his political life, whatever the difficulties to which this led. His vocation to enter politics was not misplaced like Marinetti's, nor did he, like Rathenau, misjudge the nature of his own talents.

'It is true in a general way,' Léon Blum wrote, 'that character is quickly formed and varies little. A man remains essentially what his youth has made him. But everywhere, in normal cases, a man's sensibility becomes disciplined and limited bit by bit under the necessity for action. Between thirty and forty he reaches the practical age when the most stormy, like the most nonchalant natures, turn towards the regular occupations of life.'[2] All three of these men remained essentially what their youth had made them; but the First World War and its attendant circumstances prevented them from following Blum's rule, and changed the course of their lives. Blum found a new occupation as an administrator and as an active politician; Rathenau was forced out of his self-imposed personal isolation; and Marinetti was caught up into a political movement over which he had no control, and which was to deprive him of such originality and influence as he had once had.

It was not, however, just the accident of the First World War which changed their lives; at a deeper level, all three men were primarily concerned with the problems presented by the mechanised industrial society of the twentieth century. 'The present generation,' Walther Rathenau wrote in 1909, 'has a more difficult legacy than that of 1880. It is the first since the creation of the world which was born and grew up among the bustle of mechanical transport, in the noise and dazzle of the great city. There may already be children today, conceived in the *wagon-lit*, born under anaesthetics, fed from sterilisers and cradled in automobiles, who have entered the world of electric current and department stores.'[3] Rathenau was concerned in his writings, as well as in his practical life as head of a vast electrical combine, with the effects of this mechanisation; and, although he saw the possibilities that it opened up for material improvement, he was deeply worried about its social and moral results. Marinetti, on the other hand, welcomed the machine age enthusiastically. He preached, as a fundamental part of Futurist doctrine, the beauty and aesthetic significance of the machines that were transforming men's lives, and urged that they should become an integral part of the art of the twentieth century. Both Rathenau and Marinetti realised the change of values that this implied, although the conclusions they drew from this were different. 'A racing automobile is more beautiful than the Victory of Samothrace,' Marinetti proclaimed in the Futurist Manifesto; and Rathenau, with a striking similarity of language, wrote about the worker in the twentieth century that 'an automobile is more important to him than the Parthenon and a boat race more interesting than Schiller's *Maid of Orleans*'.[4]

Blum was, like Rathenau, worried about the way in which the social structure of mechanised industrial society had developed. 'For a worker to rise to be a bourgeois is a miracle; for a bourgeois to sink to manual labour is a tragedy,'[5] Blum wrote, while Rathenau expressed the same thought in much the same way: 'The separation of classes is so sharp with us that in thirty years I have only once known of a case of a worker, the son of a worker, who has risen to a high position in the *bourgeoisie*'.[6] It was to the rectification of this injustice that Blum's political life and much of Rathenau's theoretical writings were devoted; and it is ironical that one of the causes of Blum's political failure in the 1930s was the fact that French industrial and economic life had remained obstinately old-fashioned, and that French industrialists had, for the most part, refused to take advantage of the possibilities of mechanisation which Rathenau had analysed so acutely and Marinetti praised so lyrically.

Any study of a Frenchman, a German and an Italian in the first quarter of the twentieth century is bound to bring out the differences between their countries, as well as certain un- expected similarities between their ideas and careers. Blum could not have been anything but French, Rathenau anything but German, Marinetti anything but Italian. Indeed, for all their originality, each can be described in terms of the stock adjectives commonly applied to each nationality: Blum was logical and rational, Rathenau obscure and metaphysical, Marinetti impulsive, noisy and vivacious. Blum and Rathenau, however, were both deeply influenced by the fact that they were Jews; and the difference in their attitudes to their Jewish heritage throws light both on their characters and on the position of the Jews in France and Germany. Both identified themselves with their native country; but, while for Blum assimilation was easy and natural, and hardly caused him any personal anxiety, even if it was at times a political disadvantage, for Rathenau his Jewish origins and his sedulous cultivation of Prussian traditions were in constant conflict, and added yet another rift to an already deeply divided nature. Rathenau's death was directly due to the fact that he was a Jew; but it was not until the Germans had conquered and corrupted France that Blum's life was in danger for the same reason.

Blum was a figure in the literary and theatrical world of Paris where Marinetti made his first appearance, and, indeed, it is perfectly possible that they might have met when Marinetti was associated with the Théâtre de l'Oeuvre and Blum a leading theatrical critic. Blum was, to the surprise and disapproval of some of his friends, on good terms with Gabriele D'Annunzio. When Italy entered the war on the side of France, in May, 1915, after a propaganda campaign in which Marinetti, Mussolini and D'Annunzio had all played their parts, Blum wrote to D'Annunzio and showed as much enthusiasm as any of them: 'Unceasingly during this fateful fortnight I have been thinking of your *Gloria*. Happy is the man who can realise the dreams of his youth.'[7] Rathenau was happier in the company of poets, writers and painters than when he was with his fellow financiers; and his friendship with writers of international reputation such as Hofmannsthal, Rilke and Stefan Zweig made his circle of acquaintances very unlike that of most business men or politicians.

There was one man who knew Blum, Rathenau and Marinetti and left his impression of each of them in his diary. This was André Gide. Blum had been a friend of his in his youth, and was one of the first critics to recognise his talents; and, although they went in different directions later, they were, at the end of their lives, when both were old and famous, still on terms of mutual respect. Marinetti had called on Gide in Paris, and Gide had not been impressed; he found Marinetti 'stupid, very rich and very conceited', though he was later to admit his vitality and charm. Rathenau met Gide in 1920, staying with mutual friends in Luxemburg. It was Rathenau's first unofficial trip outside Germany after the end of the war, and Gide was surprised and a little taken aback by the enthusiasm with which Rathenau greeted him, and, understandably, did not know what to reply when Rathenau said 'I attach the greatest importance to our meeting'. The importance for Rathenau was that it enabled him to convince himself that his true role was that of a writer and not a politician or financier, and the enthusiasm with which he followed up this first meeting with Gide is a pathetic example of Rathenau's misplaced sense of vocation.

However, these essays were written independently of each other, because of the intrinsic interest of the men who are the subject of them, and not in order to force comparisons or contrasts. They originated in a study of Léon Blum, who is an obvious example of the intellectual in politics; and consideration of his career led on to wondering about comparable figures elsewhere in Europe. This book is, therefore, an attempt to give accounts of the character, ideas and influence of three Europeans, born into the apparently stable world of middle class commerce and industry in the second half of the nineteenth century, who realised that that world was changing, understood the nature of the changes and helped influence their course.

I

LÉON BLUM

THE INTELLECTUAL IN POLITICS

'*Il me reste à mes yeux un admirable représentant
tout à la fois du sémitisme et de l'humanité; tout
comme il sût être, dans ses rapports officiels et
politiques avec l'étranger, un excellent représentant de
la France (quoi qu'en puissent penser les nationa-
listes) et pour le plus grand honneur de notre pays.*'

André Gide: *Journal*, 9 January, 1948

LÉON BLUM

THE INTELLECTUAL IN POLITICS

1

'THERE ARE FEW books in the world that I should be as pleased to have written.'[1] It is with these words that Léon Blum opened his review of a French translation of Jane Austen's *Mansfield Park* in 1899; and it might seem a surprising judgment from someone who was to attempt a social revolution in France and to become one of the most controversial of European statesmen. Yet perhaps the paradox of Blum's career is only a superficial one, for both his thought and his political behaviour were singularly consistent. Léon Blum was an intellectual in a country where to be an intellectual is a title of praise. And it is the intellectual quality of his thought and action that made him both a supremely disinterested political figure and, at the same time, someone for whom the shifts and expedients of day to-day political life in France were disagreeable. Yet, although his decisions, both to enter politics at all and then to follow the course he did once he was a prominent statesman, were taken on intellectual grounds and deduced from general principles, it would be wrong to depict him, as some have done, as a doctrinaire unwilling to modify his beliefs in the light of experience. He never minded admitting he was wrong. His failure, if he failed, was due as much to the nature of the French institutions he was trying to reform as to his own political and personal limitations. He certainly was not one of those utopian reformers for whom a single simple solution would make everything come right. 'In principle, one must never try to spare anyone the difficulties of life or to soften them for him,'

3

he wrote as a young man.[2] 'Realism, properly weighed, is the only possible idealism.'[3] These early beliefs were carried over into his political life. 'We have, so to speak, one foot in the real and one in the ideal,' he told the Socialist party congress in 1919.[4] His optimism, which he never lost, was not that of someone who did not see difficulties, but of one who saw round and beyond them. Moreover if his political action was sometimes hampered by personal scruples and hesitations, this was just because for him socialism was 'a system of morals and almost a religion as much as a doctrine,'[5] and because the transformation of society for which he was working had to be as much a moral as a material one; and, accordingly, ends could never justify means.

However, it was not as a politician but as a literary critic and man of letters that Blum made his name. And if one is tempted to say of him, as he said of Victor Hugo, 'His work falls into two parts; the first of which is good in so far as it makes one aware of the second,'[6] it is because his political career can only be judged in relation to the beliefs and standards of his intellectual youth. Moreover, concentration on his political career should not obscure the considerable merits of his literary work.

Léon Blum was born in 1872 in the rue Saint-Denis in Paris. Although later in life he liked to recall that his childhood had been passed 'in a popular quarter where the memory of republican insurrections still hung in the air,' in constant contact with 'the sons of republican artisans,'[7] he in fact came from a middle class background, though, in spite of the rumours later spread by his enemies, he was never a man of great wealth. What is more important, however, than the influence of the district of Paris in which Léon Blum grew up was the fact that his family were orthodox Jews. It is against this background that much of his thought must be set. The *fin-de-siècle* was a period of revolution against orthodoxy of all kinds; and the ideal of the radical lay republic was one that appealed to Jews who had thrown off their traditional religion, just as it did to the young men who had liberated themselves from Roman Catholicism. Yet in both cases early beliefs left a permanent mark on habits of thought. Blum never forgot that he was a Jew, even though it was perhaps only anti-Semitism that made him think of himself as a Jew rather than as a Frenchman. In 1923, for example, when he was already a deputy, and the Royalists in the Chamber shouted 'Go back to Jerusalem' and 'There's only room for Frenchmen here', Blum replied 'I am indeed a Jew. . . . It is no insult to me to remind me of the race of which I was born a member, which I have never denied and towards which I feel nothing but gratitude and pride'.[8] But he believed that a Jew, once enfranchised from the restrictions of religious beliefs and practices, could in fact be assimilated into non-Jewish society and a non-Jewish state. Indeed, as a young man, he perhaps over-estimated the ease with which this could be done, and was inclined to dismiss the problem of anti-Semitism too lightly as an affair of 'the clubs and the racecourses,'[9] which the Jews should not make too much fuss about. Later in his life he realised that he had been too optimistic, and, in his *Souvenirs de l'Affaire*, an account of the Dreyfus case written in 1935, he attacked those Jews who would not take a public stand when their fellow Jews were being persecuted: 'Rich Jews, middle class Jews and Jewish civil servants were afraid of the struggle on behalf of Dreyfus just as they are today afraid of the struggle against Fascism. They thought only of lying low and remaining concealed. They thought that anti-Semitic passions could only be warded off by pusillanimous neutrality. They secretly cursed those who by exposing themselves handed them over to their age-old sufferings. They did not understand, any more than they do today, that no amount of precautions and dissimulation would deceive their adversaries, and that they would be the first victims to be offered up by the anti-Dreyfusards or the Fascists if they triumphed'.[10] However, for all his solidarity with other Jews in times of trouble, Blum found his personal solution of what to him was scarcely a problem, in complete assimilation. Thus, while he supported the Zionist cause and the creation of the state of Israel, he never felt that he himself needed to act as anything other than a Frenchman. 'A French Jew,' he wrote to a prominent Jewish Frenchman not long before he died, 'born in France of a long line of French ancestors, speaking only the language of my country, mainly nourished by its culture, refusing to leave at the moment when I faced the greatest dangers, I sympathise whole-heartedly with the admirable effort, so miraculously transported from the plane of dreams to that of reality, which henceforth assures that all Jews who have not the good fortune to find it, as I did, in the land of their birth, will have a free, just and worthy country.'[11]

Yet Blum's Jewishness went further than a feeling of sympathy with other Jews in their sufferings or political support for the Zionist cause. It is not only that others were constantly drawing attention to Blum's Jewish origins—both his political opponents, and, on occasion, his friends. (André Gide, who had known Blum for a long time, once complained, in a bad-tempered passage in his *Journal*, that Blum 'considers the Jewish race as superior, as called upon to dominate'.[12]) In fact, Blum himself recognised that there were elements in his thought that were part of a Jewish inheritance and not just a reaction against anti-Semitism in others. Even if he had abandoned the Jewish religion, there were ideas in it which would find their place in the new faith that would replace the old. 'The Jews have made a religion of Justice as the Positivists have made a religion of Facts and Renan a religion of Science. . . . The idea of inevitable justice is the only thing which has sustained and united the Jews in their long tribulations. . . . And, unlike the Christians, it is not from another existence that they expect reparation and equity. The old Jews did not believe in the immortality of the soul. It is this world . . . which must one day be ordered in accordance with Reason, and make one rule prevail over all men and give to each his due. Is this not just the spirit of socialism?'[13]

Blum's education was that of the ordinary clever young Frenchman of his generation—the Lycée Henri IV followed by the Ecole Normale Supérieure, that most formidable forcing ground for an intellectual *élite*. It was, however, at this point that he showed signs that his career was not going to be entirely orthodox, for he suddenly gave up the Ecole Normale and the automatic assurance that a course there gave of a solid academic or administrative career. In fact, he took up law, and, although this was never his main preoccupation, it was as a successful lawyer—working in the Conseil d'Etat, the supreme administrative court of France, until the First World War, and, for some years after 1919, as a private company lawyer—that he supported himself and his family. It was at the Ecole Normale that he met Lucien Herr, the librarian there for many years, 'the good giant' with a gentle voice, who was the chief political influence on successive generations of students, and who converted them to socialism and inspired and guided them for all their life.[14] Through Herr, Blum was to meet the man who was the greatest single influence on him, Jean Jaurès. As yet, however, politics were not the main interest of Blum's life; and it was not until 1898 or 1899 that he became actively involved in the Socialist movement and that his intimacy with Jaurès began. For the moment, still in his early twenties, careful, even dandified, in his dress, with a flower in his button hole and, with his smooth skin and soft voice, looking younger than he was, he was beginning to be a figure in the literary world.

It was a world of great brilliance, where the pathetic figure of Verlaine was still to be seen, and where Edmond de Goncourt still held court, while the new voices, Marcel Proust, André Gide and Paul Claudel were beginning to make their impact, and disturbing, perverse minds, like that of Maurice Barrès, were contributing to an atmosphere in which, surrounded by the solid bourgeois comfort of the Third Republic, the intellectual and political values of an older generation were being questioned and overthrown. Innumerable literary reviews were founded, discussed, and abandoned, so that the young writer, even if he could not make any money, could always get into print. Léon Blum, in fact, was soon—from the age of 19— involved with one of the most enterprising and durable of the literary and intellectual publications, La Revue Blanche, to which many of the best writers of the younger generation were contributing, and where all forms of art were discussed and analysed. There was even a sporting column; and for a while in 1894 it was Léon Blum who was providing the copy on horse racing and bicycle racing, football and lawn tennis. His main regular contribution, which he continued till 1900, when he was succeeded by André Gide, was as permanent literary critic. He was already enormously well read, and could recite by heart long passages from his favourite authors, Pascal, La

Bruyère, Saint-Evremond; it was the moralists who perhaps attracted him most. At the same time he was quick to recognize new talent such as that of Proust and Gide. When, for example, Marcel Proust's *Les Plaisirs et les Jours* appeared in 1896, he could already see something of what the author of that affected and precious little book might achieve, and, while praising its elegance and polish, he awaited his next book 'with great impatience and tranquillity'.[15]

Blum's literary criticism ranged over a wide field, but what attracted him most was the discussion of ideas, and, above all, clarity of style. Indeed, for Blum it was impossible to separate the manner from the matter; lucidity of expression involved clarity of ideas and vice versa. 'One can appreciate,' he wrote in praise of a work of political theory, Henry Michel's *Idée de l'Etat*, 'the qualities we find most rarely in books today: an impartial consideration of ideas and respect for the true meaning of words.'[16] It was this passion for clarity, this desire to be free from illusions and to explain the relations between man and the society in which he lived that made Stendhal one of his favourite authors; and his essay on *Stendhal et le Beylisme*, published in 1914 at the end of his literary career, is perhaps his best book. What interested him about Stendhal was the combination of a masterly style with great psychological insight: 'Stendhal often says such and such a sentiment was the motive for the action of Clélia, Fabrice or the Duchess. But this sentiment is completely expressed in ten short words which entirely cover it and preserve its flavour, which the reader can then dissolve at his ease.'[17] Above all, Stendhal was concerned with describing the emotions of an age when values were shifting and when the traditional structure of society was breaking down. All his novels deal with the ways in which a sensitive and perhaps timid hero (or heroine, in the case of *Lamiel*) comes to terms with this fluid world, and, while despising it, attempts to use it for his own ends, and perhaps ruins himself in the process. The hero is as much a victim as the people who suffer for becoming involved with him. Julien Sorel, for example, is not the calculating ambitious monster he is sometimes represented to be; he is a young man whose character, like that of Stendhal himself, was formed by the unhappy circumstances of his childhood and early education, and whose natural tenderness of heart is only partly masked by a self-imposed contempt for his fellows, and whose very viciousness 'is passionate, and belongs to the moment when aspirations, born of his first awareness of himself and the first contact with the world, are still full of the spontaneity and disinterested ardour of youth, its enthusiasm when faced with greatness or beauty'.[18]

Stendhal et le Beylisme was the result of over twenty years meditation on literature and society, and it reflects accurately Blum's preoccupations throughout these years. 'Stendhal is the man for periods of confusion, of social fluidity, of periods of disorder. Whenever, in the formation of the character of the individual, sensibilities are sharpened without discipline and without purpose, every time in the natural course of history that social classes are mingled on the surface and separated at their foundations, large numbers of young men will adopt the same equivocal poses when faced with the world, and will run the risk of following the same painful road.'[19] It is a phenomenon familiar enough in the England of the mid-twentieth century.

Throughout Blum's literary work the themes which interest him are the structure of society and people's psychological reactions to it; what he admires is clear analysis and a limpid style—both qualities which the best of his own work has. But throughout the period from 1897 on, this interest in society and in ideas was leading him away from pure literature into a growing preoccupation with politics, and some of his friends did not like it. 'Oh, if politics did not deflect his thought to such an extent, what a subtle critic he would be!' André Gide noted early in 1907. 'But he judges people and things according to his opinions, not according to his taste. . . .'[20] The judgment is not entirely fair, for Blum retained his taste for the nuances of style till the end of his life, but his opinions were becoming the most important thing in his writing, and Gide's comment indicates the way in which Blum, while still actively involved in literature and the theatre, was moving away from his non-political friends and becoming increasingly 'engaged' politically.

The work which reveals this process most clearly is the *Nouvelles Conversations de Goethe avec Eckermann*, which appeared in the *Revue Blanche* between 1897 and 1900. 'Should I sign the

New Conversations of Goethe with Eckermann—I mean put
my name on the cover alongside that of Goethe?' Blum asked
Jules Renard when the conversations were to appear in book
form. 'Why not?' Renard replied. 'Your audacity does not lie
in signing the book but in having the idea of writing it.' 'Yes,'
said Blum, 'what you say is most disturbing.'[21] There was
indeed a touch of conceit in taking the figure of Goethe and
making him comment on the world of the late nineties in terms
that are simply the expression of Blum's own views. Yet as a
literary device it was ingenious, and it is executed with great
skill. It enabled Blum to comment on anything that interested
him—literature, society, or politics—and to review the issues
of the day in a detached fashion; and it is characteristic of the
breadth of his own interests as well as of his own estimation
of himself that he should have chosen Goethe, the universal
humanist, as the figure into whose mouth he was going to put
his own opinions about everything.

The *Nouvelles Conversations* do not provide a systematic exposi-
tion of Blum's beliefs, but they are full of remarks that illustrate
his ideas about society, and which foreshadow his later political
practice—so much so that he was glad for the book to be
reprinted in 1937 when he was Prime Minister. It is possible
to find in the *Nouvelles Conversations* much that is typical of his
approach to politics, and many phrases which occur again
word for word in his writings and speeches of thirty or forty
years later. Blum believed that the reform of society depended
on the reform of the individuals who compose it; and he was well
aware of the tragic dilemmas and disappointments this might
cause. At one point he makes Goethe sketch a *Faust Part III*,
in which Faust is a socialist agitator (with many of the traits of
Jean Jaurès), who has 'eloquence, charm and a magnetic
power that makes each member of a crowd believe in his
strength, sincerity and goodness. He is optimistic; he proclaims
his belief in honesty and natural generosity; he believes that
man is just and that only poverty and false civilisation have
perverted and corrupted him'.[22] The tragedy lies in the fact
that at Faust's side, his comrade and colleague Mephistopheles,
the tempter who is 'that pernicious influence which by imperceptible deviations distorts and perverts all actions,' constantly

scores off Faust's scruples and hesitations, his hatred of violence
and love of peaceful persuasion, so that Faust risks failure in
the present, even if in the long run he is to lay the basis for
results in the future. The *Third Faust* was never to be written;
and the Blum of 1898 was still uncertain how it was going to
end. The Blum of 1936 was to live through some of the drama
himself.

In the *Nouvelles Conversations*, Blum first makes clear his ideas
about the way in which political and social changes come
about. While firmly believing in human progress and improvement and in the rational solution of political problems, he was
forced—perhaps rather reluctantly—to face the question of
revolution and violent change. 'Peaceful and continuous
evolution is not the only law of natural development. In the
formation of the physical world, just as in the constitution of
societies, results of exceptional importance have never been
obtained by a regular peaceful process of evolution, bit by bit,
progressively. You must have a sudden eruption of latent
energy, an upheaval, the terrible *fracas* of a revolution. Of
course a revolution has never blown up ground which is not
already mined; and it only breaks out on the appointed day
when the secret expansion of its force can no longer be contained. Thus evolution prepares the way for revolution but
cannot replace it.'[23] It is a dualism from which Blum never
escaped and which explains much of his political action. He
was never quite certain whether he was working for the
evolution that prepares for revolution or whether he was
making the revolution itself.

The years in which the *Nouvelles Conversations* were appearing
were those in which Blum was becoming increasingly involved
in politics. It was the Dreyfus case that turned his growing
theoretical interests into something more practical; he was an
active member of the group of intellectuals who led the
campaign for the vindication of Dreyfus, and he put his legal
services at the disposal of Labori, the eminent barrister who
defended Zola when he was prosecuted after the publication
of his article *J'Accuse*. Blum was recruited as an active Drey-
fusard by Lucien Herr: in September, 1897, he was staying
in the country just outside Paris, and Herr bicycled over to see

him nearly every afternoon. 'He suddenly said one day "Do you know that Dreyfus is innocent?"' [24] Even more important, however, than this introduction to political agitation was the fact that it was at this time, again through Herr, that Blum got to know Jaurès well, at a moment when he was becoming the undisputed leader of French Socialism. Although Jaurès was an intellectual—he had been a brilliant student of the Ecole Normale and a professor of philosophy at Toulouse— the two men were very different. Jaurès was thirteen years older than Blum, and, although he had lived and worked in Paris for many years, he had never lost a certain provincial quality, a directness and total lack of pretension that were unusual in the political world of the capital. The shabbiness and simplicity of his appearance contrasted with the splendour and vividness of his oratory; 'In prose, he is the equal of Victor Hugo,' Blum once said. [25] What attracted Blum was the mixture of intellectual power and candid honesty, and the combination of a deep feeling for the poor and suffering with an exuberant optimism about the possibility of improving their condition and of completely reorganising the world. Moreover, although Jaurès' views about society and the course of history had been much influenced by Marxist ideas, he was never wholly a Marxist. His socialism was based on an older, more liberal revolutionary tradition, and his philosophy owed as much to Kant and to a belief in the importance of the individual conscience as it did to dialectical materialism.

Although Blum was at times attracted by the intellectual rigour of the Marxist deductive system, he was both too sensitive and too honest to adopt it completely. His view of the world was to be influenced by Marxism but never dominated by it. From Marx he got his belief that the revolution was to consist in a change of ownership of the means of production; and from Marx he got, perhaps unfortunately—for he was never very good at economics—certain economic doctrines such as the labour theory of value. But the substance of his political beliefs derived from Jaurès. Jaurès' insistence on the necessity of moral and intellectual improvement as well as on economic reform, his feeling for social justice and his awareness of the liberal and rational revolutionary tradition of France, were all attitudes with which Blum already sympathised. Léon Blum summed up his attitude to Jaurès and to Marx when, in 1941, at the most terrible period of his career, imprisoned, and with all the causes he believed in apparently defeated, he reflected on his political principles and took up again the general problems which had concerned him at the time of writing the *Nouvelles Conversations* over forty years earlier. 'I ask myself after so many years devoted to action, after so many months of scrupulous meditation: does the fault not lie with the leaders whom the working class had chosen? Did they really understand their mission? Did they grasp sufficiently the meaning of the effort by which Jaurès transformed Marxist deduction? Marx had given the most invigorating and powerful reinforcement to the working class in their struggle; I mean the conviction that historical destiny was working for them. But what is determined by fate does not necessarily satisfy critical reason and moral consciousness. Jaurès then showed that the social revolution is not only the inevitable consequence of economic development, but would be at the same time the goal of the eternal demands of reason and of the human conscience.'[26]

Blum soon became a personal friend of Jaurès, and both he and his wife seem to have taken considerable pleasure in entertaining him and in giving him meals (Jaurès was noted for his neglect of his own needs and comforts), while letting him talk politics to their friends. As early as 1899 Blum attended his first Socialist Congress—one of the many abortive attempts to achieve unity among the various Socialist groups—and sat among the representatives of the *Parti Socialiste Révolutionnaire*, the party of Edouard Vaillant and of the tradition of insurrection which derived from Blanqui. But he soon became a follower of Jaurès, first in the *Parti Socialiste Français*, and, after 1905, in the party newly united under Jaurès' leadership, the *Section Française de l'Internationale Ouvrière* (SFIO). His political interests, however, once the battle for the revision of the verdict on Dreyfus was over, were still mainly those of an onlooker. He attended Socialist congresses regularly—his little book, published in 1901, on *Les Congrès Ouvriers et Socialistes Français* is still a valuable source for the intricacies of French Socialist history in this period—he listened to the debates in the Chamber regularly, and had an accurate knowledge of how each deputy had voted in every division. Yet, even though he was not yet himself an active politician, Blum's increasing interest in politics and his personal association with Jaurès inevitably led him away from some of his old friends. The breach with Barrès had come over the Dreyfus case. He had been the most brilliant and stimulating of Blum's literary friends ('Scarcely anyone today is a better judge of intellectual matters* than M Barrès,' Blum had written in 1896[27]). They both regretted the breach, as their ways grew increasingly divergent and Barrès developed into the chief spokesman of romantic nationalist reaction in France. Over the next few years, too, Blum and André Gide grew apart. Gide was trying to solve the problems of his conscience and of moral behaviour in terms of the individual and his relation with God alone, so that the social and political framework within which these personal battles were fought out was of little concern to him. 'Léon Blum's *thought* has lost all interest for me,' he wrote in his *Journal* in 1906; 'it is only a subtle tool which he uses to serve the demands of *his cause*.'[28] Although there was never an open breach between the two men, they grew far apart, and it was only at the end of their lives, when both were old and famous, that they were on terms of mutual respect and esteem again.

In fact, however, there was little difference in the outward forms of Blum's life in these years. Although he began to contribute articles on social and political questions to Socialist papers, it was still the world of the theatre and of literature that was his main concern. He was writing regular theatrical criticism for *Comoedia* and other papers, and, later, for *Le Matin*; he was to be seen at all opening nights, and was, unsuccessfully, to start writing a play, *La Colère*, himself. His literary talents were not however creative, and he seems soon to have recognised this. Jules Renard, himself a successful playwright and one of Blum's friends whose political sympathies had developed in the same direction, wrote of him: '*Léon Blum, très intelligent, et pas un grain d'esprit. C'est agréable pour ceux qui comme moi, se croient de l'esprit et ne sont pas très sûrs de leur intelligence.*'[29]

*'choses de l'esprit'.

Blum's greatest friend was now, perhaps, Georges de Porto-Riche, a successful dramatist over twenty years older than himself, whom he saw almost daily, and to whom he remained deeply attached until Porto-Riche's death in 1930. Porto-Riche's work showed considerable wit and some psychological insight, and dealt with problems of love, and, especially, marriage, in an outspoken and sometimes brutal way. It was perhaps Blum's interest in the work of Porto-Riche and his friendship with the author, together with his awareness that *La Colère* was not going to be satisfactory, that led him to write his most important work between the publication of the *Nouvelles Conversations* in 1901 and that of *Stendhal et le Beylisme* in 1914. This was *Du Mariage*, published in 1907.

It is not, perhaps, a very convincing work (though more so than Gide's *Corydon*, which it resembles in some respects), but it shows Blum's characteristic rationalism and his desire to fit particular cases into a general theoretical framework, as well as his considerable insight into the cases themselves. Some of the examples he quotes might, indeed, be the synopses of the plots of plays by Porto-Riche. Blum's thesis was that marriages in contemporary society break down because they do not recognize the fact that most men and women have instincts that drive them towards polygamy, and that it is only when these instincts have been satisfied that they can settle down contentedly to a monogamous existence. There should, therefore, be in youth a great degree of sexual freedom, so that young men and girls can get over their polygamous phase before settling down to marriage and fidelity to a single partner. Improved methods of birth control will make this possible without creating problems about children of these early temporary unions, and eventually husband and wife would come to a stable marriage with their eyes open and aware of the problems involved. The interest of *Du Mariage* does not, however, lie in its somewhat dubious general theory nor even in the many penetrating psychological judgments it contains. It is important because of the light it throws on Blum's beliefs. Above all, it is a plea for honesty and reason in human relationships; by facing the fact that most people are attracted to more than one other person and that their wife or husband may not satisfy them, and by reorganising social institutions accordingly, we will, Blum thought, get rid of the necessity for deception in marriage, and so get rid of the lies and deceit which wreck or corrupt so many marriages in our society. A reform of social institutions would carry with it, therefore, a guarantee of improvement in moral behaviour.

While the book was denounced as immoral and subversive, both when it first appeared and, still more, when it was reprinted in 1937 while Blum was Prime Minister, it is not an incitement to immorality, but a plea for a reform that will increase morality. It is characteristic of Blum that he should have authorised its republication when he was a famous and highly controversial political figure, and when it was obvious what an opportunity for invective it would give his opponents. Blum never believed that stating or restating what he felt to be true could ever do any harm. Sooner or later men would agree on rational reforms of society, and moral improvement would necessarily follow; in the meantime the more discussion there was of the issues the better. One point only he was anxious to make clear, and that was that the book was an impersonal one. It was dedicated to his wife 'wishing to signify by this that neither disappointment nor bitterness have entered into the conception of this book, but on the contrary a feeling of gratitude, and that it has been written by a happy man'.[30]*

In the years before 1914, therefore, Léon Blum, around the age of forty, seemed to be settled into a pattern of life as a successful lawyer and distinguished critic, whose Socialist views drove him to support the Socialist Party, and, on occasion, to participate in its activities. There was still no sign that he was destined for political leadership. 'It is true in a general way,' he wrote at this time, 'that character is quickly formed and varies little. A man remains essentially what his youth has made him. But everywhere, in normal cases, a man's sensibility becomes disciplined and limited bit by bit under the necessity for action. Between thirty and forty he reaches the practical age

*Blum's first wife died in 1930, leaving one son who became a successful engineer; soon afterwards he married one of her great friends, and, after being widowed a second time, married, during his captivity in the Second World War, his third wife, who survives him.

when the most stormy, like the most nonchalant natures, turn towards the regular occupations of life.'[31] It is true that Blum remained essentially what his youth had made him; but at the age of forty he had not yet started on what was to be his regular occupation.

2

ON 31 JULY, 1914, Jaurès was assassinated in a Paris café
by a young nationalist fanatic. On 3 August Germany declared
war on France. These two events were to transform Léon
Blum's life. Jaurès' death left the French Socialists without a
leader at a most critical moment, and there was no one with
the prestige and personality wholly to take his place. At the
same time, the party had to take decisions that were bound to
affect the whole course of its subsequent development. Socialists
for the first time found themselves faced with the duty of taking
their place in the government, in order to give expression to
the unity of France in the face of the invader, and in order to
prosecute the war effectively. There was, at this stage, no opposition to the proposal that two Socialists should enter the government; and within a month of the outbreak of the war, two of
them were ministers: Jules Guesde, the veteran Marxist who
had been the champion in earlier days, as against Jaurès, of
the group who held that it was in all circumstances wrong for
Socialists to enter a bourgeois government, and Marcel Sembat,
who, in the previous year had published a book pleading for a
reconciliation between France and Germany, and proving that
a Republican government was not competent to wage a war.
The question of whether Socialists should serve in non-socialist
governments had been one of the most controversial points in
the history of the Socialist parties of Europe; and it was to
be taken up again after the war and be a central theme in
their debates for another twenty years. For the moment, however, there was no discussion or hesitation, and there is little
doubt that Jaurès, had he been alive, would have taken his
place in the government.

It was a view that Blum shared without question, and he
himself was soon actively involved in working for the government. His eyesight was too bad for him to be called up in the
army, and, when the Socialists went into the government,

Marcel Sembat asked him to join his personal staff as *chef de cabinet* in the Ministry of Public Works. Sembat was a man who had much in common with Blum. He was a member of the moderate wing of the Socialist party and a man of intellectual and artistic interests. He was actively interested in contemporary painting, and published a book on Matisse, while it had been he who had risen to the defence of the Cubist painters when one of his Socialist colleagues in the Chamber of Deputies had protested against their having their works shown in the officially recognised *Salon*. During the period Sembat was at the ministry, from 1914 to 1917, Blum worked closely with him and thus acquired his first experience of administration and of the workings of government. As might be expected, he was extremely competent as well as very observant. He not only acquired a detailed knowledge of the way in which the French railway transport system worked, but he also reflected on the functioning of the whole governmental machine. As soon as Sembat resigned in 1917, over the issue of whether the French Socialists should be allowed to attend the proposed international Socialist congress in Stockholm, Léon Blum published his conclusions anonymously in the *Revue de Paris*, under the title *Lettres sur la Réforme Gouvernementale*.[32] His analysis covers what has since become familiar ground in all discussions on the French constitution—the need for strong parties, the need to give the Prime Minister real authority, the need to prevent delays in the actual legislative procedure, and the problem of producing a strong and stable government. Blum ranges over the whole political and administrative field, and deals with points that he took up again in the constitutional debates after 1945, for, indeed, neither the Third nor the Fourth Republics went very far towards dealing with the problems he analysed.* And when Blum came to power himself he was to be the victim of many of the constitutional defects he had recognised at the outset of his active political career.

When, somewhat against his will, for he seems to have

---

*After 1945 one measure Blum had recommended was adopted in the provision of a proper office staff for the Prime Minister, so that he could work independently of a particular department and exercise a general control, in theory at least, over the actions of the government.

believed that the Socialists should continue to play a part in the government for the duration of the war, he resigned his post in 1917, he had to decide what his future was to be. There was little incentive in 1917 to return to his old life as a man of letters; he had acquired a taste for practical administration, and, at the same time, the Socialist Party was facing a major crisis. As the war dragged on, the unity of 1914 was breaking down; a minority in the party and in the trade unions had become convinced that the war must be stopped and that they had all made a mistake in accepting the *Union Sacrée* in 1914. The success of the Russian Revolution gave an enormous impetus to these ideas, and, although the example of the vindictive peace imposed by the Germans on the Soviet government early in 1918, and Clemenceau's stern measures to check defeatism, temporarily restrained the new militant left wing of the Socialist Party, as soon as the war ended the party was faced with a possible split between the revolutionary group and those who believed in the possibility of piecemeal reform within the constitutional structure of the Republic. In 1919 the debate on these issues could not be postponed any longer, and the first post-war party congress was devoted to a discussion of these fundamental questions of political beliefs and tactics. The unity, for which Jaurès had worked so hard and sacrificed so much in 1904-5, seemed about to be shattered, and his loss was felt more acutely than ever.

In these circumstances, Blum was drawn inevitably into active political life. Both his loyalty to the memory of Jaurès and his experience of government during the war pointed the same way, and in 1919 his mind was made up. In that year he emerged as a figure of importance at the Socialist Party Congress, and, shortly afterwards, he was elected to the Chamber for a Paris constituency. While one can understand the personal motives that led Blum into a political career at the age of 47, it is at first sight harder to explain the reasons for his rapid rise in the Socialist Party. He had few of the qualifications generally thought necessary for a popular leader of a working class party; he never gave up the way of thinking, or, for that matter, the appearance and manner of an intellectual. He had not the physical equipment to be a successful demagogue: 'I have naturally a very weak voice,' he told the stormy party congress of 1920, 'I am also, like you, very tired and it would be materially impossible for me to overcome disorder and violent interruptions by the strength of my throat and lungs.'[33] Yet he was able to hold mass audiences and to win the devotion of thousands of French working men and women. His success in this, indeed, seemed to justify his faith in democracy, for it was based on the power of his intellect and the sincerity of his actions. Like Gladstone, he was never afraid to put moral and intellectual issues squarely before the people, in the confidence that they would understand and support him. His honesty and disinterestedness, even if they sometimes inhibited action, yet gave Blum himself his peculiar position among French, and, indeed, European statesmen of the twentieth century. There have been few politicians who have discussed and explained the reasons for their political actions as publicly and as freely. He kept hardly any private papers, which he regarded as useful only for those politicians who were interested in personal feuds and vendettas. Yet in his speeches, pamphlets, and, above all, in the day-to-day journalism on which he was now to embark, it is possible to follow every nuance of his thought, every hesitation as well as every conviction. The lucidity and honesty of his literary criticism were transferred to the political plane; and his sincerity won the devotion of his followers as well as the respect of the respectable among his opponents.

For Blum himself his decision meant a breach with the past and an abandonment of what had been the main interests of his youth. *Stendhal et le Beylisme* had appeared at the moment of the outbreak of the war in 1914, and, when it was republished some fifteen years later, Blum wrote: 'I have since changed my existence almost as completely as it is possible for a man to do. . . . Is it really by me? It is by a me to whom I am attached by everything, yet whom I scarcely recognise. It seems, indeed, like digging up the posthumous work of a dead brother.'[34] In fact, however, Blum's character and beliefs changed very little, and, although he acquired practical political experience, his principles did not alter, so that, when, in his old age, he came to reconsider them, he was able to fall back again and again

on phrases he had used in his youth. His dilemma as a statesman was, in fact, to be that of combining his rigid principles
and firm intellectual convictions with the suppleness required
of a practical politician. He has, as a result, been denounced
by some as an ineffectual doctrinaire, and, by others, as an
over-subtle intellectual, selling out the working class for the good
of his own soul.[35] There is perhaps some truth in both criticisms.
Yet Blum's very hesitations and mistakes are sympathetic,
because they arose out of his feeling for the effects his actions
would have on others (and he was extremely sensitive and
thoughtful in his private relations as in his public life) and from
his understanding of the complexities of the world, just as
his occasional rigidity derived from the strength of his intellectual convictions and his unwavering belief in the application
of reason to human affairs. The interest, and, indeed, the
tragedy of the career of Léon Blum lie exactly in this dilemma,
and raise the question whether a man of intellectual honesty,
moral principles and personal sensibility can, in fact, ever make
a successful politician in the twentieth century.

When Blum entered active politics, it was largely with the
aim of carrying on Jaurès' task of keeping the Socialist Party
united. 'I have only entered public life in the party,' he told
the 1920 party congress, 'on two occasions, fifteen years apart.
I entered it in 1904-5 to work for unity and I returned in 1917
at a moment when unity appeared threatened. I have only
remained for that purpose.'[36] He was over-optimistic about the
possibility of achieving his aim. At the first post-war congress
in the spring of 1919, he was still hoping that differences might
be transcended, and that they were merely the expression of a
diversity of temperaments united on the ends they were to
pursue. 'When we feel ourselves sometimes hemmed in by
divisions, discussions or intrigues, there is only one thing to
do, to rise a bit higher, to climb a little and look at our goal.
And then we shall see that we are in perfect agreement. We are
like travellers in the mountains, who cannot see for the cloud
and mist. Well, there is only one thing to do: climb, climb
higher, and when you climb higher you will find the air pure,
the light undimmed and the sun shining.'[37] However, Blum
was soon forced to realise that the differences that divided the

group which wanted to accept the leadership of Moscow and to join the Third International, from those who still believed in the republican, liberal, reformist socialism of Jaurès, was too great to be bridged by rhetorical appeals of this kind, however sincere. In fact, he was one of the first people to realise what was happening in Russia, and to understand the true nature of the Communist régime. His speech at the Tours congress of the Socialist Party in 1920, when the breach finally occurred and the French Communist Party was founded, contains, among other things, a far-sighted criticism of Communist beliefs and practice, and a clear intuition of where they were bound to lead. 'What will this new party be which you want to create? Instead of the popular will at the base, going up through the party step by step, your centralised régime will involve the subordination of each organ of the party to the organ which is its hierarchic superior; at the summit there is an executive committee on which everything depends, and which is a sort of military command formed at the top and transmitting its orders down through the various grades until they reach the rank and file. . . . We tell you that your dictatorship [of the proletariat] is no longer just a temporary dictatorship which will allow you to put the finishing touches to the construction of your society. It is a stable system of government which you regard as almost normal, and beneath the shadow of which you want to do all your work. . . . You conceive of terrorism not just as a last resource, not as the final measure of public safety to be used against bourgeois resistance, not as an act of vital necessity for the Revolution, but as a means of government.'[38]

At the 1919 and 1920 party congresses, Blum elaborated his own position. It derives logically from the distinction he had made in the *Nouvelles Conversations* between the preparation of a revolution and the actual revolution itself. 'Those actions which can at present remodel the capitalist society of today as thoroughly as possible in the direction of the collectivist society of tomorrow are at the same time those that prepare for the revolution most effectively and most completely. . . . Thus the party is in evolution, in constant movement between two points, two fixed poles: one is the future society which we foresee, which we predict, which we want to realise; the other is present society, out of which we want to carve that future society. We have, so to speak, one foot in the real and one in the ideal.'[39] Blum was, like Jaurès, always stressing that the revolution was a means not an end. The seizure of power, by whatever means, legal or illegal (and Blum was fond of quoting a remark of Guesde's about using all means 'even legal ones'), was only a step towards a change in the ownership of the means of production, and this, in turn, was only a step towards a more just and harmonious life for everybody, in which the proletariat would not only have their economic needs met, but also 'all the pleasures of culture, all the pleasures of art'.[40]

In 1919 and 1920 these general considerations were of little help in uniting the party; but they were to provide the starting point for subsequent socialist policy, and were to be the basis of Blum's rapid rise to leadership. Perhaps the only thing that could have kept the party together would have been the presence of a leader of the prestige and capability of a Jaurès; and no one had emerged to take his place. Of the older generation, Vaillant had died during the war, and Guesde and Sembat were both to die in 1922. None of the generation immediately after them appeared really outstanding, even though there were among them intelligent and sincere men like Pierre Renaudel and Albert Thomas. Thus Léon Blum found himself the spokesman of a small group who attempted to make quite clear the principles that separated them from the Communists, and who were opposed to adherence to the Third International under any circumstances. In fact there never was a straight vote on this issue; and it is a sign of the revolutionary temper of the 1920 congress that the vote, when it came, was between those who were in favour of joining the Communist International without qualification, and those who were in favour of joining 'with reservations'. The former won by a 3 to 1 majority; and Blum's tiny minority refrained from voting. Blum had realised what the result would be, and had ended his speech with the words: 'It is doubtless the last time that I shall address many of you, and it is for that reason that I shall say this. We are all, though divided, Socialists in spite of every-thing; let us remain brothers, brothers separated by a bitter quarrel, but a family quarrel, who may yet be reunited in a single home.'[41]

In fact, Blum's uncompromising clarity about the aims and methods of the Communists was to have immediate confirmation. Within a few hours of his speech against adherence to the Comintern, a telegram arrived from its secretary, Zinoviev, calling for immediate expulsion from the party of those who had sponsored the motion of criticism of the Third International, limited though the criticism was. It was on this issue that the breach finally came; and, although the majority was still in favour of joining the Comintern and of expelling dissidents, many of those who originally supported this course now saw how hopeless their attempt to keep some liberty of action and of conscience had been, and they promptly left the congress. The majority soon afterwards constituted themselves the French Communist Party. They remained in control of the Socialist Party machinery and funds, and of Jaurès' old paper *L'Humanité*.

It was a terrible moment for the minority who had remained loyal to their old name, tradition and beliefs. And it was in these circumstances that Léon Blum, who had impressed them by his unfailing clarity of judgment and his freedom from illusions during the bitter days at Tours, became the most important of the party leaders. During the next year or so, Blum and the other leaders of the minority were gradually reconstructing their party, trying to finance it and starting a new newspaper, *Le Populaire*. Above all, they were concerned to win back their mass support from the Communists. In all these tasks, Blum's legal and administrative experience and his unwavering purpose were invaluable. He became the director of *Le Populaire*, a post he was to hold continuously, during the period the paper was published, until his death;* he was the acknowledged spokesman of his party in the Chamber, while, at the same time, he was obliged to go into private practice as a lawyer in order to earn his own living. The task of winning support for the Socialists, and of preventing the Communists from becoming the only representatives of the

---

*Le Populaire appeared fortnightly at first, and in 1925 and 1926 had to suspend publication for lack of funds, but appeared as a daily from 1927 until 1940 and was started again in 1944.

working class and the only revolutionary party, dominated Blum's political thought in this period. The position was a difficult one. On the one hand the Socialists were a parliamentary force of some importance (they had 105 deputies in the 1924 elections); on the other hand, they had to show that their rejection of the Third International and of the leadership of Moscow did not mean that they were just another bourgeois party with no real ambitions to change the existing order of society.

In this situation Blum developed a doctrine that would, he thought, enable the party to continue its day-to-day criticisms, and, on occasion, support, of the government, without committing himself and his colleagues to the actual acceptance of ministerial posts in a non-Socialist government. One or two Socialist ministers in a non-Socialist administration would be as powerless to introduce a truly Socialist programme as Millerand (a ghost as potent in the French Socialist Party as Ramsay Macdonald in the Labour Party) had been twenty-five years earlier.* Blum's doctrine was based on a distinction between the 'conquest of power', the 'exercise of power' and 'participation' in a bourgeois government.[42] The conquest of power would, in fact, be the Revolution, the moment when the Socialists would take over the whole of the existing state and remodel society in accordance with their programme and ideals. But there might come a moment before this when the Socialists were the largest party in parliament, and might be summoned to form a government under the normal workings of the Republican Constitution. If they were then to accept, this would be the 'exercise of power'; and it was a possibility that Blum never ruled out. If the Socialists came to power in this way, then the important thing would be for them to be strong enough to pass some of the measures which would prepare the way for the eventual transformation of society; and in these circumstances they would be justified in taking office and in working loyally within the existing constitutional framework.

*Alexandre Millerand, at that time an independent Socialist deputy, had accepted office in Waldeck-Rousseau's government in 1898 without consulting his colleagues. He was subsequently expelled from the Socialist group, and ended up as a conservative President of the Republic, 1920-24.

But, although Socialists might 'exercise' power without 'conquering' it, it would be a situation full of dangers; and, indeed, some of Blum's fears were to be justified when he did come to exercise power in 1936. 'The danger of the exercise of power,' he said in 1926, 'is precisely that it may be confused with the conquest of power, so that the proletariat is encouraged to expect from the former the totality of results which can only result from the latter.'[43] These dangers were even greater in the case of Socialist 'participation' in a non-Socialist government, and in that case they would outweigh the advantages; the only circumstances that would justify Socialists joining a government they did not control would be when the participation was 'negative', 'when the programme is above all one of defence against something'.[44] This was, in fact, the line Jaurès had taken after the Dreyfus case; and it was the justification of the Socialists' participation in the wartime governments.

These were general principles that it needed considerable restraint on the part of the Socialist leaders to apply. On several occasions—after the swing to the Left in the 1924 elections, for instance—they were offered government posts by the Radicals and others who were hoping to find a parliamentary majority on the Left; and, each time, while promising limited support in the Chamber, they declined to join the government. It is Blum's rigorous insistence on 'non-participation' in the 1920s and early 1930s that has earned him the reputation of an ineffective doctrinaire theorist, just as it was his maintenance of the rigid distinction between 'exercise of power' and 'conquest of power' in 1936-37 that led people to accuse him of losing an opportunity of making the Revolution. Yet, in both cases, his intellectual analysis had a firm empirical justification. In the 1920s, the Socialist Party, if it was to recover from the blow it had suffered at Tours, had to overcome the danger of allowing the revolutionary initiative and glamour—and consequently much mass working class support—to pass to the Communists. At the same time, the party had to play its part in the Chamber and show that it could influence policy without becoming just another opportunist group bargaining for portfolios in a succession of coalition governments. Non-participation was not just an intellectual dogma; it was, in Blum's mind, a necessary part of an attempt to build up a revolutionary party which would one day be able to take over power and launch the social revolution.

The years between 1920 and 1934, when Blum was preaching non-participation and elaborating the distinction between the exercise of power and its conquest—itself a development of his old dichotomy between the preparation of the Revolution and the Revolution itself—were for him years of hard routine work, in the Chamber, in the party headquarters and in the editorial offices of *Le Populaire*. In the Chamber, the Socialists were a force to be reckoned with, even though Blum had written a few years earlier 'I know of few more painful spectacles than the details of parliamentary life. What an expenditure of time, goodwill and illusions! What is most striking is the waste of effort, or at least the disproportion between the labour and the result'.[45] In fact, Blum himself was an accomplished parliamentarian, and won the respect even of such inveterate opponents as Poincaré. ('He is one of the most intelligent and estimable men in parliament,' Poincaré once told Count Sforza.[46]) Blum lost his seat in Paris to a Communist in the 1928 elections, but was later provided with a safe seat by the loyal Socialist deputy from Narbonne who resigned in order to let Blum be elected. He took his duties to his electors seriously, and was popular with the miners and agricultural workers in his new constituency in the South, in spite of his Parisian intellectual origins, and they returned him with increased majorities in 1932 and 1936. Indeed, the Socialists' votes were increasing almost everywhere, and they were winning back a great deal of support from the Communists. In 1920, after the split, the Socialist Party had been left with only 30,000 members, as compared with the 130,000 of the Communists; but by 1932 Socialist voting strength in the elections was more than three times that of the Communists; nor had the Communists been successful in winning control of more than a small part of the Trade Union movement.

Yet there were people in the Socialist Party for whom this slow building up of Socialist strength was unsatisfactory, disappointing and unrealistic. Individual members resigned on specific issues, and in 1933 there was a more formidable

revolt against Blum's leadership, with the result that a group
left the party altogether and founded a 'Neo-socialist' Party.
This was a personal blow for Blum, for the Neo-socialists
included Pierre Renaudel, his old colleague from 1920, slightly
incongruously placed among men like Déat and Marquet
whose desire for a strong centralised corporate state was eventually to lead them to welcome the Nazi conquest of France. But
politically this revolt was of small importance; the 'Neos'
became just another small left-of-centre political party which
soon lost its significance. Blum's policy of waiting for the right
moment appeared once more to be justified.

In the elections of 1932 there was a swing to the Left—and
an increase of support for the Socialists as well as for the
Radicals. This at once raised, as it had done in 1924, the
possibility of the Socialists joining the Radicals in the government. And, again as in 1924 and for the same reasons, Blum
still refused to compromise. It was largely this refusal that
cost him the support of Renaudel and the Neo-socialists; and
it might well have seemed that Blum was reserving the right
to criticise all governments without ever being willing to assume
any administrative responsibility himself. If he had died in
1933, Léon Blum might have been regarded, perhaps rightly,
in spite of his achievement in preserving and restoring the
Socialist Party, as the typical intellectual in politics, ready with
ingenious general theories and trenchant particular criticisms,
but playing a purely negative role. In fact, however, Blum's
patience, restraint and uncompromising refusal to enter any
government he did not control were eventually to place him
in a strong position. In 1933 the problems of France, both
internal and external, were growing, and a succession of weak
governments were unable to deal with them. By the end of
the year the Stavisky affair, a financial scandal which had led
to ever louder accusations of complicity being levelled at
members of the Radical Party, had produced an atmosphere
of open hostility to the government and to the Republic itself.
It was a crisis that was to shake French society profoundly,
and to give Blum the chance to put some of his ideas into
practice.

3

IN OCTOBER 1933, Léon Blum led his followers in the Chamber to vote unexpectedly against the government of Edouard Daladier. Daladier turned white with rage; his government was overthrown, and the two men did not speak to each other for months. Yet Blum's attacks on the Radical governments of Daladier and his successor Chautemps were mild and impersonal compared with those of either the Communists or the Right. If there was impatience with the régime and with the particular politicians in power, this was, in his view, due to deep-rooted causes that could not be dealt with by outbursts of personal rancour or blind spite. 'The revolt and the anger of public opinion are defensive reflexes of human morality against the absurdities and monstrosities produced by the existing social system, and we should encourage them as such,' he wrote in Le Populaire.[47] He was never personal in his politics, although he had experienced personal attacks of great bitterness himself, and was to have to face still worse ones.

The Communists, in particular, had never forgiven him for the way in which he had rallied a Socialist Party which they thought had been about to fade away in 1920. In 1928, however, they had had their revenge; for Blum's defeat in the general elections of that year in the Paris constituency he had represented since 1919 was due to the fact that the supporters of one of the candidates of the extreme right had switched their votes in the second ballot to the Communist candidate, rather than let Blum win. L'Humanité's campaign had been particularly violent, and had included cartoons which would not have been out of place in the German anti-Semitic press of ten years later. Blum responded by writing: 'The [Socialist] Party is firmly convinced that working class unity has as a necessary condition the destruction of the cadres of the Communist Party,' even though he added the typical qualification: 'It is by our own action and our own doctrine that we must fight to defeat Communism.'[48]

Thus, at the beginning of 1934, Blum and the Socialists appeared to be isolated. The Radicals had no reason to count on their support, while the gulf that separated them from the Communists seemed unbridgeable—the more so since the Executive Committee of the Communist International had declared as lately as December 1933 that 'the question of how soon the rule of bankrupt capitalism will be overthrown by the proletariat will be determined by the successful work of the Communist Parties in undermining the mass influence of Social Democracy'.[49] The situation, as far as Blum was concerned, changed overnight on 6 February 1934. It is still a matter of controversy whether the riots in Paris on that afternoon and evening were the result of a serious attempt by the Right-wing 'Fascist' organisations to make a *coup d'état*, in order to overthrow the government and set up a dictatorship.[50] What is important from the point of view of Blum's actions is that he believed it, and continued to do so for the rest of his life. And, in the Chamber of Deputies, where the new Prime Minister, Daladier, who had just returned to office, was making his first appearance at the head of a new government indistinguishable from its predecessors, Léon Blum launched an appeal for Republican solidarity. 'If the government wages the struggle with enough energy, with enough faith in the will of the people, they can count on us. If they fail in their duty, it is we who will launch an appeal throughout the country to the republican forces and the mass of workers and peasants. . . . The national climate must be purged and renewed. The deeper causes of the trouble are unemployment, the experience of suffering today, anxiety about tomorrow, the grave apprehension caused by events abroad. If the government were not to understand this, its success would be limited to this Chamber and to this day alone. Civil liberties can only endure through the confidence and enthusiastic support of the mass of the people. They are endangered as soon as they no longer guarantee security of life and peace. . . . In the battle now engaged, we claim our place in the front line. The Fascist reaction shall not pass.'[51] For Blum, in fact, it was just such a

situation as had confronted the Socialists at the time of the
Dreyfus affair. With the apparent danger of a Fascist revolt at
home, and the real danger presented by a Germany in which
National Socialism was more than the passing phase in the
death throes of capitalism which the Communists—and some
Socialists—believed it to be, the moment had come when the
Socialists could think of joining a government whose programme
would be, to use Blum's own phrase eight years earlier, one of
'defence against something'. Accordingly, the next morning,
after the Chamber and the streets had quietened down enough
for the deputies to go home for the night, Blum offered Daladier
Socialist participation in the government, in order, as he said
a few days later, 'not to give him the feeling in such grave
circumstances that he was being abandoned'.[52] But Daladier's
nerve had gone; and the new government, when it was formed,
was one predominantly of the Right. The moment when, at
last, the Socialists might have joined the Radicals in a government of the Left was past; and it was to be outside Parliament
that Blum had to take the next steps if his ideal of Republican
solidarity was to be realised. 'When the Republic is threatened,
the word Republican changes its meaning,' he declared to a
vast audience on 12 February. 'It regains its old significance,
historic and heroic.'[53]

The occasion of this speech was a meeting organised jointly
by Socialists, Communists and the Trade Unions, and it was
the first time since 1920 that Socialist and Communist leaders
had appeared on the same platform. In practice, however, it
took nearly two years of tough negotiations to achieve any real
cooperation between the two parties.[54] Blum's own position
was a difficult one; but his attitude remained consistent. He
was intensely suspicious of the Communists: their personal
attacks on him and the other Socialist leaders continued for
several months after the Sixth of February; and when the
Communist line changed, and they seemed to want a genuine
agreement with the Socialists for common political action,
Blum was worried, characteristically, because the shift lacked
'an absolutely satisfactory intellectual explanation,'[55] though
he surmised that it was due to Russia's need of allies in the face
of the German threat. For whatever reason, during the latter

part of 1934 and throughout 1935, the Communists were working whole-heartedly for a Popular Front—a political alliance
that would embrace not only Socialists and Communists,
but also the Radicals—and this policy was formally endorsed
by the Comintern at its World Congress in the summer of
1935.

The change in Communist policy had produced in Blum 'a
complicated mixture of hope and anxiety'.[56] On the one hand
he saw that united action at this moment might really enable
the Socialists to 'exercise' power and to introduce some of the
economic, social and administrative reforms which, he felt,
were long overdue in France, as well as helping the Republic
to resist the threat of Fascism at home and abroad. On the
other hand, he felt that, however much they changed their
tactics, the Communists were aiming at regaining the popular
support which the Socialists had been winning during the years
when Blum had been carefully and painfully rebuilding
the Socialist Party. As he wrote at the start of the prolonged
negotiations, the Communists' behaviour might arouse the
suspicion that 'the current towards unity might be transformed
into a current towards Communism'.[57] Yet unity was desirable;
and the Left wing of the Socialist Party were putting increasing
pressure on the party leaders to work, not only for agreement
with the Communists on a common programme, but also for
'organic' unity—an actual fusion between the two parties.
Blum was by now too experienced a tactician not to realise that
the Socialists must keep the initiative if they were to realise
a genuine Popular Front which should not be dominated by the
Communists. '*Pour animer les masses, il faut montrer aux masses
que vous êtes des animateurs,*' he told the 1935 party congress.[58]
Once he had made up his mind that cooperation with the
Communists and the creation of a Popular Front were necessary, he concentrated on making sure that the terms of agreement were sufficiently specific and the principles on which they
were based sufficiently clear to prevent the Communist leaders
from using the movement to their own advantage.

Blum was therefore concerned to obtain a common programme which could be put into immediate practice if the
Popular Front was successful in the 1936 elections and, as a

result, called upon to exercise power. Thus, in the negotiations between Socialists, Communists, Radicals and the other groups who were willing to adhere to the Popular Front, it was the Socialists who appeared the most doctrinaire, since they were anxious to get agreement on theoretical first principles and a positive general programme, while the Communists assumed the role of pragmatic politicians ready to compromise in the interests of immediate effective negative action against the existing government. It seemed, in fact, almost easier for the Radicals—many of whom had long disliked the Socialists, and had been unable to understand the latter's puritanical refusal of the ministerial portfolios they had repeatedly proffered to them—to reach agreement with the Communists than with the Socialists.

In spite of his own doubts about the wisdom of attempting to cooperate with the Communists, Blum nevertheless succeeded in moulding the Popular Front to a large extent in accordance with his own ideas. The proposals of the Socialists on the left who wanted immediate fusion of Socialists and Communists into a single party were firmly rejected (even though the rival Trade Union movements succeeded in uniting), while the programme of the Popular Front, when it finally emerged from the long negotiations in January 1936, contained a large number of measures which had long been part of the Socialist platform, and which went far beyond anything the Radicals had ever dreamed of. The programme of the Popular Front was, in fact, an outline for governmental action and not just the series of propaganda points the Communists would have liked to make it. As Blum put it, 'In the eyes of the electors the Popular Front means cohesion against a possible attack by Fascism. It means a joint effort to govern and to govern at once, immediately after the electoral victory, so as to be able to lessen the miseries and injustices in which Fascism finds its breeding ground'.[59] Yet, for all the care in the drafting, and although the Popular Front appeared to involve the Communists in unequivocal support for a government which would put the programme into effect, one vital point was still uncertain. Would the Communists in fact be prepared to enter such a government and take their share of responsibility for the success or failure of this first essay in the exercise of power?

The elections, which were held on the last Sunday of April and the first Sunday of May, 1936, were an enormous success for the Popular Front, and a personal triumph for Blum. The Socialists, with 146 seats, were the largest single party in the new Chamber, and the Communists had increased their number from 10 to 72, while the Radicals had fallen from 159 to 116. In the circumstances, it was obvious that the President of the Republic would ask Blum to form a government. The moment had come for the exercise of power. 'How can I tell how I will do a job I have never attempted before?' Blum is reported to have said with his usual candour on assuming the Premiership.[60] The tasks were certainly formidable; and two facts immediately showed just how hard in practice the exercise of power was likely to be.

First of all, the Communists refused to enter the government, though protesting their adherence to the Popular Front and their support for Blum. Blum therefore took office with a cabinet composed of Socialists and Radicals. He was aware of the danger that the Communists might use their freedom from responsibility to criticise the government and to dissociate themselves from it in the event of failure. Nor can it have been very reassuring for him that the Communist spokesman most enthusiastic in his expressions of loyalty to the Popular Front was Jacques Duclos, who had defeated him in the bitter election campaign of 1928. However, Blum had to take the Communists at their word; and he comforted himself and his party by pointing out that, even if not members of the government, the Communists were too far committed to the Popular Front to be able to reap any benefits from the possibility of its failure.

Secondly, in many areas, and especially in the Paris region, the workers behaved just as Blum, ten years earlier, had foreseen they might: mistaking the electoral victory, and the prospect of the exercise of power within the existing system by a government of the Popular Front, for the beginning of the Revolution itself, they had, in the weeks that elapsed between the elections and the assembly of the new Chamber, declared a series of strikes, occupying their factories and refusing to move out.* Blum saw both the reasons for this and the danger it represented. 'It is perfectly natural and perfectly explicable,' he told the congress of the Socialist Party that met on 31 May, 'especially after a long period of hardship and suffering, that the victory achieved in the political field should create in the working class a feeling of impatience to see realised those reforms for which the electoral victory allows them to hope.'[61] When Blum finally took over, early in June, there was much talk among his opponents of the impending revolution; the strikes, rumours of the government's intentions and a genuine dismay at the extent of the Popular Front's electoral success had combined to produce a mood of financial and commercial panic. Blum had gone out of his way to try and reassure opinion; he had tried to show that the government would need an atmosphere of calm if its programme was to succeed, but it was only once he was Prime Minister that he was in a position to take effective action. The day after his first overwhelming vote of confidence in the Chamber, he invited representatives of the Trade Unions and of the employers' organisations to meet at his office; and within five hours agreement was reached on terms which, it was hoped, would put an end to the stay-in strikes.

It was Blum's first great practical success; and it is hard to over-estimate its importance. By the 'Matignon Agreements' (so known because the Prime Minister's office was in the Hotel Matignon), the workers got full recognition of their right to be represented by their Unions, the right to collective contracts about wages and conditions of work, an immediate rise in wages of twelve to fifteen per cent, an undertaking from the employers to cooperate in putting into effect the government's social legislation, and a promise of no reprisals against the strikers. Bit by bit, over the next weeks, work was resumed in the factories and other concerns where it had stopped, such as the great Paris department stores. It was a triumph for Blum's diplomacy; he had impressed the employers by his own modera-

*Suggestions have been made that these strikes were deliberately engineered by the Communists to embarrass Blum, but they appear in fact to have been spontaneous, and to have surprised the Communists as much as everyone else.

tion and used their real alarm to get them to make concessions; he had avoided the necessity of clearing by force the factories which the workers had occupied; and he had won genuine gains for the impatient supporters of the Popular Front.

He was quick to follow up this success and the atmosphere of relief it produced, by hurrying much of the Popular Front's programme through the Chamber and even the Senate. The measures were voted as obediently as when the United States Congress had endorsed the first measures of Franklin D. Roosevelt's New Deal in not wholly dissimilar circumstances. When the Chamber adjourned for the summer recess, Blum was able proudly to claim that the immediate programme for legislation which he had laid before the Chamber at the beginning of June was already law: a forty-hour week, holidays with pay, the establishment of a central marketing organisation for grain, a programme of public works, the reform of the Bank of France, nationalisation of the armament industry— all these measures had been passed in a little over two months. A long overdue effort to improve the condition of the French working class had been started; and it looked as though the exercise of power was producing just the sort of results Blum had always hoped it would, in alleviating distress and preparing the way for a more radical transformation of French society.

Many of these reforms were permanent—or at least were taken up again without question after the Liberation in 1944-45. Because of them, working class conditions in France were never to be as bad again. (Some of the workers never forgot; when Léon Blum was back in France after his return from imprisonment in 1945, he sent a suit to the cleaners; it came back with a note in the pocket from one of the work people: '*Merci des congés payés*'.) But, in the situation of 1936, reforms of this kind brought their own financial, economic and political difficulties with them. While Blum's opponents on the Right were recovering their nerve and preparing to resist any further reforms, and, if possible, overthrow Blum, events in the international field were dividing him from a large number of his own supporters.

On 18 July, 1936, a military revolt led by General Franco, broke out against the government in Spain. The links between the French and Spanish governments were close; the Spaniards

had also formed a Popular Front, and, in the previous January,
the Left had been as successful in the elections as the French
Popular Front was to be three months later. The natural
reaction of the Spanish government, therefore, was to look for
active support from the French Popular Front; in particular
they needed to buy arms, the more so as the revolt was backed
by the regular army. In the early stages of the rebellion, the
Spanish government was reasonably confident that, provided
the rebels had no help from outside, they would be able to deal
with the situation. In the meantime they asked the French
government to sell them the arms they needed. Blum at once
agreed. He was due to visit London on 22 July—forty-eight
hours after the first news of Franco's rising had been received—
for conversations with the British government that had been
planned before the Spanish revolt started. Before he left, Blum
arranged with Daladier, his Minister of Defence, for the
supply of military material to Spain to begin. In fact, this at
once became known to the Right-wing press, since the Spanish
military *attaché*, like many other members of the staff at the
Spanish embassy in Paris, was on the side of Franco. While
Blum was in London a major political crisis was developing
as a result of these disclosures.

In London, too, Blum found the British government anxious
to avoid any further international complications at a moment
when they had just succeeded in sliding out of the sanctions
that had been imposed by the League of Nations on Italy after
the attack on Ethiopia the previous autumn. When Eden, the
British Foreign Secretary, visited Blum at his hotel to say
good-bye, he asked him if it were true that the French government were going to supply arms to the Spanish Republicans.
When he learnt that this was so, Eden said 'It's your business,
but I beg you to be careful'.[62] Blum's Radical colleagues were
more categorical. When the Prime Minister got back to Paris,
he was surprised to find Chautemps, the Radical vice-premier,
waiting for him at the aerodrome, and from him he heard the
first news of the extent of the storm that was brewing. The
Radicals were anxious to avoid trouble; and when Blum con-
sulted Herriot, their most respected leader, now President of
the Chamber (and a man who had been against the idea of a

Popular Front in the first place), Herriot said firmly '*Je t'en prie, mon petit, ne vas pas te fourrer là-dedans*'. During the next two weeks the Cabinet discussed various ways of helping the Spanish Republic, such as selling the arms nominally to the Mexican government, but it was clear that the Radicals were determined to stop the direct delivery of material to Spain, and that the help to the Spaniards would therefore lose much of its effectiveness. During the discussions, too, it became clear that the Italians were preparing to send help to Franco and the rebels. At one moment Blum was ready to put the issue to the Chamber, even though it almost certainly meant the defeat of his government and the abandonment of any hopes of further measures of social reform. He was only deterred from doing this by the arguments and, indeed, the tears of Fernando de los Rios, the representative of the Spanish government in Paris, who said that the fall of the Popular Front government in France would be a far more shattering moral blow to the Spanish Popular Front than the practical disadvantages caused by the loss of some material assistance.

Blum made attempts not only to get his Radical colleagues to agree to help the Spaniards, but also to persuade the British government to change their policy. The one senior service chief in France who seems to have shared Blum's view was, somewhat ironically in view of his subsequent career, Admiral Darlan, the Chief of Naval Staff, and he tried to get Lord Chatfield, the British First Sea Lord, to ask the First Lord of the Admiralty to demand that the British cabinet be summoned to consider the matter. But Chatfield was reluctant to disturb his civilian colleague's summer holidays, especially for a cause with which he personally probably had little sympathy, and the British government remained firm advocates of complete non-intervention in Spain. It was in these circumstances that Blum decided, early in August, that the adoption of a policy of non-intervention was the only possible one for France too.

At a moment when it still seemed likely that the Spanish government could deal with the revolt, provided that Franco could be stopped from getting any help from outside, the idea of preventing such help by an international agreement not to assist either side was perhaps a reasonable one. Moreover it had the advantage of being the policy for which the British government were now pressing; and solidarity between France and Britain was consistently one of the principles of Blum's foreign policy. Thus, for a few weeks in August 1936, non-intervention looked like being the right policy to pursue. In the event it turned out to be a tragic sham, and it is a mistake for which Blum has been bitterly blamed. Within a very short time it became clear that both the Italians and the Germans were breaking the non-intervention agreement, the former on a large scale; and the material help the Republicans were able to get from Russia did not offset the advantage Franco thus gained. Although Blum was extremely uneasy and unhappy, he decided not to change the policy of non-intervention on which he had embarked; and thus he was forced to stand by and watch the slow defeat of the Spanish Republic, though he was later to try and get round some of the effects of non-intervention by authorising a limited amount of smuggling of arms over the frontier under the supervision of a retired inspector of customs. In addition to his desire to keep the government in power so as to complete their programme of reforms at home, Blum seems to have been influenced by the wish not to break with the British, who were less troubled than he about the hypocrisies in which the non-intervention policy involved them; and, as the war in Spain grew in intensity, there was the haunting fear that the divisions in French society would lead to a comparable breach in France, and that the people on the Right who coined the slogan 'Better Hitler than Blum!' meant what they said.

There was perhaps no issue which caused Blum more personal suffering and no point in his career where a policy, adopted on rational grounds, even if it did not wholly accord with his own instinct, led him more obviously into the kind of dilemma with which a sensitive and intelligent man in politics is likely to be confronted. Blum had to use his own personal credit with the Socialist Party to persuade many of its members to accept his policy: he made a dramatic appeal to the most critical of them on 6 September, 1936, when revolt in the party was rising, and ended with the words: 'There are two things I can never be reproached with—lack of courage and lack of loyalty.'[63] His Spanish policy led him into a position in which both his courage and his loyalty were to be called in question by the critics in his own party, and, more especially, by the Communists. Yet examination of the circumstances of August 1936 shows neither cowardice nor bad faith; and even Blum's analysis of the situation was not wholly mistaken. On the one hand, he could have resigned and thus admitted that the exercise of power had been a failure, without doing his Spanish friends any good. Or, on the other hand, he could have adopted a policy of intervention in Spain, broken with his British allies and run the risk of splitting French society to an extent that, even if it had not resulted in civil war, would certainly have paralysed the country at a moment of internal and external crisis. The tragedy of all political action is that some problems have no solution; none of the alternatives are intellectually consistent or morally uncompromising; and whatever decision is taken will harm somebody. In the case of Blum's Spanish policy it was perhaps Blum himself who was the first and principal victim.

The opening months of Blum's government were the most successful. By the end of the year, although unemployment was diminishing and there was less labour unrest, the financial problems of France, endemic since 1919—how to balance the budget, how to check the rising cost of living, how to stop the flight of capital—were still unsolved; and a twenty-five per cent devaluation of the franc shook the confidence of the middle classes even if it had a tonic effect in other directions. Blum realised clearly the difficulty of combining a policy of expensive social reform with a policy of deflation; but in his New Year's Eve broadcast to the French nation, he looked back with satisfaction on achievements that had, he felt, been moral gains as much as material ones: 'Hope has returned, a taste for work, a taste for life. France looks and feels different. Her blood flows faster; her body has been rejuvenated. Everything makes you feel that in France the condition of man has improved. . . . Six months ago everyone was saying things must change, and already you can see that something has changed.'[64] At the same time he was increasingly worried about the divisions in the country, and stressed that the Popular Front government, while remaining loyal to its origins and its mandate, set out to be 'a national government in the highest sense of the word'. It was the achievement of this national unity that was to pre-occupy him more and more over the next two years. The most urgent problem, at the start of 1937, was to restore sufficient confidence among the financiers, who were his natural opponents, to stop the flight of capital from France, and to win their cooperation in dealing with the immediate financial problems. To this end, Blum's Radical colleagues were pressing for an orthodox financial and economic policy, a curtailment of public expenditure and an end to experiments.

Accordingly, in February 1937, Léon Blum announced a 'pause' in the programme of the government: 'We have completed a body of legislation that in normal times would have been the result of years of work, and after such a rapid race, we must get our breath'.[65] While this satisfied the Radicals, and won an occasional word of approval from the less prejudiced members of the Right, it was inevitable that the 'pause' should arouse criticism among the Communists, who were continuously grumbling about Blum's Spanish policy, as well as inside the Socialist Party itself. It involved the postponement of various measures of social insurance and unemployment assistance, as well as obliging the government to appeal to the workers' organisations not to press their claims for a rise in wages, since one of the aims of the 'pause' was to check inflation and rising prices. Blum was, in fact, ready to speak to the workers in tones that did not altogether please them: 'I would remind the workers' organisations,' he said in the Chamber, 'that they have grown in power, but that all power in this world involves duties. . . . They cannot limit themselves any longer to the defence ... of particular interests. They must bring them in-to harmony with the general interests of the nation, . . . with the interests of the reputation and prestige of French democracy.'[66]

The Communists, without actually breaking up the Popular Front, had been increasingly critical of Blum for some months; now, in an atmosphere of renewed industrial agitation, they became more openly hostile. On 16 March, for example, they created serious disturbances in the Paris industrial suburb of Clichy, on the occasion of a comparatively harmless meeting organised by one of the extreme Right wing parties which had replaced the now illegal Fascist leagues; and André Blumel, the head of Blum's private secretariat, was seriously wounded when he arrived on the scene to see what the trouble was. Blum refused to be deterred by these threats and hints on the Left, any more than he was by the more open hostility of the Right; but by May, 1937, it became clear that his difficulties were almost insuperable. He himself saw very clearly what they were. 'The difficulties of the Popular Front government,' he told a meeting of state employees on 29 May, 'lie in the following terrible contradiction: to make simultaneously in a country like ours an attempt at socially just reforms demanded by the people, and an unprecedented effort of military preparation imposed by the international situation on a country which has not yet recovered from the ravages of the last war.'[67]

The burden and expense of rearmament were a nightmare to Blum. All his instincts, rational and optimistic as he was, were against it. Throughout his political career he had consistently supported the League of Nations and consistently advocated disarmament; and he regarded himself as bound to carry on Jaurès' work of Franco-German reconciliation. It was only gradually that he had come to see the danger of National Socialism; and, although disapproving of it, he had hoped that it might remain a German internal matter, and not trouble the peace of Europe. When the Germans in March, 1936, had sent troops into the Rhineland and denounced the Treaty of Locarno, in which they had agreed to recognise the Rhineland as a demilitarised area, Blum had been out of action, recovering from the serious injuries inflicted on him by a group of Right wing toughs who had spotted him in a car as they were coming away from the funeral procession of the Royalist writer, Jacques Bainville. When he recovered, however, he was relieved that the crisis had passed without war, and fully supported Eden's efforts at combining a formal condemnation of Germany's action with an attempt at a settlement of outstanding disputes. It was not, probably, until 1938 and the German occupation of Austria that Blum finally came to see that there was nothing to be done with Hitler, and that all hopes of reason prevailing or of the League of Nations becoming more effective must be abandoned. It was perhaps the only time when he clung to illusions longer than the evidence justified. He had not, however, allowed the hopes which he still entertained when he took office, of a return to a system of security and disarmament through a restored and revived League of Nations, to prevent his government from embarking on a considerable programme of rearmament, though some—notably General de Gaulle—have criticised him for not giving the details of its execution more personal attention, and for leaving these to Daladier, the Minister of Defence, and Gamelin, the Chief of Staff. (It was a mistake that Blum himself admitted in his evidence to the Parliamentary Commission of Enquiry after the end of the Second World War.)

Blum was sufficiently interested in de Gaulle's ideas to send for him in the late summer of 1936, when de Gaulle was still a Lieutenant-Colonel. He had been critical of de Gaulle's concept of a professional army; but he now cross-questioned him closely on his views about armoured warfare and the necessity of France having an adequate offensive force, instead of waiting behind her fortifications for a German attack. When de Gaulle criticised the government for ordering the wrong kind of aircraft and the wrong weapons, Blum said that the use of the credits voted was a matter for Daladier and his service advisers. De Gaulle disagreed with this; but he himself suggests one reason for Blum's inability to deal with the question personally. 'During the conversation,' he recalls, 'the telephone rang ten times, turning Léon Blum's attention to trifling parliamentary and administrative questions. As I was taking my leave and he was called to the telephone again, he made a weary gesture. "You see," he said "how hard it is for the head of the government to concentrate on the plan you are outlining when he cannot spend five minutes thinking about the same thing." '[68]

Blum himself gave another explanation of the failure of French rearmament. Writing in prison in 1941, in the shadow of the defeat, he said: 'The execution of a rearmament programme, itself conceived by the senior officers of the Staff with too little inventiveness or boldness, revealed the insufficiency or obsolete nature of our tools, the dearth of specialists, whom technical education and a well-conceived system of apprenticeship ought to have supplied in profusion in a country like ours.'[69] The defects in French armaments in 1940 were due to the defects of French society as a whole, and not to particular policies or individual politicians. They were only one aspect of France's inability to adapt her economic and social structure to the needs of the twentieth century. One of the tragedies of Léon Blum's government was that it was the first administration since 1919 to attempt to carry out this adaptation.

Blum's government fell, in part, because of the inherent weaknesses of the political system which he had analysed twenty years earlier in the *Lettres sur la Réforme Gouvernementale*, and which he was now trying to reform. What Blum was experiencing in 1937 was the difficulty that any strong Prime Minister in France was bound to have in putting into execution a consistent programme. He not only lacked the executive means of controlling policy; he was also dependent on parties not his own. It was a combination of these two factors that forced his resignation in June 1937. In order to stop the flow of capital from the country Blum needed to impose a measure of exchange control (of a kind that has been taken for granted in the post-war world), and for this purpose he needed special powers from Parliament to issue the necessary decrees. While he obtained these without difficulty from the Chamber, his proposals were rejected by the Senate; and at 3 a.m. on 21 June, Blum resigned, a little over a year after the essay in the exercise of power had started. His fall was received with satisfaction, and not only by his opponents; for the Radicals it meant a governmental reshuffle of the kind they were familiar with and from which they would emerge with more offices, while for the Communists it was an opportunity to exploit their freedom from responsibility in order to try and discredit the Socialist leadership.

Blum's defeat placed him before the most difficult choice he had had to face since the decision about Spain the previous August. He himself, with his usual realism and clarity, analysed the alternatives before him when the national council of the Socialist Party met on the day after his defeat. There were, he said, three possibilities; he could capitulate to the Senate's vote; he could remain in power 'resting on the support of the popular masses, a course which ran the risk of endangering the re-establishment of the national economy by provoking grave unrest';[70] or he could work for the formation of a new government under different leadership, but with the participation of the Socialists. There were plenty of people at the time— and there have been many since—who felt that he should have adopted the second course. As one of them put it at the meeting on 22 June, 'We must above all respect the will of the masses. We must not give way before the Senate. There is something more important than the parliamentary crisis: it is the will of the mass of workers and peasants'.[71]

Blum in fact chose the third course, and became Vice-Premier in a new government headed by the Radical, Camille Chautemps. It was perhaps one of the few inconsistent steps he had ever taken, for this appeared to be 'participation' of the kind the party had repeatedly declined in the 1920s, and which would lack the possibilities of real reform that the exercise of power under Socialist leadership had had. The previous year, just before taking office, Blum had told the Socialist congress 'The question is whether it is possible, within society as it exists today, to procure sufficient relief for those who suffer. . . . I do not for a moment envisage the possibility of failure . . . but if it turned out that we were to fail, if it turned out that insurmountable resistance obliged us to face the fact that it is impossible to improve things within present society, that it is impossible at present to put into operation the rescue work necessary for the nation, then I declare I shall be the first to come and tell you. I shall be the first to tell you: it was a myth, it was an empty dream, there is nothing to be done with society as it is at present.'[72] This was not what Blum did when defeated in 1937; and his action needs an explanation.

The one he himself gave was simply that he did not think the Socialists should break up the Popular Front by refusing to join the Radicals in the new government. He refused to admit that his government had failed, and insisted that the Popular Front still had work to do, and that the dangers it had been formed to meet were as pressing as ever. At the same time, during the next nine months, he was becoming more than ever convinced that, if France was to meet these dangers, there must be a real effort to transcend party differences and create a feeling of unity in face of the growing threat of war.

He knew the dangers that such a policy involved for him personally, and was determined to avoid the suspicion that by becoming a 'national' politician he was abandoning his own principles. He had given his reasons, in February 1937, for not at that time attempting to form a 'national' government, and had seen how easy it would be to gain personal prestige by abandoning his own party and beliefs. 'I would have been greeted by public opinion as a true statesman,' he told the Chamber, 'since, in current language the definition of a true statesman is the man who, once he has won office, abandons the principles he represents and the friends who brought him to power.'[73] (Was he perhaps thinking of Ramsay Macdonald?)

In fact, the second Popular Front government under Chautemps, though it lasted till January 1938, did very little to forward the Popular Front's original programme. By the end of the year it had become apparent that it was no longer really a Popular Front government, and that Chautemps was pursuing policies indistinguishable from those of any other Radical Prime Minister. He had obtained from the Senate, in June 1937, the full powers which had been refused to Blum, but had used them for a conventional deflationary programme that made the Socialists and Communists increasingly restless. When, in January 1938, he was again asking for emergency powers, but undertook not to introduce the exchange control Blum had wanted to impose the previous June, the Socialist Party, apparently against Blum's own advice, though not, one cannot help feeling, against his own wishes, decided to leave the government.

In the ensuing political crisis, Blum once more made an effort to form a united national government. 'I am trying to make a kind of political Matignon agreement,' he said. There were two reasons why this failed: first, the personal animosity which many of those on the Right felt for Blum, so that to them he appeared as a symbol of the divisions rather than of the unity of France. Secondly, Blum himself realised that a national government would have to include both the Communists and those men of the Right 'known for their attachment to democratic liberties,'[74] even though he personally had little reason for liking or trusting either group. But the hope of bringing Conservatives and

Communists together in the same cabinet was a vain one. It was to be disappointed again two months later, when, in March 1938, Blum made another attempt at forming a government extending 'from Thorez to Mandel'. There had been no stability since the Popular Front had broken up in January, and, at a moment of the greatest possible international crisis, when Hitler was preparing to invade Austria, France was actually without a government. The intervening months had been a time of personal suffering for Blum, too, because his second wife had just died, and he had in fact been away in the country until a few days before he was called on to form a government.

Now that the German threat to the whole of Eastern Europe was clearer than at any time before, and in the expectation of a Nazi move against Czechoslovakia at any moment, Blum made one more appeal to the Right; and once again they refused to sit in a government with the Communists. The inclusion of the Communists was something on which Blum insisted; he was determined to maintain the unity of the Left wing parties, and, if possible, to restore the Popular Front, and he felt that, at a moment when he was trying to form a widely based government, he could not exclude the representatives of a million and a half voters, any more than, as he pointed out to his Right wing critics, he could exclude the Communists from mobilisation in the army if war came. In the event, he was forced to form a government of Socialists and Radicals, and it only lasted three weeks. Once again it was the Senate who overthrew Blum, by refusing to accord him the special powers they had accorded to everyone else who had asked for them.

Léon Blum had to justify his conduct of affairs as Prime Minister or deputy Prime Minister on two occasions—before the Vichy court at Riom, and before the friendly but not wholly uncritical parliamentary commission of enquiry of 1947, which was investigating what had gone wrong in France between 1933 and 1945. After the fall of the Fourth Republic, perhaps we can judge more sympathetically than after the collapse of the Third the inherent difficulties that confronted any attempt at strong government within the existing constitutional and administrative framework of France. Blum did not succeed in what he set out to do; the reforms he achieved were only a part of his programme; the ideas of general disarmament and international security in which he believed proved unattainable; the divisions in French society seemed unbridgeable. In spite of his prodigious memory, his speed of assimilation and his capacity for work, he had not been able to attend to all the details of administration; and perhaps he took too much for granted the technical competence of his advisers, such as General Gamelin, in fields for which he himself had little interest or sympathy. He had no professional knowledge of economics, though he had been quick to understand the significance of President Roosevelt's New Deal. Yet, if he had worked within a system that could have given him firm parliamentary backing, and at a time when the international situation was not growing rapidly worse, he might yet have created a France that was more ready to resist the shocks and challenges that confronted her.

As it was, his immediate reaction after his failure to produce a united strong national government was one of understandable pessimism, almost of lassitude. From the spring of 1938 until the disaster of 1940, Léon Blum was able to be little more than an anxious spectator. He summed up his political position in June 1938 as follows: 'We must not consider the exercise of power or participation in power as a normal stage in our action. . . . We must accept the fact that power is held by others, even if they do not entirely satisfy us, because we prefer to see them there rather than someone else; because we know the dangers of political instability. . . . Our difficulties will start again because we are acting in the midst of inextricable events, because we are caught between a society we cannot yet destroy and a society we cannot yet construct'.[75] Moreover, as the international scene grew increasingly gloomy, old divisions began to develop again inside his own party. The Munich crisis divided Blum from Paul Faure, the party secretary, and a colleague since the days of Tours. For Paul Faure the pacifist tradition of the party was too strong; and any humiliation seemed preferable to war. Blum's speech in the Chamber after Munich betrays the uneasiness he felt at having, at the instigation of the majority of his party, to condone a policy about which he felt the gravest personal doubts; and, while expressing his relief that war had been avoided, he besought the government to review its international obligations and to decide now which it was going to keep. While he still remained optimistic about France's military prospects in a war, he had, ever since the annexation of Austria, been convinced that war was coming and that France must be ready; and so he continued his modified support of the government of Daladier, while, at the same time, he refused to break finally with the Communists in spite of their criticism of him. '*On ne fait pas de la politique avec des ressentiments.*'[76]

When the catastrophe came in 1940, Blum, whose will to resist was unswerving, found himself the object of violent hatred. Few politicians in a democracy have been so detested as Blum was by his opponents; even President Franklin D. Roosevelt, who inspired something of the same feeling among men of property, was never subject to quite the same virulent personal attacks. These had not stopped short of personal violence; and Blum would have been killed by the gang of Royalists who attacked him in February 1936, if he had not been rescued in time by some workmen nearby and by civil servants in the War Ministry who saw what was happening. One of his friends and colleagues, Roger Salengro, the Mayor of Lille and the Minister of the Interior in the Popular Front government, had killed himself, hounded to death by the attacks of the gutter press of the extreme Right. In the moment of defeat and panic in the summer of 1940, Léon Blum, a Jew, a Socialist and a free-thinking intellectual, was an obvious scapegoat. 'His life is really in danger,' Georges Mandel told Sir Edward Spears, the British liaison officer with the French government, on 3 June 1940. 'To many who yearn for a capitulation and hope to make friends with Hitler, he stands for that section of the population which will fight on at any cost. That is a dangerous position to be in today.'[77]

It was, however, also a position that brought Blum new friends among his former opponents. Chief of these was Mandel himself; a Jew and a neighbour of Blum's in Paris, this man of the Right, who felt himself to be the heir of Clemenceau and whose cynicism only strengthened his determination to resist the Germans, was to be Blum's companion in captivity. Another was Paul Reynaud, who had been one of the bitterest critics of Blum's financial and economic policies in 1937, but who had remained on personally friendly terms with him and was now equally determined to fight on. These new friendships could not make up, however, for the loss of old friends who turned against him, and for the fact that many of his own party, led by Paul Faure, were determined to capitulate. When Blum arrived in Bordeaux from Paris—leaving his apartment on the Ile Saint-Louis to be ransacked by the Germans on their arrival, and thus losing the few personal papers he had kept he was made bitterly aware of the hostile atmosphere that surrounded him in the hotel where he was staying with a number of other deputies, and he moved to the house of a local socialist colleague. 'Was I not already,' he recalled a few months later, 'a source of embarrassment as well as a subject of anxiety for many of my political friends, perhaps without their being clearly aware of it ... I wondered whether the unpopularity which was growing up round my name had not already made my actions sterile—even harmful—to the ideas I should have liked to support, to the companions who defended them. To feel oneself not only a heavy or a dead weight, but one which, thrown into the scales, tips the balance to the enemy's side; to be aware that one's presence and words discredit the cause one wants most passionately to serve, these are cruel impressions, and they started to take possession of me.'[78]

It was these scruples that convinced Léon Blum that he must remain silent in the public debates about the surrender and the new constitution for France—and he has been criticised for not playing a more active part. He would not leave France; and to the surprise of his enemies and the dismay of some of his friends he appeared at Vichy, and tried vainly, behind the scenes, to make a last effort to rally the Socialist Party against Laval, who was engineering the end of the Third Republic and his own elevation to power. Blum was, for all his silence, too dangerous to be left at liberty, and he was arrested on 15 September, 1940. The years of prison began, first in France, and then, from March 1943, in Germany. He had to face the trial of the Third Republic leaders which the Vichy government staged at Riom—where his skill and eloquence enabled him to justify his own political conduct and to discredit that of his accusers, so much so that they were obligèd to abandon the whole pretence of a trial. In Germany he had to overcome the daily fear of death: Georges Mandel, the other inmate of the house at Buchenwald where he was interned, was handed over to the French collaborationist Militia and shot.

Yet these were years which Blum spent in writing and reflecting. It is interesting to see how, seventy years old and apparently defeated, he turned again to examine his basic assumptions about politics and society as well as his own past conduct. Certain ideas, and even phrases, from his youth still haunted his memory and provide a key to his deepest convictions. Above all it is the idea of justice that recurs again and again—justice in the sense of the rule of law and the safeguard of individual liberty, and justice in the shape of a fair distribution of economic benefits. 'The human race has created knowledge, science and art. Why should it be powerless to create justice?' he was fond of saying.[79] And Blum repeated word for word in *A l'Echelle Humaine*, written in 1941, a phrase he used in the *Nouvelles Conversations* written over forty years earlier: 'For a worker to rise to be a bourgeois is a miracle; for a bourgeois to sink to manual labour is a tragedy.'[80] It was because the French bourgeoisie had shown itself incapable of putting an end to this unjust situation and had lacked the vision and initiative to convert French society into a real social democracy that it had also shown itself unable to meet the German assault, spiritually as well as materially.

Yet Blum refused to despair. Both the fragmentary *Memoirs* and *A l'Echelle Humaine* are full of real optimism and hope, both for France and the world. He saw at once in 1940 the importance of de Gaulle's gesture; and in the letters which, in 1942, he tried to smuggle to his Socialist friends with the Free French in London, he insisted on his confidence in the General's good faith and on the necessity for continuing to support him; and he drafted for de Gaulle personally a memorandum to be shown to Churchill and Roosevelt in which he urged that full recognition be given by the Allies to de Gaulle's position. He remained convinced of the virtues of democracy, and he

addressed de Gaulle in terms that are as applicable in 1960
as in 1942: 'There can be no democratic state without parties.
They must be given a moral basis, and revived, not eliminated.
A state without parties is necessarily a one-party state, that is
to say a totalitarian state, that is to say an autocracy.'[81]
Because parliamentary government had apparently failed in
France there was no need to condemn democracy, still less to
adopt Fascism. 'Suppose that the German or Italian state had
been modelled on our unfortunate democracy which people
today denounce with so much arrogant contempt, would not
the peace of Europe have been sure and lasting?'[82] Moreover,
in spite of the disasters which Germany had brought on France
and on Blum himself, he refused to give up hope of a new
united Europe in which the Germans would take their place.
In 1944, when the end was in sight, though Blum's personal
fate still uncertain, he wrote: 'I do not believe in races made
up of the fallen and the damned. I do not believe it any more
of the Germans than of the Jews. . . . A very slight shift in
circumstances is enough to revive the brute in man, in every
man. But I am above all convinced, and herein lies my fundamental optimism, that men—all men—are susceptible to a cure
made up of kindness and reason, firmness and confidence, that
there exists in them, alongside the age-old savagery, a sense
of fraternity which can also be revived by acting at the same
time on their sentiments and on their interests. . . .'[83] Some
would say that this view is too easy to take—though they
should remember that these words were written within sight
and hearing of the main camp at Buchenwald. Some thirty-
five years earlier André Gide had complained that Blum, in
his book on marriage, 'misunderstood completely the value
of resignation and constraint, and implies—and this is monstrous—that the tree never produces as much or as fine fruit as
in its natural state'.[84] Between Gide's Protestant insistence on
the struggle of the individual conscience with the burden of
original sin and Blum's belief in the ultimate goodness and
rationalism of man was a gulf that separates two ways of
looking at the world. Yet Blum, even if sustained in the darkest
moments by a belief in man's fundamental goodness, could
still be appalled by his potential wickedness. 'You are already

conquerors in this respect,' he said of the Germans in 1945; 'You have ended by communicating to the whole world your hatred and your cruelty.'[85] Such moments of bitterness were rare; and they were forgotten in the warmth of the welcome which Blum received on his return to France in May, 1945. 'The proofs of friendship which pour in in every form from my friends in France and abroad make up in a few hours for the long years of trials I have just finished.'[86]

Although Blum took up many of his pre-war activities immediately on his return to France—he was writing the editorial in *Le Populaire* within two days of arriving—his position had changed. He was now an elder statesman, respected, after his behaviour in the war years, even by his opponents. His sincerity, his disinterestedness and his serenity had won their reward. Yet he remained actively involved in politics, even though he did not stand for election to the Chamber again. In 1945 his influence was decisive in ensuring that the Socialists rejected the Communist offer to form a united party, and the party congress of that year gave him the opportunity for a final review of his own Socialist doctrine. He rejected suggestions that he did not accept the main teachings of Marx, though with reservations about the concept of the class struggle and about the wholesale application of materialist philosophy outside the realm of historical explanation. But once again he showed how far he was from any purely materialist interpretation of the concept of revolution or of the dictatorship of the proletariat. 'I not only think that the capture of power, even if it takes the form of a political revolution by means of an insurrection, even if it gives complete power to the working class, is only the Revolution insofar as it permits the accomplishment of the transformation of society; but I also think that the transformation of society in itself is not the final goal, but the means, the necessary condition—but only the means and the condition —of the transformation of the condition of man . . . I mean that the object of the Revolution is not only to liberate man from economic and social domination and all the forms of servitude accessory to it; but it is also to ensure for him within the collective society, all his fundamental rights and all freedom to follow his personal vocation. . . . Our true aim in the society of the future is not just to make human beings more useful, but happier and better.'[87] While recognising Communist services in the Resistance and the heroism of the Soviet Union, he remained as convinced as he had been in 1934 that the Communists were not to be trusted unless they gave very positive proof that their aims and methods had changed. It was Blum's personal stand on this question that, in 1945 and the immediately following years, overcame the objections of those (such as M Guy Mollet) who wanted the Socialist Party to be based on a more rigid Marxism.

Blum had a last brief experience of the actual exercise of power at the end of 1946 and beginning of 1947. It was a moment of emergency and parliamentary crisis; the new constitution had been voted, but had not yet come into operation, and neither the President nor the Council of the Republic had been elected. In the elections of 1946, the Communists had emerged the largest single party (and the Socialists had lost twenty-seven seats and three-quarters of a million votes). The National Assembly had failed to produce a majority either for a government led by Thorez and the Communists or for one under Bidault and the Catholic MRP. In these circumstances, Blum—not himself a member of the Chamber—was asked to take office for one month. As in 1938, Blum failed to form a broadly based coalition government, and was forced to fall back on a government of Socialists alone. He knew how limited the possibilities were, with no real parliamentary majority (though his investiture had been voted almost unanimously), and he realised that all he could hope to do in the short time available was to administer what he called 'a psychological shock', in the hope of stopping the rise of prices and dealing with the immediate problems of government. He had no illusions about his task; and the last Blum government, though it did succeed in temporarily halting price rises, left little behind it except a repeatedly implied warning, too little heeded, that the irresponsibility of the political parties would lead to the collapse of the Fourth Republic as it had contributed to that of the Third.

Blum himself did not like the role of 'a consultant specialist to whom serious cases are submitted', as he put it. And it is perhaps unfortunate that his contribution to the Fourth Republic could not be a more positive one. The last years of his life were still active; but they were necessarily a period of retirement from day-to-day political life, and his imprisonment had left him in frail health. They were passed at his home near Paris; he continued to write regularly for *Le Populaire* and to advise, restrain and encourage his Socialist colleagues; and he continued working and writing to the end. He died on 30 March 1950. His last words were: 'It's nothing; don't be afraid for me'.

The career of a man who never quite achieved what he hoped, or what his talents might have led him to accomplish, is always hard to assess. Blum was not a wholly successful politician; nor was he a really original thinker. Yet there have been few men of equal intellectual gifts in twentieth century politics. It was not just his lucidity, his freedom from illusions or his power of synthesis that made him outstanding. (He could compose a leading article for *Le Populaire* in his head and dictate it word-perfect over the telephone.) Nor was it his personal scrupulousness and sensibility, which appeared to give him a certain reserve and shyness—qualities which, when combined with extreme short-sightedness, were sometimes mistaken for arrogance—that made him unusual, uncommon though they are in professional politicians. What is remarkable is the consistency throughout his life of his moral and intellectual attitudes. The story of his life is a fascinating one, not only because of the circumstances which turned the young aesthete and dandy of the nineties, devoting his life to literature and the theatre, into the elder statesman, imprisoned by his countrymen and handed over by them to the Germans, but also because it is a remarkable example of the application of reason and the intellect to private and public problems, and of a man who preserved in the hurly-burly of political life the intellectual and moral standards of his earlier years. His epitaph might well be, in the words of the person closest to him in his last years, '*Il etait fidèle*'.

II

WALTHER RATHENAU

PROPHET WITHOUT A CAUSE

'*C'était Parsifal qui parlait.*'

André Gide: *Feuillets*

WALTHER RATHENAU

PROPHET WITHOUT A CAUSE

1

IN 1881 EMIL RATHENAU, an engineer and businessman in Berlin and a member of the orthodox Jewish community, acquired Edison's patents for the manufacture of electric light bulbs. It was the foundation of a fortune and of a commercial, financial and industrial success outstanding even in the Germany of the last quarter of the nineteenth century. The *Allgemeine Elektrizitätsgesellschaft* (AEG) rapidly became one of the large industrial combines typical of German economic life in the reign of William II, and its founder a man of great wealth. It was a period of enormously rapid economic expansion in Germany, as in the United States, and the men who profited by it, Krupp, Stinnes, Ballin and the rest, were emerging not only as the representatives of the most highly developed form of centralised capitalism, but also as a class that was claiming a share in the political management of Germany, hitherto mainly in the hands of the old land-owning nobility. Yet, while the vulgar buildings being put up in Berlin symbolised one aspect of this new, brash prosperity, there were also memories of an older, more sober Prussian tradition, just as there were challenging new voices attacking all the premises on which German society at the end of the century rested.

Walther Rathenau, Emil Rathenau's elder son, was born in 1867, and was 16 years old when his father founded the AEG. He had grown up in an atmosphere of financial uncertainty— 'I grew up,' he was later to write, 'in an atmosphere not of want, but of anxiety'[1]—and his father, for all his decisiveness

and the effectiveness and ruthlessness with which he built up
his vast enterprises, was a man of moods, swinging from boundless optimism to depths of black, all-embracing pessimism.
Moreover, Walther Rathenau's family links, like his own
nature, were not just with the world of big business and
technological progress to which his father's life was dedicated,
and it was by no means obvious that he was going to follow an
industrial career like his father. His father's mother had
belonged to the cultivated Jewish middle class which, in the
Berlin of the 1830s and 1840s, had kept alive the values of
Goethe and the German Romantics. Walther's grandmother
had moved among people who had been friends of Goethe's
protégée, Bettina von Arnim, of the formidable Rahel von
Varnhagen and the young Ferdinand Lassalle and Franz
Liszt. Walther Rathenau valued these links with the intellectual
life and culture of an older generation, and he was never to
lose his veneration for the world of Goethe, who always remained for him 'one of the four evangelists of German culture'
(the others were Shakespeare, Rembrandt and Bach). When,
later, he began to appear in fashionable society, he was introduced to an old lady who remembered the 1840s. 'Her mother
was Schubert's "*Schöne Müllerin*" . . . she told me how Tieck
read, how Sontag sang and Elsler danced. . . . To me it is something rare and strange that I, the little electrical engineer,
should actually touch with my fingers the magic ring of the
Romantics.'[2] There is, of course, some affectation in this; the
'little electrical engineer' was, by 1902, when this meeting took
place, already a successful man in his own right and a director
of the AEG. But his devotion to the Romantic age was genuine
enough, and much of Walther Rathenau's time was spent in
the company of writers and painters whom he believed to
embody the values of the age of Goethe.

There was, too, another aspect to his cult of the past. If the
Romantic age represented the life of the arts and the intellect
to which one part of his nature responded so warmly, it was
the Prussia of the Napoleonic period, of the age of Stein,
Hardenberg, Fichte and the great movement of national reform,
which embodied the moral values he respected most. This
German Jew's cult of Prussian traditions and his attempts to

combine the Jewish and Prussian elements both in the German
Empire and in his own nature is the key to his character and
actions, and the source of much of the frustration and tragedy
of his life. He was a passionate admirer of classical Prussian
architecture and was able, in 1910, to buy a country house,
Freienwalde, which had been a royal residence of the house of
Hohenzollern, built by the architect Gilly at the end of the
eighteenth century. Both here and in the house he built for
himself in the fashionable Berlin suburb of Grunewald, the
rooms reflected the cool, refined, restrained taste of the Prussian
late eighteenth century, which suited the pose of impersonal
and impassive detachment the owner had come to adopt.
The taste for Prussian classical architecture symbolised a more
profound enthusiasm for Prussia and Prussian life. Although
Rathenau realised the limitations of the blond-haired, bone-
headed Prussian of tradition—'When has a man of the blond
type of the Nordic gods ever achieved greatness in the world
of art and thought?' he wrote[3]—it was nevertheless this
physical type that aroused his most intense admiration. It was
the plains and woods of Brandenburg that were his favourite
landscape, which he evoked in a poem written, on the eve of
the First World War, to commemorate the Prussian War of
Liberation of 1813:—

> Blond und stahlblau Korn und Lüfte
> Himmelsaugen heiliger Seen
> Dunkler Kiefern Waldesgrüfte
> Blasser Dunen Schaumeswehn. . . .
>
> Musste sich der Mensch verschliessen
> Dass das Herz umpanzert bliebe,
> Endlich darf es überfliessen
> Land, mein Land, du meine Liebe.[4]*

*Blond and steel-blue corn and air
 Blessed lakes the eyes of heaven
 Wooded vaults of dark fir
 Spindrift of pale dunes. . . .

 Even if a man has had to lock himself up
 So that the heart should remain well-armoured,
 At last it may overflow
 Country, my Country, thou, my Love.

The one person who remained a constant source of strength in the midst of the conflicting trends to which Walther Rathenau was exposed—the claims of his father's successful business, his artistic and intellectual tastes, his Jewish heritage, his admiration for an idealised Prussian type and tradition—was his mother, Frau Mathilde Rathenau. She came from a Frankfurt banking family, and seemed to embody the Jewish family virtues; dignified, reserved, strong-willed, perhaps a little puritanical and severe, her deep affections were centred on her husband and three children, and, in particular, on Walther. Throughout his life, whenever he was in Berlin, he visited her almost every day, and one of his favourite, and characteristic, recreations was to play piano duets with her. The member of the family to whom Walther was closest, however, was his younger brother Erich. His letters to Erich are full of a spontaneous affection and even gaiety that are to be found nowhere else in his writing, and Erich's death in 1903 deprived Walther of the one person with whom he perhaps felt wholly at ease. Erich depended a great deal on his brother's advice, and Walther was able to satisfy his constant desire to advise and devote himself to someone younger than himself, without the fear, which he so often felt in other cases, that he was laying himself open to exploitation and disillusionment. Throughout his life he remained a pedagogue *manqué*; and his great ambition was to influence the young. 'The noblest and most gifted Germans should consider it their good fortune and their highest honour to become educators of young men,'[5] he wrote; and the book he regarded as his most important work, *Zur Mechanik des Geistes*, was dedicated 'to the younger generation'.

Inevitably, Walther Rathenau's relations with his father were complicated and difficult. It was only towards the end of the older man's life that they came close to each other. 'We discovered each other late,' he wrote at the time of his father's death in 1915. 'First came respect, then friendship and finally love. Now we are very closely united; I feel that the last shreds of misunderstandings have fallen away, and feel calm and secure in his presence.'[6] They were very different in temperament; Emil Rathenau was suspicious of his son's artistic and intellectual interests and remained sceptical of them. 'He is a tree which bears more blossom than fruit,'[7] he is reported to have said; and when Walther's philosophical works were appearing, he said, truly enough, 'Walther's books are far easier to write than to read'.[8] Walther himself summed up his father's character well, and suggested the differences between them when he wrote 'He thought in terms of things, not of concepts and values'.[9]

It was presumably this sense of uneasiness in his relations with his father that made Walther determine to make himself financially independent as soon as possible, and he was prepared to go to considerable lengths to achieve this. It meant, first of all, the abandonment of any ideas he might have had of an artistic career. He not only was a competent pianist, but he drew sufficiently well for the painter Max Liebermann—a cousin on his grandmother's side—to encourage him to take up painting professionally. As a student at the University of Strasburg he wrote a play called *Blanche Trocard*, which he submitted unsuccessfully to the director of the municipal theatre at Frankfurt, and which was, in fact, a drama of marriage and personal relations, of a kind which Léon Blum might well have been reviewing in the Paris theatre a decade later.

In fact, however, Walther, after an unremarkable and not very distinguished school career, turned himself into a competent and well-qualified technician in the field of electrical engineering, and became a specialist in electro-chemistry. He studied mathematics, physics and chemistry at the Universities of Berlin and Strasburg, though he also took a course of philosophy with Dilthey, which seems to have left strangely little impression on his own later thought. He graduated in 1889, at the age of 22, with a thesis on *Light Absorption by Metals*. There followed the hardest part of his apprenticeship—ten years of solitary provincial life, first working at an aluminium factory at Neuhausen, near Schaffhausen in Switzerland, and then managing the electro-chemical works at Bitterfeld, not far from Leipzig. There is little evidence about this period; but there is no doubt that it marked him profoundly and permanently. His youthful letters suggest a boy full of high spirits and humour. The personality that emerges from the years at Neuhausen and Bitterfeld is grave, serious, somewhat remote, humourless, though not without an occasional touch of irony, and expresses itself in an elaborate, highly-wrought and perfected prose style. Only an occasional hint of the reasons for this change emerges from the published letters and in Count Harry Kessler's admirable but discreet biography. There were difficulties of a practical kind to be overcome; there was the problem of getting himself accepted on his own merits, and not as heir to his father's business; there is a suggestion of a love-affair that was broken off. Certainly, Rathenau disliked intensely serving in a subordinate position, and the passion for independence was one of the reasons which made him, later in life, reluctant to enter politics. There is a typical letter to his father from Neuhausen: 'You know me well enough to realise how much I suffer in a subordinate position. I would never of my own free will be a dependent official in any business. I have a more than average hatred of having my work allocated to me every day by a superior who comes in from time to time to see whether I am doing my duty and to whom I owe an account of everything—a man who can give orders, who praises and blames me, whom I must answer when he speaks to me, and who leaves me when he has had enough of me. . . .'[10]

Walther Rathenau had, even as a student, disliked the cruder forms of sociability. 'I don't have the ability to get drunk,' he wrote to his mother after a student party at Strasburg in 1887, 'so I at least have a clear head on the morning after, but during the evening itself I don't have the right kind of naive pleasure and can only at best amuse myself at the others' expense.'[11] However, the complete isolation in which he found himself at Neuhausen drove him to a sort of Stoical cult of solitude. 'Living here in solitude and quiet costs me less effort than you might believe,' he wrote to his father. 'I can very easily do without what is known as "pleasure" and as for "society"—admittedly none at all is rather little, but it can be endured.'[12] His mother seems to have been worried by his deliberate detachment from ordinary human feelings. 'You must not believe that I am fighting against feelings and instincts,' he told her when replying to her good wishes for his twenty-fifth birthday, 'but living among passionate men— which is what we all are by nature—has warned me against excess. . . . And you yourself would admit that one does well to get rid of real sentimentality. Otherwise what a wretched state I should be in today! As it is, I feel calm and contented and grumble about my work and look forward to the evening as on other days.'[13]

As important, however, as the personal emotional experiences of the years at Neuhausen and Bitterfeld was the constant reflection on what it meant to be a Jew. 'In the youth of every German Jew there comes a moment which he remembers with pain as long as he lives: when he becomes for the first time fully conscious of the fact that he has entered the world as a citizen of the second class, and that no amount of ability or merit can rid him of that status.'[14] These words, from a pamphlet written in 1911, sum up the bitter memories of his own youth. They were repeated a few years later, when one of his aristocratic women friends urged Rathenau to go into politics. 'My business activity satisfies me, my literary activity is a vital necessity, and to add a third activity, that of politics, would not only exceed my strength but also run counter to my inclinations. But even if I did have the inclination to enter the field of politics, you know that all external circumstances would prevent it. Even though I and my ancestors have served our country to the best of our ability, I am, as you may know, being a Jew, a second class citizen. I could not become a higher civil servant, and in peace-time not even a lieutenant. I could have avoided these disadvantages by conversion, but then I would, I am convinced, have been condoning the breach of justice committed by the ruling classes.'[15]

This was true enough; and Rathenau must have been made very conscious of his position during his period of military service. Other Jews, it is true, were less sensitive, and either accepted the necessity of conversion or were satisfied with their position as leaders of finance and industry, as indeed Emil Rathenau was, and with the fact that the social barriers which excluded them from aristocratic life were gradually being broken down, as the Kaiser's friendship with the shipowner Albert Ballin and even with Walther Rathenau himself seemed to show. While Walther Rathenau was too proud, independent and sensitive to be satisfied with a compromise, his own solution

to the Jewish problem in Germany lay in asserting the specifically German quality of German Jews. The Jews were, he
constantly repeated, no different from any other Germans:
'My people are the Germans and no one else. The Jews are
for me a branch of the German nation (*ein deutscher Stamm*) like
the Saxons, Bavarians or Wends'.[16] The link between Jews,
he wrote a little later, 'does not extend beyond the sense of a
common religious past'.[17] Consequently, while German Jews
could work to get rid of the disabilities under which they were
suffering, their future lay in Germany and nowhere else.
Zionism was a movement he regarded with the utmost suspicion
and scepticism. 'The vast majority of German Jews,' he wrote
in November 1918, 'among whom there are many whose
ancestors have lived in Germany for countless centuries, have
only one national feeling, and that is German. We want to
live and die in Germany and for Germany as our fathers did
before us. Let others found a state in Palestine: nothing attracts
us to Asia. (*Uns zieht nichts nach Asien.*)'[18]

During his period of isolation at Bitterfeld, Rathenau had
started to write essays and aphorisms, and to publish them
anonymously. One of these essays, *Höre O Israel*, is full of that
peculiarly masochistic anti-semitism that is only felt by
sensitive Jews. 'In the midst of German life is an alien and isolated race of men. Loud and self-conscious in their dress,
hot-blooded and restless in their manner. An Asiatic horde on
the sandy plains of Prussia.'[19] Yet, for all Walther Rathenau's
carefully cultivated Prussian patriotism and his belief that
Jews must be 'bred and educated as Germans', he fostered just
as carefully the Jewish elements in his character and inheritance.
'I am a German of Jewish race,' he wrote in 1918. 'My people
is the German people, my home the German fatherland, my
faith the German faith that stands above the different sects. But
Nature, with a smile, in a moment of wilfulness and lordly
bounty mixed both sources of my ancient blood in a foaming
conflict: the urge to reality, the links with the spiritual.'[20] His
cultivation of the conflict within himself and his fear that his
Jewishness might lead to a rebuff sometimes went to comical
lengths. Bülow, the former Imperial Chancellor, in his malicious
and not always accurate memoirs, tells a story that has a ring

of truth, about Rathenau's first visit to him, when Bülow was Chancellor and Rathenau already an eminent figure in the financial and social world of Berlin. After Rathenau had made a low bow, ' "Your Highness", he began in his melodious voice, laying his right hand on his left breast, "before I am worthy of the favour of being received by you, I must make an explanation that is also a confession." He made a short pause, and then said, with great expressiveness, "Your Highness, I am a Jew"'.[21]

This awareness of his Jewish heritage and the emphasis on his Jewish origins contributed much to the development of Rathenau's ideas. It was in the Jewish mystics that he believed his own mysticism to be rooted, and it was in the Old Testament that he sought the justification of his own beliefs. 'The spiritual community of Judaism is the only one that is free from dogma and myth,' he wrote, not entirely correctly. 'It is pure spirit; its creed is the four words of the annunciation of God, its only commandment is the word *"Ahabta"*—"Thou shalt love". No other faith has room for the revelation of Jesus except the spiritual faith in which he himself and his young men taught and died.'[22] He took his Jewish studies seriously; he worked hard to learn Hebrew and discussed Hasidic mysticism with Martin Buber. Yet the result of his religious eclecticism was only to produce a watery *salon* mysticism that lacked both the discipline of Jewish thought and the moral insight of Christianity. It was typical that he should have chosen to make the funeral oration at his father's funeral himself, and typical, too, although his father had been a practising Jew, that Walther's speech should have contained hardly any reference to Jewish belief and should have quoted indiscriminately from Moses and Jesus. Inevitably some of his father's Jewish friends and relations were shocked and many of Walther's Christian friends felt uncomfortable. It was this desire to appear as a prophet or preacher that led to the spread of many malicious and untrue stories about him, like the one attributed to Ballin, another successful business man, who did not have much patience with metaphysical and mystical flights of rhetoric. It is repeated by Bülow, though even he has the grace to add '*se non e vero e ben trovato*'. According to this story, Rathenau once said to Ballin: 'Since the creation of the world there have been three very great men, curiously enough all Jews: Moses, Jesus—and the third my modesty forbids me to name'.[23]

While occasionally Rathenau was perhaps able to use the fact that he was a Jew to avoid doing things he did not want to do, like getting married or entering politics, his constant awareness of the Jewish part of his nature was a continuous source of tension, and his assertion of his Jewish origins and his refusal to go through the formality of conversion was a constant act of deliberate courage. Indeed, he seems almost to have gone out of his way to provoke reactions of an anti-semitic kind. One of the most curious of his friendships, for example, was with Wilhelm Schwaner, a teacher and publicist who belonged to the extreme wing of the German Nationalist movement, and who produced a 'Bible for Young Teutons' and lived long enough to see the hideous triumph of his ideas under the Nazis. Yet Rathenau was on very close terms with him, addressed him as '*Du*', and, while denying his racial theories, admired and envied his work as a teacher of young blond Germans. Rathenau, indeed, seems to have taken a perverse pleasure in the blows which his friendship with Schwaner inevitably inflicted on him. Schwaner had the habit of sending on to Rathenau letters from his nationalist friends full of abusive attacks on Jews in general and Rathenau in particular, so as to give Rathenau a chance to reply. But in each case, Rathenau refused to take any action, as when he wrote in 1916: 'I know no one by whom I would rather be defended than by you . . . so it is not arrogance when I say I want no protection against unfriendly or hostile men. . . . Why does anyone seek his happiness in the persecution of his neighbour? Because it consoles him and increases his self-esteem to place himself above others. Your correspondent expresses it openly: "If this man Rathenau has helped us, it is a scandal and disgrace." Christ would not have understood that. . . . I know that the Jews in general have their enemies and it is no business of mine to change this. To be fought against is for the majority an element in their education; perhaps these men are destined for a task for which it will take another few hundred years to prepare them.'[24] And again, in 1918, after another similar attack, Rathenau writes to Schwaner: 'I respect your friend because he is your friend. . . . I beg you, dear Wilm, let every-one speak and write about me as he thinks fit and is prepared to take responsibility for. I have no wishes, for my work is done. If it is the fate of my work and of what remains of my life to be persecuted, so be it. That will also be best for our country'.[25]

When Rathenau returned to Berlin from Bitterfeld in 1899, he was not yet as pessimistic as he was to become during the war, but his basic attitudes and ideas had been determined by the long period of isolation and meditation on his own personality, ideals and heritage. But if the period had been important for his intellectual and emotional formation, it had also laid the foundation of his practical business success. He had shown himself a good technician and an imaginative factory manager. He had established his claim to be taken seriously as an industrialist in his own right, independently of his father's achievements. Henceforth his financial and professional independence was assured, and he was quickly to show that he was at least as inventive and enterprising a business man as his father. He later wrote that, on leaving Bitterfeld, he had decided to retire and to devote himself to literature. If he did take this decision, it was short-lived, for he immediately accepted a directorship in his father's firm, the AEG, and became responsible for the construction of power stations in Germany and abroad, including those in Manchester and Genoa.

His success, intelligence and personal charm soon made him a figure in fashionable Berlin society, as well as in the world of artists and writers he preferred to frequent. Count Harry Kessler, his friend and biographer, recalls him at the time of their first meeting. 'Anyone who met him then will remember a slim and very tall young man, who startled one by the abnormal shape of his head, which looked more negroid than European. Deep-set eyes, cold, fawn-coloured, and slow measured movements; a deep voice; and a bland address—these formed the somewhat unexpected, and, as it were, artificial setting for a dazzling display of intellect.'[26] And Stefan Zweig, the Austrian writer, who had been impressed by Rathenau's occasional published aphorisms, remembered, like so many others, above all Rathenau's voice and way of speaking. 'He spoke fluently as if he were reading from an invisible sheet of paper, and yet each single sentence was so well-rounded and clearly formed that, if his conversation had been taken down in shorthand, it would have been a completely finished *exposé* of his theme.'[27] Outwardly, Rathenau's career seemed set for success, financially, socially and intellectually. Yet the inner contradictions in the Germany in which he found himself were mirrored in his own nature, and the tragedy of his life was inextricably entangled with that of the German Empire.

2

'IT IS HARD to over-estimate how strongly the last generation was formed by the influence of Richard Wagner, not so decisively by his music as by the gestures of his characters, by his ideas. Perhaps, though, this is not quite true: perhaps, on the contrary, the gestures of Wagner were the echoes of what pleased his age, for he was as great a listener as composer. It is easy to evoke a gesture, hard to describe it: it was the expression of a kind of theatrical, barbaric military pomp. It expresses itself in the monuments and buildings of Berlin, in the modes of behaviour and cults of certain groups, and was looked upon by many as being truly German. There is always someone— Lohengrin, Walther, Siegfried, Wotan—who can do everything and knock everything down, who can release suffering virtue, punish vice and bring general salvation, striking an exaggerated pose, with the sound of trumpets, and lighting and scenic effects. A reflection of this operatic manner could be seen in politics, even in the use of expressions like "Nibelung loyalty" (*Nibelungentreue*). People wanted the word of salvation to be spoken on every occasion with a great gesture, people wanted to see historical turning points presented before them, they wanted to hear the clash of swords and the flapping of banners.'[28]

This was how Walther Rathenau, on the eve of defeat in 1918, looked back on the Germany of his youth, and, for all his misunderstanding of Wagner's symbolism, it was a fair comment on the false and theatrical nature of German politics, particularly in the reign of William II, who came to the throne in 1888, five years after Wagner's death. The Kaiser himself, whose histrionic nature and desire to strike attitudes constantly overcame his own natural intelligence, set the tone. 'For sovereigns every day is a fancy dress ball,' one of his friends said. 'The surprising thing is that they like it.'[29] There were plenty of members of the public ready to respond, either by

tolerating the sycophancy of a court that its critics described as
'Byzantine', or by applauding a foreign and naval policy based
largely on the search for prestige, and executed by means of
gestures whose purpose and effects were never fully understood.

Rathenau, while constantly critical both of the Kaiser's
behaviour and of the institutions of the Empire, yet had a
certain sympathy with William II, whom he saw on a number
of occasions, and whom he described as 'a true prince; conscious of the impression he was making, forcing his nature so
as to give it dignity, strength, mastery. There was scarcely an
unselfconscious moment; the only unconscious thing, and that
was where he began to be a touching human being, was the
struggle with himself; a nature set against itself without its
knowledge'.[30] When Rathenau applies to the Kaiser words
which are not an inaccurate description of himself, it is easy
to see why he felt sympathy for a monarch many of whose
actions he criticised violently. A visitor after the war and the
Revolution noticed a chair in Rathenau's office with a cord
across it to prevent anyone sitting on it: 'Is that the chair your
father used?' he asked. 'No' was the reply. 'That is the chair
on which the Kaiser used to sit.' Rathenau's attitude to the
Kaiser was typical of his ambivalent attitude to the society of
his time.

There was no doubt of Rathenau's ability to profit by the
opportunities which the German, and, indeed, the international economy presented at the beginning of the twentieth
century. After three years as director of the AEG, Rathenau
went into banking and joined the board of the *Berliner Handels-
gesellschaft* in 1902. He rapidly became involved in one of those
networks of interlocking financial and industrial enterprises
typical of capitalist organisation in Germany. As a banker he
was responsible for the financing of industrial undertakings:
as a director of the AEG he was interested in firms which
supplied raw materials for the electrical industry (metals, glass,
chemicals, for example) as well as in those enterprises which
used the products of the electrical industry—telegraph companies, tramways or power stations. He soon branched out
into other new and expanding fields such as motor cars, aviation
and ship building, and his interests included not only important

European undertakings, among them the electricity supply of Genoa or the tramways of Seville, but also mines in Africa and electric railways in South America. 'Electricity is . . . not an industry,' he wrote in 1907, 'but a complex of industries, a sphere of the economy. It includes lighting and power, transport undertakings, the machine tool industry, the steam engine industry, centralisation and decentralisation of the production and distribution of power, and it links up with nearly all the other well-known fields of industry today.'[31] By 1909 he was more or less permanently associated with eighty-four large concerns, and had, at one time or another in the decade before the First World War, been closely involved with eighty-six German companies and twenty-one foreign ones.[32] There was no doubt about his position among the 'three-hundred men, all acquainted with each other', who, according to him, controlled the economic destiny of the continent.[33]

Inevitably, all this activity made Rathenau very rich indeed. His attitude to money was as ambiguous as his attitude to most other things. He affected to despise luxury, and genuinely hated the ostentation in which so many of his fellow-financiers lived. When he bought Schloss Freienwalde, he was at pains to point out that he was only doing so in order to preserve a historical and artistic monument from the speculative builders. He claimed that his house in Berlin was a 'decent middle class' home (*bürgerlich anständig*).[34] What he never realised was that the carefully cultivated simplicity and restrained elegance in which he lived were in fact refinements only possible to the very rich, with each piece of furniture carefully selected, each object an exquisite example of its kind.

Rathenau was sometimes very generous; but more often his wealth made him suspicious of other people's motives in their relations with him, and it became yet one more barrier between him and the outside world. He became, as presumably all rich and prominent people must, very skilful at refusing requests. 'I cannot refrain from pointing out,' he wrote to a "Society for the Improvement of Convicts", 'that your name offends my sensibilities. It does not correspond to my ideas that one part of mankind should proclaim of itself that it has the intention of improving another part.'[35] And to someone who asked him to lend his support of Bacon's claims to have written Shakespeare, he answers urbanely: 'I do not feel myself called upon or capable to take sides in the great Bacon controversy. Questions which learning has made its own I must leave to researchers, among whom I do not count myself; the layman must refrain from hypotheses and judgments based on emotion.'[36]

Requests from individual friends and acquaintances were harder to deal with; and it was a subject on which Rathenau was even more suspicious. 'Friendship is almost impossible for those whose situation presupposes that they can fulfil certain kinds of wishes,' he noted.[37] Among his letters in the spring of 1918 there are some to a certain Herr E. in Zurich which reveal how profound this attitude was. This gentleman had written to Rathenau, sending some of his writings, and clearly asking for some sort of help. Rathenau's reply is revealing, both in its suspicions, and in the underlying desire for understanding and intimacy. '. . . What do you want from me? You know of me that I am considered a man with money: that I write books and consequently understand a language that is not the language of money. . . . I am fairly old. Years ago I was inclined to make a present of my heart. A kind word unlocked me. Although a Jew, I am not suspicious but easily trusting. When I saw that people wanted to use me as a means to an end, I was shattered, dishonoured, humiliated, betrayed. I would gladly have given help of my own free will: but to be a tool, abused, despised and thought to be stupid? To be a traitor himself betrayed? Wounded vanity is very hard to heal: it took some time to recover. . . .'[38] And yet, a month later, Rathenau was writing: 'I have given instructions for a monthly allowance to be paid to you till 1 June, 1919. You will compare the sum with my income and find it small, even when I tell you that this income is not inherited from my father but has been earned, and I do not regard it as my property. So now for a time a third person is working for you, a person who up to now has worked not for me, but through me for others. The world is poorer than you think, and allows its scarce goods, which are being terribly squandered today, to be wrested from it less easily than you think. You will call this remark tactless and out of place; I cannot help that; I am finally finished as a means for you. But you are not finished for me. For I take an interest in your existence and your troubles. I beg you sincerely, work, even though it is hard for you. If I had not worked hard years ago, near you in the aluminium factory at Neuhausen, for a salary of two hundred francs, I would not be able to offer you some modest assistance today.'[39]

It is a curious and tantalising fragment of correspondence, but it shows much of Rathenau's attitude to his own riches— the fear of being exploited, the pride at having made his fortune independently of his father's, as well as his extreme sensibility and touchiness in his relations with other people. Yet his wealth was, as Count Harry Kessler suggests, also a means of protecting himself from people, a way of ensuring that he was treated with respect and consideration. What is surprising about Rathenau is not so much that he made money, but that he went on making it. In fact the activity of running a vast business was something that was for him satisfying in itself. 'I should like to stress,' he wrote, 'that anyone who thinks only of making money for himself can never be a great business man.'[40] Elsewhere he spoke of the satisfaction resulting from having created new industries. 'When I saw newly founded villages grow to towns filled with men who extracted power from the depths of the niggardly earth, when a thousand machines turned their wheels and a hundred factory chimneys made their offerings of smoke, then I was pleased to remember that it was a bold idea to start mines in this despised place, and I was glad, looking back, at all the trouble and worry with which each foot of this land had to be fertilised.'[41]

If, on the one hand, Rathenau wanted riches to enable him to lead the kind of independent existence he needed in order to protect his own sensitive nature, the making of them must have required qualities other than those of the philosopher and mystic he believed himself to be. He was familiar with every detail of his businesses; he was a tough and shrewd negotiator; he would carry out unheralded and meticulous inspections of his factories. As an employer, he was just, remote and urbane. He took a paternal interest in individual workers: 'I have long been in correspondence with gifted workers,' he told the War

Minister in 1917. 'The unsatisfied longing for intellectual things, for nature and life, is astounding.'[42] But he bitterly resented any interference in his relations with his workers, whether by individuals or by trades unions. 'I consider it neither as an advantage nor as a favour when anyone, however high his intellectual position, takes it on himself to speak for my workers,'[43] he wrote in 1913. He expected from his staff and workers adherence to his own standards of seriousness, devotion and hard work. 'The Englishman,' he wrote, 'prosperous, healthy, enjoying his strength (*muskelfroh*), loves work, but he does not sacrifice himself to it. He demands weekdays off, hours off during the day, country life and sport. The German loves his work above everything, is insatiable of knowledge, and, if his love of work fails, there is his inflexible conscientiousness which redoubles his sense of duty.'[44] The only thing, he went on to say, that hampered English industry was the Trade Unions; and he remained all his life an enemy of the Trade Unions in Germany as well as of the Social Democratic Party. Thus, however critical he became of the existing social system, to the workers he inevitably remained one of the bosses. His own view of the way to handle subordinates is expressed in a letter to a friend: 'Men are bad almost only because of inner or external anxiety. A man who bears a grudge against you is a poor fellow who is unhappy, and who believes, wrongly, that he will be happier if he makes your life difficult for you. On the contrary you must talk to your own people—frankly, in a friendly way, as man to man.'[45] One cannot escape the suspicion that a frank talk from Rathenau might well have turned into a metaphysical or ethical lecture.

While Rathenau was often forced into the company of his fellow business men and of politicians, he avoided public life, even though his wealth and his friendly relations with the Kaiser and with both Bülow and Bethmann-Hollweg might have given him opportunities, in spite of his being a Jew. The only public service he performed before 1914 was, at Bülow's request, to accompany Bernhard Dernburg, the Colonial Secretary, on two tours of Germany's African colonies in 1907 and 1908. It is not clear what the purpose of these trips was; perhaps, as Kessler suggests, Bülow wanted, at a moment when German colonial policy had been severely criticised by the Liberals, Catholics and Social-Democrats, to give an appearance of detached, impartial interest in colonial problems by sending a non-political economic and financial expert to Africa. In fact, Rathenau's African expeditions left no mark on German colonial policy nor on his own ideas, and they remained an isolated excursion into public life. In spite of his growing financial success and influence, it was as a man of letters and a philosopher that he thought of himself. The people he saw most were novelists, playwrights and poets—Frank Wedekind, Gerhart Hauptmann or Richard Dehmel; during the war he got to know Rilke; his portrait was painted by his friend, the Norwegian expressionist painter Edvard Munch. (It was a picture of which Rathenau said, with one of those ironical comments on his own character that occasionally shake the composure of his own view of himself: 'A nasty fellow, isn't he? That is because when you have your picture painted by a great artist, you become more like yourself than you are'.)[46]

Yet, when he was with original creative artists, he was more interested in talking to them about his ideas than in listening to theirs. When he first met Rilke, on a walk in the Tiergarten, Rilke, always an elusive man, could not get a word in. Rathenau wanted to be taken seriously as a writer, and he seems to have wanted to establish that he was the equal of the writers whom he knew. He exchanged telegrams in verse with Hauptmann and Dehmel; he gave Wedekind advice about the construction of his plays; he quoted Plato in Greek to his admirers, and on one occasion, after reading aloud a translation by Rilke of a sonnet by Louise Labé, he was so enthralled by his own performance that he insisted on going off immediately to a friend's house to repeat it. He had begun to publish essays and articles in the nineties, mostly anonymously, and in 1908 he published under his own name a volume of *Reflexions*, in which he collected some of these writings. The book was expensively and elaborately produced, and Rathenau was bitterly hurt and disappointed when it was not taken seriously by the critics. The result was to make him devote himself with renewed energy to producing his next two books, first *Kritik der Zeit*, published in 1912, and then *Zur Mechanik des Geistes*, which he considered a major piece of philosophical writing, and which appeared in 1913.

Rathenau's friendship with writers and artists, some of whom, such as Wedekind and Munch, represented the most advanced trends of the day, left surprisingly little impression on his own tastes and interests. He remained consistently hostile to modern art. Although his cousin Max Liebermann had done so much to introduce the taste for French Impressionists into Germany, for Walther Rathenau Watteau remained the greatest French painter, and, although his mother possessed a picture by Vuillard, nothing so contemporary decorated the walls of Freienwalde or the house in Grunewald. He rarely went to the theatre, and indeed had strong views on the difference between art and entertainment, which banished into the latter category much of the most interesting contemporary work. 'Art has nothing to do with pleasure. Art enriches the soul, pleasure gives it the illusion of escaping from its poverty.'[47] In his attitude to art, as in everything else, Rathenau was torn between his admiration for spontaneous insight and feeling—'Dons are there to prove things,'* he once wrote[48]—and his desire to analyse everything in terms of his own active intellect and include it in a comprehensive rational system: 'aesthetic enjoyment arises when a concealed orderliness is discovered.'[49]

Although Rathenau cultivated the company of writers and painters, his relations with them suffered from the same inhibitions that made all his friendships so precarious and unsatisfactory. Someone once called him 'the Don Juan of friendship'; and, all through life, one has the impression that he was looking for some ideal relationship he was never able to find. People of all kinds would be taken up with enormous enthusiasm only to be dropped again; one would conform to Rathenau's ideal of a blond Prussian physical type; another would seem for a moment to be the one person who really understood his ideas; and it seemed impossible to find anyone who combined both aspects. André Gide, who met Rathenau in 1920, gives a vivid account of the almost embarrassing

*'Zum beweisen sind die Privatdozenten da.'

effusiveness with which he greeted a promising new acquaint-
ance: 'I was at first a little embarrassed by the extreme
affability of this huge man who at once took my arm to lead me
along the garden paths.'[50] And, again, on their second meeting:
'I find it very difficult not to be embarrassed by the over-
cordial way in which he takes hold of one; his hand hardly left
my arm during our whole conversation, the refrain of which
was "All Europe is heading for the abyss".'[51]

Early in his life, Rathenau seems to have decided not to
marry, but women were among his closest and most constant
friends—always provided that they did not expect more than
an exchange of poetical, sentimental or metaphysical letters.
Minka Grönvold, the wife of a Norwegian painter, Lore
Karrenbrock, Fanny Künstler, a feminist writer, Lilli von
Mendelssohn, the daughter of old friends, for whom he felt
avuncular affection, and, most important of all, Lili Deutsch,
the sister of the banker Otto Kahn, and the wife of one of
Rathenau's colleagues, all played an important part as sentimental or affectionate friends. But Rathenau made it quite
clear both to Fanny Künstler and to Lore Karrenbrock what
the limits of such relationships were. 'Thank you for your dear
letter, the warmth and goodness of which touched me deeply,'
he wrote to Fanny Künstler. 'In early years my desires were
strong and my need for human contact great. I was filled with
the urge to express myself, to feel confidence in, to enjoy, to
live with another person, not only in cases of passion, but also
in everyday life. Even today I am still subject to passion,
but a change has begun. It is as if two men were living in me,
of whom one is growing, the other dying. The one that is dying
is the acquisitive one who rejoices in the external world, and
with him is dying much that is lively, colourful, frank, and
joyous, and the other, whom I can scarcely call me any more,
is growing up. For the latter does not worry any more about my
destiny, he wants things that are impersonal and makes me the
servant of powers which need give me no account of their
actions.'[52] And to Lore Karrenbrock he wrote in 1920: 'Union
exists only in the realm of the senses, and this is but fleeting
illusion. But souls fall one behind another like shooting stars
and cannot leave their orbits and do not meet. If that were to

happen, it would be like running into the sun, a disintegration into atoms. For your heart there is only one thing: to give it to those who need it; men are so much poorer than you know, and every child, I think, needs your heart. . . .'[53]

Even in the case of Frau Deutsch one cannot help wondering whether the fact that she was safely and, apparently, happily married did not make Rathenau's relationship with her easier. It certainly seems to have been the closest and most spontaneous of his affections. Moreover, they did not always see a great deal of each other, though, when they did, Rathenau was always ready to see difficulties and take offence: '. . . Your image has always been with me,' he writes in a letter of 1913. 'Your image—for our actual meetings are no longer a success. When we meet among other people I feel a tension and an embarrassment which makes every word constrained. For a few moments you control yourself with effort. I feel it—and then comes a movement, a look or a word which wounds me to the quick, which—forgive me for speaking so freely—infuriates me. And then against my own nature I become suspicious and prone to take offence. . . . When we are alone, on the other hand, other things are blown aside like a breath, as if they were lies and foolishness. I remember you once saying to me: "But come, we can't talk about botany"—and then nothing remains but the I and the Thou: however, even then we are not united and the atmosphere remains troubled and threatening.'[54]

In this atmosphere of troubled, intense relations, of friendships quickly made and quickly dropped, there were a few people who knew how to deal with Rathenau and retain his affection. There was Ernst Norlind, a Swedish painter and writer, who was introduced to Rathenau in 1915 by Gustav Landauer, the writer and anarchist politician. Norlind had the advantage of being a Swede, for Rathenau felt Sweden to be one of the few countries where his works were really understood; and the distance between Berlin and Sweden made the relationship all the easier since it was possible for them not to see too much of each other. Norlind quickly saw the paradox of Rathenau's life, and thought it odd to be talking about religion and metaphysics over smoked salmon and good Rhine wine, but by September 1919 Rathenau was writing to him: 'Since my father and brother died—they are not dead for me—there has been no one of whom I could say in the highest sense that he is my friend—except you. This is something I had to say to you.'[55] (The high-flown sentimental tone of so many of Rathenau's letters to his men friends strikes an English reader as odd, but that it was not an unusual epistolary style in the Germany of William II is shown by the published correspondence between Hugo von Hofmannsthal and Eberhard von Bodenhausen, an industrialist nearly as successful as Rathenau himself.) Another great friend was Gustav Steinbömer, one of the most curious and sympathetic figures of his age, an officer of the Prussian general staff and a childhood companion of the Crown Prince, whose understanding of the theatrical side of military life made him after the war an assistant producer in Reinhardt's theatre, and who, on leaving the army, took a degree in art history and became a writer. His autobiography *Herren und Narren der Welt*, published under the pseudonym of Gustav Hillard, not only gives an affectionate and ironical picture of Rathenau but is also one of the most attractive accounts of life in Germany in the first quarter of the century. He understood Rathenau very well, and he was impressed by his charm and by his real desire for affection and friendship. They first met in 1916 in Frankfurt; and it was typical of the enthusiasm with which Rathenau flung himself into new friendships that they should have been so enthralled by their conversation that they missed their train to Berlin and travelled together, still talking, in the next one. It was a meeting that Rathenau did not forget; and in his will he left Steinbömer the gold cigarette case which Steinbömer had picked up off the floor for him on this first occasion.

As important as his complicated, difficult, exacting friendships was Rathenau's growing sense of isolation from the social and political system in which he lived. For a time this made him a friend of the most ruthless, brilliant, courageous and unscrupulous journalist of the day, Maximilian Harden. Like Rathenau, a highly-strung Jew, 'hard to define and easy to abuse', as Hofmannsthal put it, Harden used his paper '*Die Zukunft*', in which Rathenau's first literary essays had appeared, as the vehicle for a series of violent and effective attacks on the political and social life of Germany. Harden did not hesitate to attack the Kaiser himself, and it was he who started the cruel assault on the Kaiser's friend Philipp Eulenburg and began one of the most famous scandals of the age in order to discredit the Kaiser and his *entourage*, an example of Harden's methods which showed clearly the difference between them and Rathenau's general impersonal criticisms of German society. (Rathenau, indeed, on this occasion supported Bülow's efforts to get the Eulenburg case dropped.) It was inevitable that Rathenau should sooner or later quarrel with Harden, and in 1912, in circumstances that are not clear (Kessler speaks of 'a personal difference'), Rathenau actually challenged Harden to a duel which Harden refused to fight.* Although their relations were later partly restored, Harden remained bitter, and Rathenau hurt and offended.

It was Rathenau's simultaneous rejection of the values of German society and his use of that society as a basis for his worldly success that infuriated his enemies and sometimes puzzled his friends. His criticisms were at two levels; on the one hand there were shrewd analyses and comments on Germany's political and economic structure and, on the other hand, there was a mystical rejection of the whole of the life of this world and an insistence on other, profounder values. Rathenau himself would never have separated the two parts of his thought in this way, however; his plans for a new society were inextricably involved in his belief that this must be based on a new set of spiritual values.

Rathenau began to formulate his quasi-mystical beliefs on a trip to Greece in 1906, from which he returned with a sheet of writing paper on which he had written out a '*Breviarium Mysticum*'. It is worth quoting, because all Rathenau's later metaphysical writings are merely a development of these ideas in much the same terminology.

'I   Every man's picture of the world is the measure of his soul.

II   Many are born with a soul, all can achieve one.

III   The soul is vouchsafed to everyone who is *bonae voluntatis*. *Bona voluntas* means the will to what is good.

*It seems that Harden accused Rathenau of plagiarising some of his writing.

IV   The soul is the reflection of God.

V   The powers of the soul are threefold: Imagination, Love, Respect.

VI   Through imagination it grasps the world, through imagination and love living creatures, with all three the power of God.

VII   The soul serves no ulterior aim, the intellect serves an aim (*Die Seele ist zweckfrei, der Verstand zweckhaft*).

VIII In its struggle with the intellect the soul is victorious because the intellect defeats its own ends.

IX   Art and unconscious creation are the language of the soul, science and conscious creation are the language of the intellect.

X   The soul is nourished by the urge to life, the intellect by fear of death.'[56]

These are ideas developed again and again in Rathenau's later philosophical writings; and, as always when dealing with the language of personal religious experience—and this is what Rathenau thought he was expressing—it is hard to give an account of his beliefs that means anything for those who have not had similar experiences and do not already share Rathenau's view of the world. Rathenau's ideas certainly do not emerge very much more clearly from his major metaphysical work, *Zur Mechanik des Geistes: oder vom Reich der Seele* (*On the Mechanism of the Spirit: or concerning the Kingdom of the Soul*), published in 1913. It is an ambitious work which attempts both to give a psychological account of human beings and to preach a way of life for them. The basis of Rathenau's philosophy is the distinction between that part of human nature—the soul—which seeks no ulterior aim and whose activity is some sort of mystical contemplation of the other world and the achievement of unity with God, and the intellect, which is concerned only with practical goals (*Zwecke*) to be obtained in this world. Parallel with this is another distinction, already put forward in an essay of 1904, between the '*Zweckmensch*' or '*Furchtmensch*', the man whom fear drives to seek some sort of security in the achievement of worldly success, and the '*Mutmensch*', the man who has the courage to break away from the values of the world and to think only of God and the soul. It is clear that these warring elements—the soul and the intellect, fear and courage—are the conflicting forces that Rathenau recognised in his own character, and this becomes even plainer when one reads his description of the characteristics of the man of fear and the man of courage. The *Furchtmensch* is described thus: 'In order to shine he becomes talkative and exaggerates; he is far from having a disinterested and warm relationship with other people, for they are either means to an end or else just the masses. Anxiety and insecurity drive him to self analysis, fear of other people's superiority makes him critical, deprecatory and malicious. The virtues that he understands are sympathy and charity, which he practices half from fear of his own possible misfortunes and half from satisfaction at other people's bad luck.'[57] The *Furchtmensch*, in fact, represents all the aspects of Rathenau's own nature he was fighting to suppress. The qualities of the *Mutmensch*, on the other hand, are self-sacrifice, humility, truthfulness and 'transcendence'—the latter virtue apparently being the disinterestedness that seeks no worldly goal but only the self-fulfilment of the soul—, all the virtues which Rathenau believed he was cultivating.

Once this basic distinction between fear and courage, intellect and the soul, has been established it can be applied to the whole of experience. There are, for example, two kinds of art; Manet and Zola are, according to Rathenau, typical representatives of the art of the *Zweckmensch*—the man whose goals are this world—while Rembrandt embodied the art of the soul. History, too, is divided into periods in which the soul predominates, and 'intellectual' periods. 'The rule of faith, of loyalty, of war, of positive ideals, is characteristic of the periods of the soul. The rule of the material, of *raison d'état*, of peace, academic learning and analysis are characteristic of periods of the intellect.'[58]

There was no doubt about the sort of period the early twentieth century was; and the last part of *Zur Mechanik des Geistes* as well as much of Rathenau's other writing, notably *Zur Kritik der Zeit* (1912) and *Von kommenden Dingen* (1917), is devoted to an analysis of contemporary society and to suggestions as to how the rule of the soul can be substituted for the rule of material ends. Rathenau's social and economic criticism is a curious mixture of shrewd specific observations about the Germany and Europe of his day, and general recommendations so vague that it is often very hard to see what practical arrangements he would like to see made in order to realise the kingdom of the soul in this world. The imprecision of so many of his general views contrasts strangely with his practical grasp of administrative and economic detail and his genuine insight into specific situations. It was, he felt, the coming of machines that had been disastrous for the world. On the one hand, mechanisation marked an enormous step in human material progress: 'I consider that mechanisation is one of the great movements of history, comparable to the introduction of agriculture in prehistoric times, or the great discoveries of primitive times—weapons, fire and clothing.'[59] And mechanisation had possibilities for human improvement: 'It is not just crass materialism if I believe that in the new city there will be more dynamos than pearly gates.'[60] Yet, on the other hand, whatever potentialities for good mechanisation might have in releasing men from degrading and pointless tasks, its results in practice had so far been an unmitigated disaster, and had led to the virtual disappearance of the 'soul' from contemporary society.

At this point, Rathenau links his belief in the superiority of the 'world of the soul' over the world of practical ends, with his cult of the German past, and he declares bluntly in *Zur Mechanik des Geistes* that mechanisation and 'degermanisation' (*Entgermanisierung*) have come about simultaneously, so that the establishment of the kingdom of the soul will necessarily bring about the restoration of some sort of pristine German moral and social values. The effects of mechanisation have been that the labouring masses have been thrust out of the community and doomed to a lifetime of pointless mechanical work. The worker's interests are far removed from those of the educated classes, who have no idea how to appeal to him. 'The academic intellect cannot think of anything else for the education and improvement of the lower classes except the old childish means: pictures, the theatre, music, literature, the humanities. These things are without meaning for the intelligent proletarian. An automobile is more important to him than the Parthenon and a boat race more interesting than Schiller's *Maid of Orleans*.'[61] The Social Democratic Party was powerless to help the situation; it was 'a church and not a faith' [62]; it had 'never kindled the hearts of mankind, and no great and successful deed has ever been done in its name; it has aroused interests and produced fear'.[63] Rathenau consistently underestimated the efficiency and strength of the organised labour movement in Germany, and the intellectual power and attraction of Marxism. Like so many other critics of Marx's teaching, he thought that once he had proved that the labour theory of value was fallacious, he had disposed of Marx as a serious thinker.

If mechanisation had created the problem of a soulless mass of workers cut off from any true national community, it had also produced a complicated and disastrous political situation. 'It will be difficult for future writers of German history to understand how, in our time, two class systems could penetrate each other; the first is a survival of the feudal system, the second the capitalist class system, a phenomenon produced by mechanisation itself. But it will strike him as even odder that the newly arisen capitalist order had first of all to contribute to the strengthening of the feudal order.'[64] This was a true analysis. One of the difficulties of the Wilhelmine Reich and the tragedy of the Weimar Republic was that there was never a responsible Conservative party. On the one hand, the old Prussian aristocracy was determined to maintain its political, economic and social position, and to sacrifice everything rather than this; on the other, the industrialists were interested only in their profits, in their own position in the state, and in keeping the workers in their place; and they were prepared to make an alliance with the old ruling class for these purposes. This, as Rathenau realised clearly, had led to Germany being in the hands of a ruling class that was both selfish and short-sighted. 'We are not threatened by the working class, because the socialism of today lacks the power of positive ideas. Two other weak points will shatter the Prussian state: the lack of leaders (*führende Geister*) and the unfair distribution of burdens.'[65]

Rathenau's criticisms of the German state and society were to become more specific during the war. In his pre-war writings he was content to suggest how he thought Germany might be turned into a real *Volksstaat*, an organic state in which each citizen had a part, and which would embody what he regarded as the values of the 'kingdom of the soul'. Hereditary wealth was to be abolished; the hereditary class structure and restricted culture of an aristocratic society would disappear; and the vast productive power of modern mechanised industry would be available to increase production, so as to satisfy and liberate not only the German workers, but also the inhabitants of less fortunate countries. To do this, industry must be properly planned and organised; distribution must be centralised; consumption of frivolous luxury goods must be curtailed. And he ended *Zur Mechanik des Geistes* with these words: 'Thus we stand at the gates of that kingdom which is not of this world but which yet has its beginnings there, the kingdom which is known by its evangelists as the kingdom of heaven and the kingdom of God, and which in this poor worldly book hovers above us as the kingdon of the Soul'.[66]

There is nothing very original in Rathenau's philosophy: bits of Nietzsche and Bergson (although Rathenau affected to despise his work), strong echoes of Fichte, and the dehydrated mysticism of Rathenau's own eclectic religious beliefs. Rathenau was enormously sensitive to criticism and deeply disappointed that his large work—over 340 pages of elaborate prose—was not at once hailed as a masterpiece. He was gradually to win admirers, especially in Scandinavia, while his economic ideas were taken seriously abroad: a French study of them was published in 1919. But what made, and makes, so much of his economic and social analysis difficult to read is the way in which it is involved with the metaphysical and mystical speculation that was for him the most important part of his thought. Above all, it was his own worldly position—and this is at the centre of his frustration and unhappiness—which both stopped him being taken as seriously as he would have liked and aroused the enmity of many people. The spectacle of one of the richest financiers and industrialists in Europe advocating the abolition of inherited wealth, stiff taxation and the restriction of luxury production and consumption was bound to seem at least paradoxical, and, to Rathenau's fellow business men and many members of the ruling class in Germany, dangerous, sinister and subversive.

The criticism that upset Rathenau most was an article by the Viennese novelist Robert Musil in the *Neue Rundschau*, in which Musil said that Rathenau treated metaphysics 'as a patent of nobility and as heraldic speculation which suspends the discarded skin of experience from the stars'.[67] Rathenau had met Musil at the house of the Munich writer, Franz Blei, and was outraged by the attack. 'My evenings with you have become a bitter memory,' he wrote to Blei. 'For where my life's work is regarded as a failure, I can only serve to entertain, and this is a service that gives me no pleasure.'[68] If Rathenau remembered his meetings with Musil as a source of bitterness, they were impressed on Musil in a different form, and Arnheim, one of the leading characters in Musil's great novel *The Man Without Qualities*, bears an unmistakable resemblance to Rathenau. Musil's criticism of Rathenau is not wholly unjustified. There is, for all the insight of some of Rathenau's analytical and prophetic passages, a peculiar lifelessness and remoteness about his philosophical speculations. A critic, writing just before Rathenau's death in 1922, summed it up well. 'These books, in spite of their wide circulation in a period avid for metaphysics, have not exercised the slightest influence; there is not a trace to be found of real effect on the older or younger generation of really front-rank intellectuals. Today they already seem to be in the same class as the poems, architecture and music of crowned heads; works of a superior, educated dilettante of somewhat uncertain taste, who has no idea of what has been done before him or around him, without critical awareness of what he owes to others, of what is a new discovery and what is just a new formulation. . . . Compared with his essays in the field of philosophy, even a Lotze seems an intellectual giant and an Emerson a creative genius.'[69]

One of Rathenau's tragedies was a misplaced sense of vocation; his acute analytical intellect and his practical and administrative ability did not satisfy him. It is as if he felt that only by rising above the limitations of his Jewish birth and his inner hesitations and anxieties, into some purely spiritual realm, could he be taken at his own valuation. Instead, his writings only made him more enemies, and placed him in a false position from which he was never to escape.

3

'THE EPOCH IN which we were born began with a war; now it is coming to an end with a war,' Rathenau wrote to Fanny Künstler on 19 August 1914.[70] 'The new life which it befell us to proclaim is dawning, a life which will be stronger and deeper than the lamentable end of the old life. But this birth is a hard one and will take a long time; it will not be finished with the peace settlement. In the old world we were young, in the new we are old. Will events overtake us? That would be splendid. And it would still be splendid enough if we are able to see the dawn. Moses saw his promised land.' The belief that the war would be long and hard, and that because of it things would never be the same again, separated Rathenau from the majority of his fellow countrymen. For them the outbreak of the war was a moment of great optimism. Not only did the Crown Prince exhort them to a bright and jolly war (*ein frisch–fröhlicher Krieg*) but also many even of the most respectable Germans welcomed the war as an escape from the dead end of German political life, an opportunity to forget their differences and to come together in support of a great national cause of a kind there had not been since the achievement of German unity in 1870. Even as moderate a man as the historian Friedrich Meinecke could still, years after, look back on August, 1914, as 'one of the great moments of my life which suddenly filled my soul with the deepest confidence in our people and the profoundest joy.'[71] And Rathenau himself in 1918 remembered the first weeks of the war as 'great and unforgettable. It was the ringing opening chord for an immortal song of sacrifice, loyalty and heroism'.[72]

Rathenau, when he came back to Berlin from the peace of Freienwalde, where the landscape had been looking exceptionally lovely in the sun of that ironically beautiful summer, was torn between his feelings of deep German patriotism and his prophetic forebodings about the length and horrors of the war.

He immediately offered his services to Bethmann-Hollweg, the Imperial Chancellor; and, at the same time, he approached the War Ministry with suggestions about wartime economic organisation. While he never, to the last, doubted that Germany would eventually win the war, he realised that it would be longer and harder than most of those responsible for the planning of German strategy imagined. On 7 September, he sent Bethmann-Hollweg a memorandum in which he set out his reasons for believing that England, always for him the real enemy, was economically in a position to sustain a long war. At the same time he pointed out that the only hope for Germany and Europe was a negotiated peace with France that would remove England's reasons for continuing the war: 'The final goal would be the one situation which can bring about the balance of power in Europe for the future: Central Europe united under German leadership, politically and economically fortified against Russia on the one hand and England and America on the other. The sacrifice we would have to make would be the renunciation of the acquisition of French territory and a moderate indemnity'.[73] And he went on to outline the strategy which, after France's acceptance of peace terms, would be needed to eliminate Britain: 'Systematic working on the nerves of the cities by means of an overwhelming air force on a considerably larger scale than hitherto suggested: use of the western ports of France to break the Atlantic blockade: a threat to the English position in the Mediterranean, especially in Egypt, Gibraltar, and Suez: above all the economic unity and liberation of central Europe'.[74] It is a strategic programme not far from that adopted by the Germans in the Second World War.

However, while Rathenau was thinking about the peace terms and the subsequent economic reorganisation of Central Europe, he was also aware of more immediate and pressing economic needs. He soon convinced the War Minister that, unless Germany's stocks of raw materials were properly controlled and use made of the stocks captured in Belgium and northern France, Germany would soon run short of certain essential things—notably saltpetre for the manufacture of explosives. Accordingly, Rathenau was very soon made head of a specially

constituted department of the War Ministry responsible for
the supply of raw materials. The months he spent in this post
were, from a practical point of view, extremely successful; and
his work, backed by the technical ability of Wichard von Moel-
lendorff, a former official of the AEG, contributed to preparing
the German economy to withstand a long war and an effective
blockade. Rathenau's experience of the higher administration
from the inside did not lessen his misgivings about the future
or reassure him about the way in which the German state was
being run. But it did for the time being satisfy his need to be of
some use to the German cause, in which, for all his doubts
about the future, he never ceased to believe. 'You look after
hearts and I look after weapons,' he told his propagandist
teacher friend Wilhelm Schwaner. 'Harder times are coming,
for before victory is granted to us much must be purged
away. Sometimes I cannot sleep for tiredness.'[75] And to Stefan
Zweig, who had thrown himself passionately into the campaign
which Romain Rolland was waging from Switzerland for an
end to the war and the maintenance of humane international
standards, Rathenau wrote: 'I could not live if I had not created
an activity for myself which enables me to wage a campaign
with my own hands—the campaign for raw materials. . . .'[76]

At the end of six months, Rathenau regarded his personal
part in this campaign as finished. He gave up his post in
March 1915, and handed over to an army officer whom he had
selected. He had ensured that stocks were properly conserved
and controlled and that captured supplies were put to a proper
use; he had introduced important technical innovations and
established new factories; and he had set up a new type of
private company under public control (the *Kriegsgesellschaft*)
which was, as Rathenau realised, in its 'position between a joint
stock company which embodies the capitalist form of private
enterprise, and a bureaucratic organisation, an industrial form
which perhaps foreshadows the future'.[77] Rathenau's effective
work of organisation at the War Ministry had enhanced his
position in the economic and political world; yet it had also
left its rancours. He was not an easy man to work with; he
was a Jew; he was a civilian in a Ministry mainly staffed by
soldiers, while civilian business men resented his authority over

their transactions. When he gave up his job, he was upset that he had received no word of gratitude. 'Neither of the groups concerned can forgive me that I, a private citizen and a Jew, have done the state some service of my own accord, and I do not think that this attitude will change in my lifetime,'[78] he wrote a year later to Emil Ludwig. His immediate mood after resigning was even blacker, and he told Frau Deutsch 'You must forgive me, but at present I find any but the most casual conversation impossible. I feel so sore at heart that every word which goes beneath the surface causes me pain. I try to concentrate my thoughts on some more or less distant subject and perform a few unimportant daily tasks. I hope we shall see each other when I am in the country. I was there yesterday—blossom and blue sky and death over all'.[79]

In fact, there were plenty of daily tasks waiting for him, and they were not unimportant, for, in June 1915 Emil Rathenau died, and Walther became president of the AEG. He felt more alone than ever before. 'I have been too long accustomed to inner loneliness,' he wrote to Schwaner, in September. 'It cannot now be broken. Until recently I regretted that the passionate experiences which filled my middle years did not lead to establishing a home and family life. Now that is past. What I still want is very little: to complete the series of my writings, if possible; then there is also the—probably temporary—task of helping my father's work to survive our present economic difficulties. What comes then, I do not ask. In these war years, I have gone grey; and it is something I feel inside me as well. . . .'[80] His personal loneliness was reinforced by his sense of political isolation and his forebodings about the future. 'Which of us knows if he will live to see peace?' he had written in October 1914. 'We shall live through more difficult things than we have ever seen. A hard race will grow up and perhaps it will trample on our hearts.'[81] Colonel House, President Wilson's representative, who visited Berlin in March 1915, noted the same mood. 'I met last night an able and sane man by the name of Dr Rathenau. . . . He has such a clear vision of the situation and such a prophetic forecast as to the future that I wonder how many there are in Germany that think like him. It saddened me to hear him say that as far as he knew, he stood alone. He said he had begun to wonder whether all the rest were really mad, or whether the madness lay within himself.'[82]

All the criticisms he had ever made of German society and politics now seemed to Rathenau to be justified; the chances of a just, negotiated peace, which he had hoped for in the first months of the war, seemed to have vanished, and German war aims appeared both unjust and unattainable. 'I do not believe in our right to decide the final destiny of the world. . . . This war is not a beginning but an end; ruins are what it will leave behind.'[83] In 1916 he was actually writing to a friend in the army 'If the war goes on lasting a long time and I find it quite intolerable in Berlin, it could be that I might ask you for a place. Perhaps you need a clerk or something of the kind.'[84] Nevertheless, in spite of his expressions of isolation, impotence and despair, Rathenau continued to be in touch with the men who made German policy. He was actively involved in the foundation of the *Mittwochsgesellschaft*, a club of seventy members which met each week to discuss current events, and which brought together Nationalist politicians and Right wing Social Democrats, Field Marshals and industrialists. Yet even here, though Rathenau's views were listened to with respect, they commanded little support.

There was only one person whom Rathenau still believed capable of waging the war effectively, and who, it was believed, took notice of what Rathenau said. This was General von Ludendorff, at the beginning of the war the Chief of Staff on the Eastern front. Rathenau first met him on a visit to the front late in 1915. 'I felt,' he wrote five years later, 'that here was the man to lead us, if not to victory, at least to an honourable peace, and from that day on I was one of those who did everything in their power to smooth his path to the supreme command.'[85] There is actually little to show that Rathenau contributed much to the decision to appoint Field Marshal von Hindenburg to be supreme commander, with Ludendorff as his Chief of Staff, a development that led, in effect, to the establishment of a military dictatorship and the end of civilian government in Germany. Ludendorff had impressed Rathenau by his awareness of the economic aspects of the war, and Rathenau

had supported Ludendorff's proposal to deport Belgian workers
to help in German war industries—a step which, together with the
confiscation of Belgian raw materials in 1914, made Rathenau,
immediately after the war, as much of an object of suspicion to
the Allies as he was, for opposite reasons, to German Nationalists. On the other hand, it soon became clear to Rathenau
that Ludendorff's aims and methods were not always ones of
which he could approve. Ludendorff was the advocate of
German territorial expansion in Eastern Europe, and Rathenau,
although he had seen that in certain circumstances the war
might place Germany at the head of a voluntarily organised,
united European economic sphere, and was even 'in principle'
prepared to accept the possibility of certain strategic annexa-
tions in the West, nevertheless had consistently opposed plans
for conquest in the East.

The real point of disagreement between Rathenau and
Ludendorff, however, arose at the end of 1916, when Ludendorff and the naval authorities decided that unrestricted
submarine warfare was the way to defeat England. From the
moment when, in the autumn of 1916, plans for the submarine
campaign were being discussed, Rathenau was expressing his
doubts to various military friends, such as General von Seeckt,
and to Ludendorff himself. He was worried not only by the
obvious effect on American opinion, but still more by the extent
to which the U-boat war would arouse foreign opinion against
Germany and make any sort of reasonable negotiated peace
impossible. The U-boat campaign was, he thought, 'a leap
into the abyss, which only succeeds if it succeeds one hundred
per cent. I fear that we must reckon with an unforeseeable
prolongation'.[86]

Rathenau put his views personally to Ludendorff in a long
interview in July 1917, and his failure to carry his point
marked the end of his illusions about the Chief of Staff.
His visits to Ludendorff and his public pronouncements about
the conduct of the war had led some people to expect that
Rathenau himself was preparing for a political role. In fact,
however, his attitude remained unchanged: 'I am more distant
from day-to-day politics than ever before and have no intention
of going any closer. It is sufficient for me to contribute by my

intellectual work to a remoter future; I am happy to leave
the present to those better qualified'.[87] His dislike of politics
was genuine, and his brief experience of working for the War
Ministry had left him bitter and disillusioned, so that all his old
hatred of serving in a subordinate position must have been
redoubled. It was a tragedy both for him and for Germany,
because his views about war policy and the terms of a possible
peace showed a realism and understanding of what was really
important that hardly any other leading Germans possessed.
When it came to analysing specific political and economic
situations, he showed the same clarity as in his business life;
it was only when his romantic and metaphysical ideas got the
better of him and when he was talking about his rather vague
schemes for a remote political future that the weakness of his
thought became apparent. But perhaps this misunderstanding
of his own vocation, together with the invisible barrier (Kessler
calls it a 'wall of glass'), which he erected between himself
and others, would have made political success impossible,
and perhaps he was destined to remain a prophet without a
cause.

Certainly, Rathenau's analysis of the war situation had been
largely justified. At the end of 1914 he had written: 'In this
war there is a false note (*In diesem Kriege klingt ein falscher Ton*).
It is not 1813, not 1866, not 1870. . . . What will the reward of
victory have to look like to justify so much blood and tears?
I believe in victory, but I fear the end'.[88] By 1917, when a
far higher price had been paid in blood and tears than could
have been foreseen in 1914, he was still more gloomy. Especially,
his mind was turning to the economic chaos which would be
left behind by the war, and to the new forms of economic
organisation which would be needed to deal with it. He fore-
saw the economic consequences of the war very clearly—
inflation, extension of state control, vast capital losses, a balance
of payments problem—but these could, he thought, be used to
effect a revolution in Germany's economic organisation that
would require, as a first condition, a far-reaching political
revolution. 'Now, at the beginning of the second year of the
war,' he wrote in *Von kommenden Dingen*, 'the realisation is
dawning that all economic life rests on the fundamental basis of

the state, that state policy is more important than 'business' (*Geschäftlichkeit*), that each owes his possessions and abilities to all.'[89] Both in *Von kommenden Dingen* (Of Things to Come), published in 1916, and in *Die neue Wirtschaft* (The New Economy), published a year later, there is the usual shrewdness in analysing specific economic situations, coupled with a certain vagueness about the political institutions required for economic progress. On the economic side, as on the philosophical, Rathenau starts from the changes brought about by mechanisation; but while, earlier, he had been impressed by the moral injury inflicted by machines on men, now he was more optimistic, and saw that increased mechanisation could result in increased production, and that this could be used both to repair the damage caused by the war and to remove poverty everywhere. But it would have to be an international effort; each country would need foreign capital to restore its economic life, and, more than ever before, the international economy would have to be treated as a single entity. However, as in most German plans for the unification of Europe, Germany was to take the lead, in this case spiritually as well as materially. 'Germany is a link in the chain. But it is the destiny of our German conscience to grasp what is more difficult, to wrestle with what is harder; to have insight, to rethink, to sink ourselves in the depths of the divine will, to reverse what has come to pass and to bear in its place our inner, inmost determination—that is the German mission.'[90]

Economic reorganisation meant political and social reconstruction. On the economic side there must be increased state control and direction of industry, but not state ownership. Rationalisation, standardisation, mass production were the foundations of the new economy. Firms were to be organised in vast cartels by enlightened capitalists who would plough their profits back into the business. 'A good business man will be inclined to limit his own consumption and that of his family more than is necessary, so as to produce for his firm richer resources and greater expansion.'[91] The whole mechanics of consumption and distribution must be revised. Small firms and small retailers must be abolished so as to save manpower and increase efficiency. Above all—and this is something that

Rathenau harps on in all his writings—luxury spending must be curtailed, and the money saved put to useful purposes. 'We see the racecourses and places of entertainment in a large city filled with sturdy, self-confident young men who will spend more in an hour on a horse or a dancer than a poor student, a poet or a musician dreams of as a means of livelihood for a whole year.'[92] Rathenau's own austerity was to be imposed on everyone; and he was particularly severe on women's extravagances and the whole apparatus which caters for their addiction to irrational and changing fashions. (Indeed, at one point he goes so far as to attribute the decline of artistic taste to the growing liberty of women.) Once consumption is curbed—by order of the state—money will be available both for the technical improvements which will increase production, and for the provision of the educational means which will give equality of opportunity to all and produce the technicians to run the new economy.

Rathenau did not believe that equality as such was an attainable or desirable ideal; he called it 'the meanest, most unreal and most dangerous of all modern Utopias'.[93] But he was as impressed as the Marxists were by the fact that modern mechanised industry had resulted in a kind of slavery from which there was no escape. By the abolition of hereditary and artificial distinctions of wealth and social position, the major evil of contemporary society would be removed. 'The separation of classes is so sharp with us,' he wrote to Ernst Norlind, 'that in thirty years I have only once known of a case of a worker, the son of a worker, who has risen to a high position in the *bourgeoisie*. This man had unusual technical gifts and was a dear friend of mine. I knew him when I was an official in a Swiss factory, and I was able to see to it that he ended his life at the head of a large firm in Silesia. His wife told me that when he died he had my last letter under his pillow.'[94]

There is much that is impressive in Rathenau's vision of the managerial society of the future; and some of his ideas are genuinely prophetic. An aristocracy of merit, opportunities for all through the abolition of hereditary privileges, increased production by means of rationalisation, centralisation and the control of consumption—these are familiar goals in the mid-twentieth century. Power would lie in the hands of enlightened capitalists, austere dedicated men at the head of vast cartels, staffed by the managers who had risen to positions of influence after education at the hands of the charitable foundations financed by the profits of industry. These, too, are features not unknown today. These business enterprises would not be state-owned, but the state would exercise a general supervision over the shape of the economy and determine the goals it was to serve—a situation not unlike that which was to prevail in Germany under National Socialism.

However, there are, of course, obvious flaws in this system as a pattern for the future. Just as Rathenau's philosophical views reflected his own psychological conflicts, so his economic ideas also express his own temperament. If all capitalists were like Rathenau and were prepared to work within a controlled economy for the good of the community, their only incentive being to make more money to plough back into their own firms, then such a system might conceivably work. There are men like this—perhaps more than opponents of the capitalist system would like to admit—but hardly enough to found Rathenau's new economy. Moreover, there are more serious gaps in Rathenau's plan. He never really deals with the problem of the working class, how it is to be organised or how it is to be represented. Beyond laying it down that there will be opportunities for any son of a working class family to rise to a managerial position, and beyond providing for the material welfare of the workers by increased production and fairer shares, he does not really face the problem or provide an adequate substitute for the existing structure of trade unions and socialist parties. There are hints that workers will be allowed to have a share in the control of industry, and that eventually all firms should be self-governing. 'Functional Unions' are to be the organs by which industry is to be rationalised and managed, and they are to have special recognition by the state. Their function, however, seems to be that of generally regulating and organising the industry and of looking after the relations between one cartel and another; and they are clearly not thought of as particularly responsible for representing the workers. In fact, they begin to look rather like the state-run trade union movements established by the Fascists and National Socialists.

Finally, and this is the most serious weakness in Rathenau's social and economic thinking, he nowhere makes clear just into what sort of political framework the new industrial organisation is to fit. He was perhaps deliberately vague about this, for he had little confidence in paper constitutions and academic political arrangements. 'The *Volksstaat* is not created by institutions and paragraphs of constitutions and laws, but by spirit and will.'[95] At the same time, his experience of the political parties of imperial Germany had left him sceptical of parliament, while he was, on the other hand, for all his admiration for Prussian traditions, bitterly opposed to the retention of power by the old ruling class. His political ideals remained dominated by the example of Stein and the Prussian reformers of the early nineteenth century, but, at the same time, he found it hard to reconcile his version of their ideas with the democratic parliamentary trends of the twentieth century. Consequently, just as the reorganisation of the economy required that men made in Rathenau's image should control industry, so the new society would require a Rathenau to be its political leader. 'I am a supporter of the idea of monarchy,' he wrote in *Von kommenden Dingen*, 'not just out of distaste for election jobbery and rivalry, for lawyers and publicists, but also from an innate sentiment and conviction that at the head of the power of the State, there should be a deeply responsible man, removed and withdrawn from all the desires, ambitions and temptations of ordinary life; a consecrated man, and not an *arriviste* who has made a successful career.'[96]

The conception of a state built up out of autonomous corporations serving a common ideal has much in common both, as Kessler points out, with the ideas of Guild Socialism that were being developed in England at the end of the First World War, and also with some aspects of Catholic political thought, and, more important, with the ideology of Italian Fascism. Rathenau did not live to see the application of such ideas in Germany or Italy, nor, in a form which he would perhaps have found more acceptable, in Austria under Dollfuss or in Portugal under Salazar. He certainly would have been appalled by

National Socialism, for he had always maintained the right to individual liberty and recognized the claims of learning and the arts to be unswayed by political considerations; and his idea of a *Volksstaat* was far removed from the noisy brutality of Nazi ideals. Yet the tragedy of German democracy lay in the fact that men like Rathenau, who genuinely wanted an end to the old abuses, refused to try to make the parliamentary system work. 'Our members of parliament,' he wrote during the last weeks of the war, 'are not used to responsibility and discipline, and it will take a long time before they have learnt that party considerations alone do not produce governments.'[97] The criticisms were perhaps justified; and Rathenau did at moments talk of parliament as a kind of school for administrators and leaders, but he and many other Germans refused to give parliamentary democracy time to work, and despaired in advance of reforms along conventional democratic lines, so that even their collaboration in the running of the Weimar Republic was given with a mental reservation, while their criticisms of democracy and their appeals for a renewal of German society were to be echoed by other and more sinister voices.

Rathenau's economic and social writings were far more successful than his philosophical work, partly because it was felt that, as a successful financier, he knew what he was talking about and was not the dilettante he seemed to be when dealing with metaphysics, and partly because, by 1918, there were enough people who were disturbed about the course of German political life to respond to his criticisms. At the same time, however, Rathenau's views made him more and more enemies. His attacks on inherited wealth and on the class structure of Germany alienated both his fellow-industrialists and such members of the Prussian aristocracy who bothered to think of such things. His criticisms of Social Democratic theory and practice were enough to make his ideas suspect to Socialists, especially as he had claimed, mistakenly, that *Von kommenden Dingen* 'struck at the heart of dogmatic socialism'. Rathenau's isolation in the last months of the war was as great as it had been two years earlier, when he had written: 'I feel myself painfully divided from the way of thinking of my people in so far as they believe the war to be an event that will bring salvation'.[98] And his words of the autumn of 1914 remained as true as ever: 'This precious truthful people has no positive sense of freedom. They love authority, they want to be governed, they submit and want to obey. This half-virtue is a fault in the light of eternal history. We are governed by a caste, tough and self-confident but incapable of initiative. That was all right as long as they were not ashamed of being out-of-date. Recently they have wanted to be modern, and have destroyed the old without obtaining the new, have made enemies of the world, have weakened us in our foreign relations and then let fly at a moment which we had not chosen'.[99]

By the spring of 1918, Rathenau had been proved right on several points. The old military caste was more strongly entrenched than ever; Hindenburg and Ludendorff were able to ignore the faint doubts expressed by some members of parliament, and to control with reasonable success the currents of unrest among the workers. On the other hand, their policy of unlimited submarine warfare had been as unsuccessful as Rathenau had predicted, and England remained undefeated. True, the Germans still looked like winning the war; peace had been signed with the Bolshevik government in Russia in March 1918, and the gains in the east had exceeded the wildest expectations of the most violent annexationists; American power in Europe, though growing, had not yet been fully brought to bear; Italy had experienced a humiliating defeat in the autumn of 1917, and Rumania had been knocked out of the war. When, therefore, Ludendorff's great spring offensive of 1918 failed, and advance was turned into retreat, and retreat into defeat as the summer months passed, very few Germans were prepared to face the truth, after four years of propaganda predicting inevitable victory.

Rathenau himself was in a strange mood. While he had never lost his belief in a German victory, he had always been aware of the length and cost of the war, and had been the most bitter opponent of the false optimism fostered by the German leaders, so that he had won the reputation of a defeatist. At the same time, he felt that a last-minute revolutionary effort might still avoid defeat, and that 1918 might be a second 1813. In July 1918, he published an appeal to the youth of Germany (*An*

Deutschlands Jugend), which is the most sibylline of all his writings. It is a plea for the national regeneration of Germany through the younger generation, so that, whatever form the peace might take, and whatever the machinations of Germany's enemies, she might still hold her place in the world as the leader of the new social and economic order. 'Love for our home outweighs all else, and demands that the justice and nobility of the future should come into the world as a work of the German spirit, as a gift of the German heart to the peoples of the world. . . .'[100] There could be no going back. 'Our way of life will be new, our economy, our social structure and the form of our state. The relations between states will be new, as will world trade and politics. Our learning and even our speech will be new.'[101] The war was bound to end very soon: 'The great ones have had their say, it is time for the little people to speak, before the graves and monuments open their mouths: "Friends, men, brothers, hear! It is enough. . . . You have destroyed a world in your blind madness".'[102]

On the subject of the peace treaty that would end the war, Rathenau was again prophetic: 'The coming peace will be a short armistice and the number of future wars unforeseeable, the best nations will fade away and the world will sink into misery, unless the peace settlement is sealed by the will to put these principles into practice. A League of Nations is all very well, disarmament and arbitration are possible and sensible: but it all remains without effect unless first of all an Economic League, a common economy for the whole world, is created. By this I mean neither the abolition of national economies, nor free trade nor customs unions: but the distribution and administration in common of international raw-materials, the allocation of international products, and international financing.'[103]

As Rathenau held these high, if vague, hopes that the horrors and mistakes of the war might still not have been in vain, and that the peace treaty might lead to a new international political, economic and social order, he was appalled when the end of the war was approaching and it became clear that Germany's defeat was complete, and that she would be at the mercy of whatever terms the Allies chose to impose. He still could not really believe in Germany's defeat: 'It is not Germany's destiny to perish,' he wrote as late as 30 September, 1918. 'Therefore *sursum corda*! Lift up your hearts!'[104] He was, therefore, bitterly opposed to Ludendorff's request for an armistice at the end of September; it was a step which, he felt, both deprived Germany in advance of bargaining power and would be likely to lead to chaos at home. 'The step was too hasty,' he wrote in an article on 7 October 1918. 'Negotiations must not start from weakness but first the front must be strengthened.'[105] And on the next day he wrote to Maximilian Harden—it was their final and most serious difference of opinion—'I am convinced (although I am not given to thinking in terms of catastrophes) that we are heading for civil war, a military revolt and a food strike, brought about by the disorganised dissolution of the front. We can only save ourselves by winning time'.[106] Rathenau's own proposal, again with the legend of 1813 uppermost in his mind, was for a last-minute mobilisation of all Germany's remaining resources of manpower and materials, and the arming of the nation preparatory to a mass rising—a *levée en masse*—should Allied troops reach German soil. In addition to advocating this course in the press, he addressed memoranda to the newly formed government of Prince Max of Baden, which was making a last attempt to save the Empire by introducing constitutional reforms, and pointed out that Germany was not yet at the end of her resources. The new Chancellor, who had opposed Ludendorff's demands for an immediate armistice for reasons similar to Rathenau's, was inclined to take Rathenau's arguments seriously, but they were firmly rejected both by the War Ministry and by the General Staff. Nevertheless, in the eyes of many people on the Allied side, Rathenau was now not only the man who had stolen Belgian stocks of raw materials and recommended the deportation of Belgian workers, but also the man who wanted to prolong the war unnecessarily.

On 9 November 1918, the Kaiser abdicated and the Republic was proclaimed, with the Social Democrat Friedrich Ebert as President; on 11 November the armistice came into effect and the war was over. The German Revolution had come about, and it was a revolution in which Walther Rathenau had no part. 'The revolution was necessary,' he wrote a month later. 'I welcomed it, and also do not have any doubts about our future for a moment, in spite of all the internal and external pressures on us. I realise without any feeling of sadness and resignation that I myself will not contribute to this future. My writings have made me an enemy of the old middle class: the new powers that be do not welcome me as one of themselves, but, for some reason or other that I don't know, regard me as an opponent.'[107] It looked as though the isolation in which Rathenau had shrouded himself during the last years of the Empire was going to be unbroken in the Republic; in fact, however, he was, in his early fifties, soon to embark on a new career.

4

WALTHER RATHENAU, EVEN at the moments of his life when he felt himself most isolated and alone, could not refrain from practical activity; and, indeed, his position as an important industrialist and financier made withdrawal from current affairs impossible. Immediately after the Revolution, while protesting that his work was over and that he had nothing to offer for the future, Rathenau plunged, for the first time in his life, into active politics. He began by making an attempt, though it lasted a very short time, to start a new party, the *Demokratische Volksbund*. According to Rathenau, it was not to be a party in the old sense of the word but 'a free union of opinion. Its task is to encourage social idealism in the bourgeoisie and to strengthen it in the working class, in so far as this is accessible'.[108] The idea was abandoned after a few days; it seemed too vague and impractical; and in any case, as Rathenau himself realised, the German middle classes, intent on a struggle for immediate survival, were not very interested in his ideas. Actually, another similar attempt to found a political party was being made on a rather more practical basis by a group of academic and professional figures; and on 16 November the *Demokratische Partei* was founded. The hopes that it might develop into a new, broadly-based Liberal party were not fulfilled, however, and it was to remain a minority group with more prestige than influence. Rathenau was one of its early supporters, and he was anxious to be a candidate in the elections for the National Assembly which was to launch the new republic. It was a decision that left him disappointed and bitter, and contributed much to his disillusionment with parliamentary government.

It had been suggested that he should stand for a constituency in Silesia, where he was chairman of the board of an important glass factory, but he was opposed by many local supporters of the party, partly on anti-Semitic grounds, and, although his friends were subsequently able to get him a place on the electoral list for Prussia, he was too low down on the list to have any hope of being elected. An even harder blow to his pride followed in February, 1919. After the National Assembly met, telegrams were received and read out by its secretary proposing the names of candidates for the post of President of the new republic. A group of German residents in Sweden had sent in Rathenau's name—'a well-meant but highly misguided and inopportune effort,' he called it. 'The Parliament of any other civilised state,' Rathenau wrote a few months later in his *Apologie*, 'would have shown sufficient respect for a man of recognised intellectual standing to have passed over in silence this act of bad taste. But the first parliament of the German Republic, assembled in this darkest and most solemn hour and destined to set the seal on Germany's ignominy, greeted it with roars and shouts of laughter. The papers talked of merriment lasting for several minutes, and eye-witnesses related how men and women rocked in their seats with delight at the idea. This was their way of greeting a German whose intellectual achievement they either did or did not know, as the case might be. I was certainly astonished when I read it, but it did not distress me personally.'[109]

It was the Right who had laughed at the suggestion of Rathenau's name as a candidate for the Presidency; but his relations with the Left were no better. He was excluded from the Commission established by the new government to advise on the socialisation of industry, after receiving an invitation to join it, because of complaints from the Independent Socialists, and in spite of his protests to the President of the Republic. 'I do not think,' he wrote to Ebert, 'that there are many men on the bourgeois side who, at the risk of their position with the bourgeoisie and disregarding all the hostility shown, have done what I felt it my task to be and attacked the old system without reserve, opposed the war, and presented a complete new economic system scientifically based and elaborated. . . .'[110] Nor was Rathenau much more successful in influencing opinion abroad; an open letter to Colonel House, appealing for fairer treatment for Germany, remained without effect; letters in the neutral press defending the German people while denouncing their former leaders had little visible result. The worst shock, however, was when he discovered that, at the request of the Belgians, his name had been placed on the Allied list of war criminals, because of his alleged role in the deportation of Belgian workers. The charge was eventually dropped, but Rathenau was understandably depressed and wounded that it should have been made at all.

During these months immediately after the end of the war—perhaps the hardest time of his life—Rathenau made a determined effort to find his old serenity and a stoical detachment worthy of Marcus Aurelius, with whom he liked to compare himself. 'In my own life I could not have borne this time, I could not have borne the weight of hatred and enmity that lies on my shoulders: I bear it because I have no longer any will of my own, any home, any life of my own, but I exist like a man in a fort who has his orders and mans his gun,' he wrote in November 1919.[111] Yet it was only natural that he should occasionally falter in this detachment; he engaged in what was for him an unusually sharp controversy with Wissell, the Social Democratic Secretary of State at the Ministry of Economics, whom he accused of perverting and distorting his ideas. At the same time he produced two small books—*Apologie* and *Der Kaiser*—in which he tried to defend himself against his opponents and show the consistency of his views and behaviour.

Any hopes that Rathenau had had that the Revolution might bring the realisation of his plans for the future any nearer had vanished. 'What used to be called the Reichstag is called the National Assembly. Where Bethmann sat, Scheidemann sits, on William's throne is Ebert, where Ludendorff commanded, Noske commands.'[112] All that had happened was that Germany was defeated, ruined and humiliated. 'No chains were broken by a burst of spirit and will, but one link has rusted through. A general strike by a defeated army is called the German Revolution.'[113] There was every ground for his dissatisfaction and anxiety. The Treaty of Versailles had been far more severe than had been expected. The German economy was still suffering from the effects of the Allied blockade and the disruption caused by sudden demobilisation and the loss of territory under the terms of peace. The Republic, linked in the minds

of most Germans with the shame and hardship of defeat, had
few positive supporters and was openly threatened by the
nationalists on the Right and by the new Communist party
on the Left. Public order was only precariously assured. Karl
Liebknecht and Rosa Luxemburg, who had led the Communist
rising in Berlin in January 1919, had been dragged from their
prison and murdered. Kurt Eisner, the Socialist Prime Minister
of Bavaria, had been assassinated. The Free Corps—irregular
bands of fanatical nationalist ex-service men—were openly
tolerated by the military authorities. In March 1920, there
was an attempt at a *coup d'état* by Wolfgang Kapp, a retired
senior civil servant, and a few officers. It failed because Kapp
did not have the support of the army, and, in particular, of its
commander, General von Seeckt; at the same time, the Trade
Unions organised an effective general strike. Kapp's *putsch*
was an indication of how, in some cases at least, the old
Prussian traditions of loyalty, which Rathenau admired so
much, had not been transferred to the Republic, for it was to
Kapp that Rathenau had written eleven years earlier: 'I believe
that the greatness of a country rests first and foremost on moral
values, and among the strongest of these values in our country
I would reckon the idealism of our civil service. If this succumbs
to the attacks and temptations which are naturally strong in a
period of capitalism, unscrupulous and one-sided lack of recognition of the qualities of the Civil Service could lead to dis-
couragement and bitterness, the consequences of which we could
not foresee.'[114]

Rathenau was one of the men most open to attack by the
extreme Nationalists; and his position was made even more
difficult after Ludendorff, in November 1920, declared to the
Reichstag committee that was enquiring into the reasons for
Germany's defeat: 'I regret that I am compelled to repeat a
remark of Walther Rathenau's to the effect that on the day that
the Kaiser and his paladins on their white chargers ride
victorious through the Brandenburger Tor, history will have lost
all meaning. Thus there were currents of opinion in the nation
which did not suscribe to the view of the Supreme Command
that we must fight to a victorious conclusion, and these currents
of opinion must be taken into account'.[115] It was no use

Rathenau protesting, rightly, that this was a distortion of a phrase used in his pamphlet on the Kaiser, and that what he had meant was that the policy of Germany's leaders had been wrong just because it could not lead to victory; the damage was done, and, in the eyes of many, Rathenau had been condemned by Germany's most prominent soldier as a defeatist and a traitor. The charge, and the publicity given to the phrase about history losing its meaning if the Kaiser and his paladins rode in triumph through the Brandenburger Tor, were all the more damaging, since they occurred at a moment when Rathenau, for the first time since his political disappointments in the winter of 1918-19, was beginning to play a part in public life again.

'On occasions when the state has wished to make use of my services,' he wrote in August, 1920, 'I have never refused, and I intend to follow the same course in the future. But I do not like the complicated ways that lead to the centre of the state machine. I have never in my life asked for anything, and I have always found that ideas prevail, even when one follows them through in an objective way and excludes personal steps.'[116] It was, however, largely through his personal connections that Rathenau was becoming involved in public life again in 1920. In March of that year, Dr Josef Wirth became Minister of Finance, and decided that a man of Rathenau's financial ability, fertile intellect and complete disinterestedness could be of great value in dealing with the question of reparations, which dominated German economic, and indeed, foreign policy at this time. The two men established a warm personal friendship. Both had received a scientific training (Wirth had been a teacher of mathematics); both were lonely bachelors; and Wirth's serious devotion to his political tasks, and his religious convictions (he was a Roman Catholic and a member of the Centre Party) commanded Rathenau's respect. Wirth's simplicity and directness, and the fact that he did not share Rathenau's tortuous and elaborate intellectual approach to politics, made it possible for Rathenau to work with him more harmoniously than with most of his previous colleagues. It was Wirth who appointed Rathenau to the second Socialisation Commission, where, after much speaking and the usual complaints of being misunderstood, he voted with the majority who rejected the nationalisation proposals of the Left.

In July 1920, Wirth invited Rathenau to go to the Spa conference as a technical adviser to the German delegation. It was an important occasion, for it was the first time that the Germans had been invited to a conference with the Allies as equals, and the aim of the conference was to try and get some agreement about the details of German disarmament and about coal deliveries by Germany in execution of the reparations clauses of the Treaty of Versailles. Rathenau was characteristically ambiguous about his personal position. 'Yes, I was at Spa,' he wrote to Wilhelm Schwaner, 'but only in the modest role of a so-called "expert" without any influence on decisions. Nor am I a *Ministerialrat* as it says in the address of your letter, nor in influential positions in the state and nation as you assume. I limit myself now as before to the field of activity you know.'[117] However, to his mother, he suggested what his true role was: 'Everything happens behind the scenes,' he told her, and, a day or two later, 'Today is a critical day, when the whole affair may perhaps go wrong. The work has been less tiring than the constant talks with fifty people from early morning to late at night'.[118]

Whatever Rathenau's doubts, hesitations and deliberate modesty about his own position at Spa may have been, his line about Germany's policy towards the Treaty of Versailles had been quite consistent. Until the treaty had been actually signed in June 1919, he had been very strongly opposed to its terms and bitterly disappointed in President Wilson and Colonel House for agreeing to them. He had maintained that the only fault of the German people had been to trust in unworthy leaders, and that it was morally wrong to saddle the whole German nation with the guilt of a few men, and to punish them with loss of territory and economic penalties. Indeed, he had even gone so far as to say not only that the German government should refuse to sign the treaty, but also that they should resign, dissolve the National Assembly and hand over the sovereignty of Germany and the direct responsibility for governing the country to the Allied powers, so that no German should be forced to bear the burden of an unworkable peace treaty. (It was the course the Allies themselves were to follow at the end of the Second World War.)

Once the treaty was signed, however, Rathenau realised that some effort must be made by Germany to fulfil its terms, if there was ever to be any hope of getting it revised. 'The injustice lies as much with the executioners as with the victim,' he wrote, 'but the injustice of the executioners is none of our business.'[119] From the start, he had gone much further than most Germans in admitting the duty of Germany to pay reparations to France and Belgium. 'The injustice which we have committed in France and Belgium is not to be denied,' he wrote in the *Frankfurter Zeitung* in January 1919. 'The much talked of demolition in the area of our retreat was also an injustice. It was unjust to destroy factories in Belgium and to deport Belgian workers. The Reich has the duty to repair the injustice by compensation.'[120] His own suggestion was the typical one that this should be met by a voluntary effort on the part of the German people, and that German workers should go of their own free will to rebuild the devastated areas. In fact, his attitude to the problem of reparations remained that it would be more easily solved by direct contacts between German and French firms and individuals than by the elaborate machinery of inter-governmental negotiations. He saw, as Keynes did on the Allied side, that the sums being discussed in Allied circles were hopelessly unrealistic, and he was determined to work for some plan that would both be practicable for Germany and, at the same time, convince the Allies of Germany's serious intention to pay something.

At Spa, the arguments inside the German delegation were as violent as those between the Germans and the French. Rathenau's chief opponent was Hugo Stinnes, the head of a vast coal trust in the Ruhr and of an industrial empire as large as Rathenau's own. Their personalities were as contrasted as their views: Stinnes liked to emphasise the coarseness and bluff directness of his character; he dressed almost like a workman; politically he was a supporter of the extreme nationalists, and did not hesitate to use anti-Semitic arguments against Rathenau, who, he said, had 'the soul of an alien race'.[121] In diplomacy he believed that the only way to deal with the

Allies was by rudeness and complete intransigence. While he became popular in Germany for his unbending attitude at Spa—and the Allies reflected on what it would have been like if a man like that had been on the winning side—Rathenau impressed the British and even the French as a man with whom discussion might be possible, and he became even more unpopular in Germany as a result. Although Rathenau's views partially prevailed at Spa, the result could not be said to be a triumph for his policy of negotiation. The Germans had accepted, under the threat of an Allied ultimatum to occupy the Ruhr, a figure for coal deliveries, but had made no effort to suggest a total reparations figure acceptable to the Allies. The Allies, on the other hand, and especially the French, were convinced that Germany would only be induced to meet her obligations by a series of threats and ultimatums.

In May 1921, a new government was formed with Josef Wirth as Chancellor. He was anxious that Rathenau should become more than an unofficial adviser to the government, and pressed him to accept office as Minister of Reconstruction, which would give him a chance both of pursuing his policy of negotiating an agreement on reparations, and of influencing the whole course of the German economy. It was the hardest decision Walther Rathenau had ever had to take. For years he had cultivated his isolation and his stoical independence; he had claimed again and again that his philosophical and theoretical writing was all that interested him; at fifty-four he regarded himself already as an old man. 'I am fifty-three years old,' he had written to Frau Deutsch at the end of the summer of 1920. 'I look backwards rather than forwards, and my work is almost done. It still keeps me going, but it is no longer a driving force. I have surmounted life's summit, and yet the peace I looked for has not come. It is not the broad valley that I see, but range upon range of mountains and the stars and horizon.'[122] There were practical arguments against accepting office, too. Rathenau had constantly maintained that Jews should not take prominent positions in public life, and he was well aware of the unpopularity and even personal danger he might incur. His mother, for this reason, was strongly against his accepting Wirth's invitation. Even more important, however, was the knowledge that by accepting office, he would have to give up his business interests. 'The dismantling of a life's work in twenty-four hours was hard,' he wrote after finally joining the government and resigning all his director-ships, 'but it means little in comparison with the task of con-struction that faces me.'[123]

It took him a long time to make up his mind: 'My internal barometer still stands far to the left of "unsettled" and near the point which indicates rain and snow—in political terms "refusal",'[124] he wrote to Gerhart Hauptmann on 25 May, and on the next day he told Schwaner: 'In these last ten days I have come more and more to the view that the objective conditions for fruitful work are hard to bring about. The immoderate attacks from one familiar side would not make me refuse; but the only thing that would make me accept would be the certainty that a clear situation could be created as a basis for my work.'[125] However, he let himself be persuaded; his friendship and respect for Wirth and the arguments of Rosen, the new Foreign Minister, combined to make him accept office, after he had been promised that financial and foreign policy should be closely linked, so that he would be given a chance of pursuing simultaneously the two aims of inter-national reconciliation and of reorganising the German economy. 'I am glad you did not have to go through all the excitement here,' he wrote to his mother, who was doing a cure at Carlsbad. 'The final decision was all the same very hard.'[126]

It was a new life for Rathenau; and he found it in some ways more exacting than he had expected. He was working till one in the morning; he had to appear before the Reichstag (of which he was not a member); he had to fulfil social obligations of a kind he detested. 'What I under-estimated about this work,' he wrote to his mother, 'is the physical side, which was a hard burden in the first days of great heat. Before, I used to sit at my desk, knew when my meetings would end and knew when I had to go and visit a factory or to meet foreigners. Now these things don't depend on me: cabinet meetings are postponed three times a day, nothing starts punctually, I have to go out to make visits, drive to the Reichstag two or three times unnecessarily, because the agenda has been changed. . . .'[127]

The Ministry, dependent, like all governments in the Weimar Republic, on the support of a coalition, only lasted five months; and, in October, Rathenau was forced to resign because the other members of the Democratic Party, of which he was nominally a member, left the government as a protest against the League of Nations' decision to award the most important part of Upper Silesia to Poland. It was a matter on which Rathenau felt strongly—he had written a year earlier 'Whoever separates German men from German soil sins against the spirit of the nations, and strikes a blow at Europe's heart which never heals'[12a]—but he was reluctant to leave the government when, he hoped, his policies were just about to have some effect. He had succeeded in negotiating an agreement with the French, which was signed at Wiesbaden on 7 October. It was an attempt to put reparations payments on a business-like footing, to substitute payments in kind for payments in gold and to avoid endless inter-governmental wrangles by entrusting reparations deliveries to private firms. At the same time, he hoped that the suspension of payments in gold would check the inflation of the German currency, which was already becoming a grave economic danger. In fact, the agreement came to nothing: French industrialists disliked the idea that the devastated areas, which they regarded as their best markets, should be supplied direct by German firms; and German nationalists objected to the fact that deliveries were to be made to France at all, particularly as the Wirth government had made an effort to prove their good intentions by making a large payment in gold in the summer of 1921, as stipulated by the London agreements of the previous spring. By the end of 1921 any sort of working agreement on reparations, in spite of the meetings at Spa, London and elsewhere, seemed as far off as ever, while the Germans attributed a worsening economic situation at home to the intransigence of the French, and, still more, to the efforts of men like Wirth and Rathenau to negotiate agreement in a more reasonable atmosphere.

Rathenau realised that the French were the main obstacle to a settlement, just as he had realised during the war that it was the British who were the chief enemy. However, it was in London that his diplomatic talents and obvious goodwill were

most appreciated, and, although he ceased to be a member of
the government in October 1921, Wirth, who formed a new
administration without the Democratic Party, continued to
make use of him on official missions. He was in London at the
end of 1921, trying, with some success, to persuade Lloyd
George to accept the idea of a moratorium in reparations
payments and indeed a reconsideration of the whole reparations problem. Rathenau and the German government were
worried at the growing inflation in Germany, and attributed
it to the necessity of making reparations payments in cash,
which severely reduced the gold and foreign currency reserve of
the Reich. Rathenau found Lloyd George a sympathetic
listener. Lloyd George was genuinely anxious for a settlement,
partly, perhaps, in the hope of restoring his own political
position at home, and he was impressed by Rathenau's intelligence and expert knowledge, as well as by his desire for agreement. He not only promised to press for a reduction in
Germany's payments in gold, but also listened sympathetically
to a proposal by Rathenau for the establishment of an international body to finance the economic recovery of Russia—a
first step towards realising Rathenau's old dreams of international schemes to finance development in backward areas.
There even seems to have been a suggestion of a pact to
guarantee the Franco-German frontier—the idea which was to
be taken up by Stresemann three years later and to lead to the
Locarno treaties.

Rathenau's visit to London naturally aroused French
suspicions that the Germans were trying to detach Britain from
France, and encouraged the people in France who were opposed
to any negotiations. For the moment, however, the French
Prime Minister, Aristide Briand, was able to ignore them, and
the conference that met at Cannes in January 1922 seemed to
have more prospect of success than its many predecessors.
Rathenau, at Wirth's request, led the German delegation, and
both Lloyd George and Briand were anxious to achieve positive
results. Briand realised that he would have the utmost difficulty
in persuading his colleagues to make any concessions to Germany, but he was prepared, on the recommendation of the
Reparations Commission, to agree to some reduction in the

immediate sum due in gold, and to discuss the possibility of a moratorium. Some of the experts working with Rathenau were in favour of immediate acceptance of any temporary reduction that might be offered, but Rathenau himself was determined to use the occasion for a full-scale statement of Germany's position and of her claims to a long-term reduction in the total sum of reparations due. He was in the process of making his speech when the news reached Cannes that Briand had resigned. Briand had, in fact, agreed with Lloyd George that France would be prepared to make some concessions to Germany, in return for a military guarantee from Britain, but, in spite of this promise, he was unable to carry either his colleagues or the President of the Republic with him, and, on returning from Cannes to Paris at the urgent summons of President Millerand, had no choice but to resign. A new French government was formed under Poincaré, the embodiment of French intransigence, whose origins in Lorraine and whose legal training combined to make him insist on the exact fulfilment by Germany of every line of the Treaty of Versailles. It was clear that the Cannes conference would achieve very little, and that Wirth's and Rathenau's 'policy of fulfilment' stood little chance of success. Rathenau spoke again before the conference broke up, and insisted again on Germany's willingness to pay up to her capacity and also proposed his own scheme for international economic cooperation for the reconstruction of Eastern Europe.

Reparations and economic reconstruction were to be the topics for discussion at the next European conference, to be held at Genoa in April. It was to be an important and wideranging meeting, and, for the first time since the Revolution, the Russian government was to be represented at an international congress of this kind. In the meantime, however, Rosen, the German Foreign Minister, had resigned, worn out by his constant meetings and wrangles with the French. Soon after returning from Cannes, Rathenau was offered his job. He found the decision even more difficult than when he had entered the government the previous year. The post was, given Germany's international position, the most important one in the country; and Rathenau's experience of international affairs over the past months had shown him how difficult it was to obtain results. He would be exposed to insults, personal attacks, and, indeed, to physical danger. Just how high the personal risk was had been demonstrated in August 1921, when Matthias Erzberger, the Centre Party politician, who had been one of the plenipotentiaries sent to sign the armistice in 1918, and a member of the first Republican government, had been murdered in cold blood as he was taking a walk while on holiday in the Black Forest; and even more sinister was the fact that there were plenty of people in Germany to applaud the crime.

Rathenau realised the danger and was not afraid; indeed there were moments when he almost seemed to welcome it. His hesitations sprang from his doubts about what he could achieve. His semi-official position gave him, he believed, more freedom in diplomatic negotiations, and he only wanted office if there were immediate tasks for him to perform. What finally swayed him was, perhaps, the feeling that the Genoa conference, in spite of all the difficulties, might give him a chance to realise some of his larger economic objectives. On the day on which he finally decided to accept, he wrote to his Swedish friend, Ernst Norlind: 'I have had to take office again, and I am entering on it with the deepest anxiety. I know how little I can achieve, but I hope that there are powers stronger than our human powers to help our poor country'.[129] And, the same evening, he wrote to Frau Deutsch: 'It is late at night, and I am thinking of you with a heavy heart. You will have heard . . . of the decision I had to make this evening. I stand before this task in deep and earnest doubt. What can a single individual do in the face of this torpid world, with enemies at his back, and conscious of his own limitations and weaknesses? I will do what I can, and if that is not enough, then I know you at least will not forsake me like the others'.[130]

He had not dared to break the news to his mother; and she read of his appointment in the newspaper. When he had lunch with her the next day, they both sat pretending to eat, until his mother could bear it no longer and said, 'Walther, why have you done this to me?' 'I really had to, Mama, because they could not find anyone else,' was his reply.[131] It was true, up to a point: he was free from political affiliations, so that his appointment did not affect the careful balance that had to be maintained in distributing portfolios in a coalition government; he had the full confidence of the Chancellor, Wirth; he had shown his ability to negotiate with the Allies and to represent Germany in a dignified and impressive way at international conferences; he had the technical financial and economic experience to deal with the question of reparations which dominated German foreign policy. Above all, he had a clear conception of the direction in which German policy should develop, and saw that it was only by making an effort to convince the Allies that Germany was prepared to meet some of her obligations, that the atmosphere could be created in which serious negotiations for a revision of the Treaty of Versailles would be possible. On the other hand, the appointment of Rathenau as Foreign Minister aroused violent protests from the Nationalists, and the clearer the lines of his policy became, the greater the danger that he would meet the same fate as Erzberger.

Rathenau came to the Foreign Ministry as an outsider; and it was a department staffed by some of the ablest professional diplomats in Europe. ('Do you really understand our Minister's books?' one of them anxiously asked a colleague.)[132] Some of them believed, as Rathenau did, that the greatest hope for Germany lay in working hard for an agreement with France and Britain; but there was an influential group inside the Foreign Ministry who were convinced that the only way in which Germany could regain freedom of action in foreign policy was by an agreement with the Soviet Union which would show the world that the countries which were regarded as outcasts were still a formidable element in the balance of power, and that Germany still retained some initiative in diplomacy. The leading exponent of this policy was Baron Ago von Maltzan, head of the department responsible for Russian affairs; and he was strongly supported by the head of the German army, General von Seeckt, who saw that there were all sorts of military possibilities in a policy of collaboration with the Soviet Union. When Rathenau took over the Foreign Ministry, plans for some sort of agreement with the Soviet government had been under discussion for some time.[133]

Rathenau's own attitude to the Russian Revolution was uncommitted and unprejudiced. He had early realised the importance as well as the horror of what was happening in Russia. 'Tolstoy's life and death, the great event of our time,' he had written early in 1918 to the novelist Hermann Hesse, 'has been made reality in the country next to ours, but it is a realisation in blood and misery that we can only view with sadness.'[134] Nevertheless, partly no doubt because of his consistent under-estimation of the power of Marxist doctrine, he never fully understood the extent to which Lenin, for all his elasticity and opportunism in practice, was actuated by theoretical principles, and was determined to maintain the impetus of the Revolution and of the transformation of Russian social and economic life. 'Bolshevism,' Rathenau was writing early in 1920, 'is today only a facade; in practice it is a question of a strongly oligarchical agrarian republic, which I believe will survive in spite of all its industrial difficulties.'[135] He had been among the many distinguished Germans who visited Radek, the chief Communist agent in Germany, when the latter had been in prison in Berlin in 1919—an encounter which was sufficient to enable his enemies to spread the wholly unfounded rumour that Radek had married Rathenau's sister—and he had always hoped that a moment would come when Germany might be able to develop economic links with Russia. When a number of German academic and public figures set up, early in 1920, a 'Study Committee for Russia' and visited the Soviet Union, Rathenau refused an invitation to go with them, but wrote that he hoped that the committee's work would lead to 'a first and decisive *rapprochement* in the economic field, to which, I hope, political *rapprochement* will be added'. 'I consider it important,' he told another member of the committee, 'that we create reasonable relations with the Soviet government, which is establishing itself more and more as a military-agrarian oligarchy.'[136] He was anxious, as he had told Lloyd George in December 1921, and repeated at Cannes the following month, for the nations of Europe to make a joint effort to assist Russian recovery, and the Genoa conference seemed an obvious opportunity for putting this policy into practice, even though the proposal was not welcomed by the Russians, who talked of colonial exploitation.

However, unlike Maltzan and his supporters in the *Wilhelm-strasse*, Rathenau believed that relations with Russia must be subordinate to relations with the West, and consequently when Chicherin, the Russian Foreign Minister, visited Berlin on his way to Genoa, although the general lines of an agreement were drawn up, Rathenau refused to make any definite commitment, for fear of alarming Britain and France, and so making impossible any agreement on what he regarded as the main question of German foreign policy, that of reparations. Maltzan, an able and determined man, although he had not been able finally to put his plans into effect when Chicherin was in Berlin, was a leading member of the German delegation at Genoa and was ready to seize any opportunity he could of pressing his policies on his Minister, and of resuming the negotiations with the Russians which had been started in Berlin.

The Genoa conference was an impressive one. Lloyd George led the British delegation, Wirth and Rathenau the German, while Facta, the last Prime Minister of Italy before the triumph of Mussolini, presided. It was significant, however, that France was not represented by Poincaré, the Prime Minister, but by Barthou, the Minister of Justice. As at all international conferences, what happened at the public sessions was less important than the private conversations between delegates, though Rathenau was able to score a personal oratorical triumph at the formal closing session, with a quotation from Petrarch— *io vo gridando pace, pace, pace!*—which was thought particularly appropriate. However, it was in the private conversations that Rathenau was disappointed. He had set great hopes on private meetings with Lloyd George, and on the possibility of winning his support for a revision of Germany's reparations payments as well as for his scheme for an international consortium to help Russia. For five days, Rathenau waited for a chance to have a confidential talk with Lloyd George without success; and, as he waited in his hotel suite between the formal meetings, watching the streaming rain outside, rumours began to reach him of negotiations between the French and the Russians, meetings between Lloyd George and Chicherin from which the Germans had been excluded. There was even talk of the French agreeing that the Germans should pay reparations to Russia as well as to the Western Allies. Rathenau was too sensitive a man not to feel that something was being plotted at his and Germany's expense, and that Lloyd George was deliberately slighting him. By 15 April—it was the Saturday before Easter—he had worked himself into a characteristic mood of black, defeatist gloom. That night he could not sleep, and when, at 2 a.m., Maltzan appeared in his room, he immediately expected bad news. 'Have you brought me my death sentence?' he asked.[137] In fact, it was the moment of Maltzan's triumph, for he had just received a telephone call from the Soviet delegation with an invitation from Chicherin to a private meeting at Rapallo, some twenty miles from Genoa, the next day.

The party—Rathenau still in his mauve pyjamas and Maltzan in a black silk dressing gown—then moved to Wirth's room to discuss their reply to the Russian proposal. Rathenau's personal reaction was to use it as an excuse for immediately seeing Lloyd George and demonstrating his Western sympathies by telling him of the Soviet invitation. He was overruled, however, when Maltzan said that this would be a gross breach of confidence, and that he would have to resign if Rathenau took this course. Maltzan used later to boast to his friends that he had 'raped' Rathenau. Accordingly, it was decided to go to Rapallo the next day for discussions with the Soviet delegation, and the German delegates drove off to Rapallo on the morning of Easter Sunday, 16 April. Rathenau, during a pause in the negotiations, took the opportunity to drive over from Rapallo to Portofino, where an old friend, Freiherr von Mumm, was living; and it was, ironically, during this time that Lloyd George at last made an unsuccessful effort to get into touch with him. In any case, the German decision was taken; and at 6.30 p.m. the Treaty of Rapallo was signed. 'Today, Easter Sunday, I made an excursion to Rapallo. More about it in the newspapers,'[138] Rathenau wrote to his mother that evening.

In itself, the Treaty was not very important, and included little except a general expression of friendship and a renunciation of any Russian claims for reparations from Germany and of any German claims to the repayment by Russia of pre-Revo-

lutionary loans Even the secret military arrangements which
followed, by which the Germans were to have the right to attach
officers to the Red Army for training in the arms denied to
Germany by the Peace Treaty and to arrange for the production of poison gas and other forbidden weapons in Russia, have
perhaps been over-estimated by historians anxious to prove a
link between Bismarck's Reinsurance Treaty, the Treaty of
Rapallo and the Nazi-Soviet pact of 1939. What was important
was that the treaty should have been made at all. It was a great
shock to Britain and France to be reminded that Germany
had more room for diplomatic manœuvre than had been
believed; and it was alarming to see the Soviet Union emerging
as a factor in conventional diplomacy. In practice, however,
the Treaty of Rapallo brought few advantages to Germany. It
destroyed all Rathenau's hopes of using the Genoa conference
for serious discussions with Britain and France, and, indeed,
although the conference lasted nearly three weeks more, no
one was very interested in it any longer, and it achieved nothing.

From Rathenau's own point of view, the Treaty of Rapallo,
for which his name is now chiefly remembered, was a failure.
In a moment of wounded vanity and neurotic depression he
had been persuaded into adopting a policy in which he did not
really believe. He lost the confidence of the Western statesmen,
and encouraged the French to believe even more strongly than
before that the Germans were untrustworthy and insincere. He
failed to bring back from Genoa any concessions from France
and Britain. The results for him personally were even worse
than the political effects of Rapallo, for now his enemies, in
addition to calling him Jew, defeatist and traitor, could also
brand him as a Bolshevik and a Russian agent. 'Rathenau has
to face the undying hatred of the Right,' Lord d'Abernon, the
British Ambassador, noted in his diary a few weeks after
Rathenau's return from Genoa, 'and he receives continually
threatening letters from the members of the extreme Nationalist organisations. As he is courageous, and indeed contemptuous
of danger, he refuses all police protection. But he has often told
me he is sure to be assassinated.'[139]

Although tired by the strain of the Genoa conference and
by a continuous effort to get Lloyd George's support for

Germany's request for a moratorium in reparations payments, Rathenau seems to have reached a point of inner calm, and, as one reads the accounts of the people who saw him in those weeks, one cannot avoid the impression of a man going knowingly and gladly to his death, a willing sacrificial victim acting in the spirit of a remark he had made towards the end of the war: 'Many must leap into the ditch before it can be crossed'.[140] In May 1922, just before leaving Genoa, he expressed his own mood clearly in a letter to Frau Deutsch: 'What a wretched sort of life is that which merely runs its course untroubled! The wonderful thing is that all true sorrow is beautiful. Only the stupidly awry and the arbitrarily distorted is ugly. In our life everything has been Law; thus were the facts and thus their predestined course. Nothing has been in vain, nothing can be thought away or given up. And, if you honestly reflect, you will find that even what seemed to be chance was really necessity. And is Chance going to have his own way now? My life has run too far along its course for that to be possible. Now at last I am free of my fellow-men. Not in the sense that I could ever be indifferent to them. On the contrary, the freer I am, the nearer and dearer—despite all—they are to me; and I joyfully recognize that I exist for them not they for me.

'The only person who exists for me, freely and consciously, without need of support, help or even thanks, and who shares completely my inmost life—that person is you, and I thank you for it.

'Certainly there is not much more that I can do. The flame burns low. But you know it is my destiny to be ready to lift from others the burden that oppresses them and to remain myself without desire. . . .'[141]

Towards the end of May 1922, Wirth received a visit at the Chancellery from a Catholic priest, and he subsequently gave Kessler an account of what had occurred: 'He informed me simply and soberly in a few sentences that Rathenau's life was in danger. I could not question him; the interview took place in absolute privacy. . . . Then Rathenau himself was called in. I implored him with all my might to give up his resistance to increased police protection for his person. In his well-known manner, with which many of his friends were familiar, he stubbornly refused. Thereupon I informed him of what had happened, and asked him whether he did not see that the step taken by the Catholic priest was a very serious affair. My words impressed Rathenau deeply. He stood motionless and pale for about two minutes. None of us dared to break the silence or speak a single word. Rathenau seemed to be gazing on some distant land. He was visibly struggling with his own feelings. Suddenly his face took on an expression of infinite benevolence and gentleness. With a calm such as I had never witnessed in him, although I had gauged the measure of his self-control in many a discussion on difficult personal or political questions, he stepped up to me, and putting both his hands on my shoulders, said "Dear friend, it is nothing. Who would do me any harm?" '[142]

Walther Rathenau was murdered on 24 June. The people who were already plotting the murder when the conversation with Wirth took place were half-a-dozen blond young Germans of just the kind Rathenau believed himself to be addressing when he wrote *An Deutschlands Jugend* four years before, and whom he exhorted: 'Be blessed in your hard and inexorable nature. . . . Be blessed with consuming love which shall strike you like fire and purge you and our country of the dross of today and yesterday, and rise like the smoke of sacrifice to the throne of him who blesses. Plunge into the struggle for the soul of our people!'[143] The eldest of the conspirators was twenty-five years old; they came from good homes; some of the older ones had been members of the Erhard Brigade, one of the most notorious of the Free Corps, and of its clandestine terrorist off-shoot, the Organisation Consul. They showed each other the famous passage of Rathenau's about history losing its meaning if the Kaiser and his paladins rode victorious through the Brandenburger Tor; they believed that Rathenau had married his sister to Radek, and that he was preparing to hand over Germany to the Bolsheviks; they doubtless repeated the jingle that had become current in Free Corps circles:

> *Knallt ab den Walther Rathenau,*
> *Die gottverdammte Judensau.**

*Shoot down Walther Rathenau, the god-damned dirty Jew.

In an atmosphere of adolescent emotionalism and passionate friendships the principal characters of the conspiracy, Erwin Kern, Hermann Fischer and Ernst-Werner Techow, made their plans. They borrowed an automatic pistol; they practised shooting in the Grunewald; they acquired a large open car and leather motoring coats to go with it. On 23 June they spent the evening together, going over the plans and drinking to heighten their resolution.

On the same day, by an unfortunate coincidence, Helfferich, one of the leaders of the Nationalists, delivered a violent attack in the Reichstag on Rathenau and on the policy he represented: 'The policy of fulfilment has brought in its train the appalling depreciation of the German currency, it has utterly crushed the middle classes, it has brought poverty and misery on countless families, it has driven countless people to suicide and despair, it has sent abroad large and valuable portions of our national capital, and it has shaken our industrial and social order to its very foundations!'[144] Nothing, Helfferich seemed to imply, was too bad for the author of such disasters. His attack was the more regrettable because, during these weeks, Rathenau had been trying to find some point of contact with his chief political opponents at home. A few days before, Helfferich himself, together with one of the other Nationalist leaders in the Reichstag, had been invited to dinner with Rathenau, and, although there seemed no possibility of agreement, the meeting was not unfriendly and they planned to meet again. On the evening of 23 June, Rathenau dined at the American Embassy; at his suggestion, Hugo Stinnes was invited in after dinner, and a political discussion, in a tolerably friendly atmosphere, went on until four in the morning of 24 June.

After a few hours sleep, Rathenau left his house in Grunewald in order to go back to the Foreign Ministry. He drove, as always, in the back of a large, slow, open car, which he had continued to use regularly, in spite of warnings from the police that they could not guarantee his safety in it. As he was driving down the Königsallee, the conspirators' car, driven by Techow, which had been waiting for Rathenau to appear, pulled level with his car. Kern shot at Rathenau with his automatic pistol and Fischer threw a hand grenade into the car. By the time any help could reach Rathenau he was already unconscious; his chauffeur drove him straight home, and soon after arriving there he died.

The murder created an enormous sensation; and Rathenau became more popular dead than he had ever been alive. The workers of Berlin organised an impressive procession to demonstrate their loyalty to the Republic and their readiness to defend it. The Reichstag showed clearly its support for the government, and Helfferich was given such a hostile reception that he was forced to leave the Chamber, while his nationalist colleagues sat white and shaken as Wirth denounced them: 'The real enemies of our country are those who instil this poison into our people. We know where we have to seek them. The enemy stands on the Right. (*Der Feind steht rechts.*)' Rathenau had become a symbol of that Republic he had viewed with such misgivings and of the liberal parliamentary government about which he had felt such doubts. For a time, at least, the shock of his death produced a reaction against the lawlessness which had made it possible, and which was to lead to unsuccessful attacks against Maximilian Harden and the Social Democrat leader Scheidemann; and, for a time, an atmosphere was created in which the Republic might have been strengthened, had it not been for the worsening external situation.

The assassins escaped from the scene of their crime, and Kern and Fischer fled from Berlin. In a castle in Thuringia, Kern was shot by the police while resisting arrest, and Fischer killed himself. (The Nazis later set up a monument on the spot.) Ernst-Werner Techow, the driver of the murderers' car, was arrested, along with his brother and a number of other young men who had been accessories to the plot. Techow was sentenced to a few years imprisonment; during the Second World War he was killed on the Russian front.* Techow's mother, the

---

*The story, given a certain currency by an article printed in the New York periodical *Politics* in January 1947, and accepted by Rathenau's latest biographer, Hellmut M. Böttcher, that Techow joined the French Foreign Legion and spent the war years atoning for Rathenau's murder by helping Jews to escape from France, though romantic and edifying, does not seem to have any evidence to support it, and was denied by Techow's brother. See Eduard Rosenbaum in *Merkur*, xii Jahrgang, Heft 8, August 1959.

widow of a respectable Berlin magistrate, was subjected to insults on the streets and in the shops during her son's trial, and, when Frau Rathenau, Walther's mother, heard of this, she wrote a letter which reflected in style and sentiment Rathenau's character and influence:

'In unspeakable grief I give my hand to you, the most wretched of women. Tell your son that I forgive him, as may God forgive him, if he makes a full and frank confession before earthly justice and repents before heavenly justice. If he had known my son, the noblest man that earth ever bore, he would have rather turned the murderers' gun against himself than against him. May these words give peace to your soul.'[145]

The tragedy of Rathenau's life and death lies in the fact that his political aims and his view of the world carried his own destruction with them. His admirable aims of fulfilment and appeasement during the brief time he held political office led directly to his death; yet he had already endangered them by his treaty with the Russians at Rapallo. His cultivation of the incompatible sides of his nature—Prussian and Jewish, capitalist and social reformer, financier and philosopher— cancelled each other out, so that he pleased nobody and achieved little. His criticisms of German society and his misty visions of the future were, for all his personal courage and disinterestedness, dangerous at a time when what was important for Germany was to make the present political arrangements work; and his own practical sense in diplomacy and business showed that he sometimes realised that this was so. What is more disquieting is the way in which his conception of the *Volksstaat*, the organic community of the future, and his romantic appeals to the younger generation to put these ideals into practice, could so easily sound like the ideals which his murderers believed they were serving. 'The younger generation was striving for something new, hardly dreamed of. They smelt the morning air. They gathered in themselves an energy charged with the myth of the Prussian-German past, the pressure of the present and the expectation of an unknown future. In the face of derision, against a world of foes, they gathered round a flag which they thrust into the future and in which they firmly believed. . . .'[146] They are sentiments and even language not far removed from Rathenau's own. The words were written in 1933 by Ernst-Werner Techow, one of his murderers.

III

F. T. MARINETTI

FUTURISM AND FASCISM

'*Il tape du pied; il fait voler la poussière; il jure, sacre et massacre; il organise des contradictions, des oppositions, des cabales pour ressortir de là triomphant.*

Au demeurant, c'est l'homme le plus charmant du monde si j'en excepte d'Annunzio; verveux à la manière italienne qui prend souvent la verbosité pour l'éloquence, le faste pour la richesse, l'agitation pour le mouvement, la fébrilité pour le transport divin. Il vint me voir il y a quelque dix ans et déploya des amabilités si incroyables qu'elles me forcèrent de partir sitôt après pour la campagne; si je l'avais revu, c'en était fait de moi; j'allais lui retrouver du génie.'

André Gide (on F. T. Marinetti).

F. T. MARINETTI

FUTURISM AND FASCISM

1

ON 20 FEBRUARY 1909, *Le Figaro* published a document that was headed 'Futurist Manifesto'. Its aim was to shock: '*Debout sur le cime du monde, nous lançons encore une fois le défi aux étoiles*'. It would be easy now to dismiss it as just one more of the *avant-garde* proclamations which were published constantly in Paris in the first decade of the century. Yet it is a document that is full of historical interest, both because of its content, which was to have considerable influence on European literature, painting and even politics, and because of the circumstances in which it was written.

Although its message was international, and it was to have repercussions all over Europe, its author was Italian; and one of its aims was to regenerate Italy—that Italy which had 'been too long the great second-hand market'—to 'rid it of the innumerable museums which cover it with innumerable cemeteries'. However, there was at that moment no obvious intellectual centre in Italy where such an appeal could be effectively launched. Rome, for all the symbolic value it had had when won from the Pope in 1870, had never become a cultural capital; Turin remained a provincial city, while Naples, even though Croce was to try and make it an intellectual centre, remained backward and unpredictable, a city that seemed almost foreign to Italians from the North. In Florence, it is true, there were a number of literary reviews, whose editors and contributors were as concerned as the authors of the Futurist Manifesto about the need to give Italy a living cultural present worthy of its past. These reviews, *Leonardo*, *La Voce*, and, later, *Lacerba*, were inevitably the work of a small group of people (nearly all of whom were to be influenced, at least temporarily, by Futurism) such as Giovanni Papini, Ardengo Soffici, Giuseppe Prezzolini. But, although they themselves were among the leading critics in Italy and published work by new and promising writers (including Benito Mussolini) they were, in fact, unable to make much impression on the drowsy, peaceful atmosphere of a city, which, more than any in Italy, lived for and on its past. 'I am very sorry indeed,' Papini wrote with characteristic egotism, though not without some truth, 'to think that the Florence of the first half of the century will owe to ME ALONE and to my friends, the honour of being remembered and admired.'[1]

There remained Milan, commercially and industrially already the most important city of Italy, which was, in fact, to be the centre of the Futurist movement. As yet, however, it was not a place from which a new movement could be launched with any hope of reaching a wide audience. If any proclamation was to cause a stir outside a very restricted circle in the Italy, and, indeed, the Europe of 1909, it would have to be published first of all in Paris. Paris was already an Italian intellectual centre. After all, the most famous living Italian writer, Gabriele D'Annunzio, who was regarded as a regenerator of the Italian language and of Italian literature, was as much at home there as in Italy and, indeed, was to live there permanently for some years after 1910 (though largely because his financial difficulties had made life in Italy impossible), and he wrote some of his works in French. It was in Paris, too, that the author of the Futurist Manifesto, Filippo Tommaso Marinetti, had been living, and, although his home was in Milan and the Manifesto was actually drafted there, it was in French that Marinetti's early literary works had appeared. If the prevailing literary and artistic conceptions were to be attacked there was no better place to do so than the city where contemporary art and ideas were being developed to their most refined and advanced point, and therefore it was natural that Marinetti and his friends should decide to strike their first blow for a new aesthetic in Paris.

Marinetti came of a rich, North Italian family with business connections in Egypt, and he was born in Alexandria in 1876. He was at school at the Jesuit College there—and was expelled because of his enthusiasm for Zola—and when he was 17 he went to Paris to the University. Although he later studied in Pavia and Genoa, he spent most of the early years of the century in Paris, and began his literary career there. His epic *La Conquête des Etoiles* appeared in 1902, and has little original about it, though it already shows a taste for vigorous battle scenes. Soon, however, he began to think of himself as a writer of the twentieth century, looking to a future in which all would be possible, provided that what was old and stale could be destroyed quickly and radically enough. His second volume of poems was dedicated to D'Annunzio and called, characteristically, *Destruction*. Marinetti's mind was already full of universal disasters that would purify the world: in 1906, for instance, he was invoking the avenging sea to deliver us from 'infamous reality':

> *Hola hé, hola ho! Détruisons! Détruisons!*[2]

Marinetti's most ambitious work of this period was a play, *Le Roi Bombance* (1905), a tedious and laboured satire in which a style that echoes that of his friend Alfred Jarry's *Ubu Roi* is used to attack Socialist ideas of a Utopia in which all men's material needs will have been met. None of Marinetti's writings are very interesting or very original; but certain ideas were already emerging which, ever more stridently repeated, were to be the main themes of the Futurist movement—violence, destruction, hatred of the past and its values, and, at the same time, intense excitement about the prospects of the new century that was just beginning, an awareness of the beauty of machines which could replace the more traditional objects of aesthetic satisfaction, and a realisation of the heightening of experience which new sensations of speed and mechanical power could give.

There was nothing very new in all this. The admiration for destruction was common enough at a moment when Nietzsche's influence in France and Italy was at its height, and when Georges Sorel was elevating violence into a political doctrine. Indeed, a group of minor writers and artists, who had founded in Paris a group called *Compagnons de l'action d'Art*, based on a mixture of anarchist and Nietzschean ideas, had already gone so far as to publish a Manifesto in 1907—two years before the Futurists—in which they proclaimed the necessity of resorting to violence to preserve the dignity of art, declared the inequality of man, and exclaimed 'Long live violence against all that makes life ugly!'[3]* And, as many of Marinetti's contemporaries were pointing out, Walt Whitman, Zola, Verhaeren and others had already been concerned to glorify '*les villes tentaculaires*'. In Italy the influence of Nietzsche had been as great as in France. As early as 1904, Giovanni Papini, the critic whose later adherence first to Futurism and subsequently to the Catholic Church was held by some to have conferred great prestige on both movements, had written: 'When lives have to be sacrificed we are not saddened, if before our minds shines the magnificent harvest of a superior life that will arise from their deaths. And while the lowly democrats cry out against war as a barbaric residue of ferocious ages, we believe it is the greatest awakener of the weak, a quick and heroic instrument of power and wealth'.[4] And D'Annunzio had not only taken over Nietzschean ideas, but, with the facility he always showed for picking up the latest intellectual and artistic modes, he had (in *Laudi*, for example) praised the beauties of modern life, and in *Forse che si Forse che No* (1910) he was among the first to see the possibilities of the aeroplane as a subject for literature, while, as early as the *Odi Navali* of 1892 he had addressed himself, though still in traditional romantic terms, 'To a Torpedo-boat on the Adriatic'. Moreover, at a higher intellectual level, Bergson had been teaching the importance of understanding the nature of speed and motion if we were to be able to evaluate and interpret our sensory perceptions of the world around us.

Marinetti had acquired all these ideas in Paris, where he had been associated with the group of people concerned to make

*One member of this group was a Mexican painter, Gerardo Murillo, who took the Aztec name of 'Dr Atl' and, on returning to his native land, introduced their ideas to the young painters who were to become the leaders of the Mexican revolutionary movement in painting. He was much influenced by Futurism, too, and became a practitioner of *aeropittura* which aimed at exploiting the new view of the world obtainable from the aeroplane.

the Théâtre de l' Oeuvre a centre of drama which should occupy itself with the problems of contemporary life. He had, however, also maintained his contacts with Milan, where he had helped to found a review, *Poesia*, in 1905, so that for him the artistic aims of his Paris acquaintances were combined with the violent Italian nationalism of his Italian friends. It was from this fusion that Futurism was born. In England, where, in the twentieth century, advanced artistic tastes have usually been accompanied by internationalist and even pacifist political views, it perhaps needs an effort to understand the mood of most Italian intellectuals at the beginning of the century, disillusioned at the cultural results obtained by a united Italy, and anxious for their country to be taken seriously for its present achievements and not just for its past glories. Consequently, there was a growing mood of criticism. The younger generation were anxious to break away from the disillusionment which had depressed the greatest writer of the previous period, Carducci. He had written 'The times today more than ever before lack idealism and beauty; you might say that the new generation lacks a national consciousness'.[5] In their search for a new national consciousness, the Futurists were to react against Carducci himself, yet their sense of frustration derived from similar sources to his.

The political system and the jobbery of parliamentary government as practised in the era of Giolitti were under attack from many directions. Sociologists like Mosca and Pareto were developing theoretical reasons for rejecting democracy; syndicalist leaders were preaching direct action to achieve their aims. But it was not just the internal situation that was under discussion. If Italy was to be respected for her present self, then, many people thought, it would only be when she was a great power with a foreign policy that commanded respect abroad. And consequently those writers and thinkers, like D'Annunzio and Croce, who had achieved a reputation abroad, were doubly honoured at home, so much so that some of the younger people were already beginning to resent their domination. The fact that hundreds of thousands of Italians still lived under foreign rule in Trieste, the Alto Adige and surrounding districts, was a constant reminder of Italian inferiority in the world. Trieste had become a powerful symbol for every patriotic Italian, and the young Guglielmo Oberdan, who in 1882 had planned to murder the Austrian Emperor and been executed by the Austrians, had become a national hero. Italy's alliance with Austria-Hungary and Germany was under an emotional strain long before 1914.

The Socialists, while bitterly criticising the internal regime in Italy, were committed to opposing a nationalist policy abroad, and officially put their faith in a solution of the question of *Italia Irredenta* through a peaceful agreement between international-minded Socialists. But even they could not overlook the problem. The serious young Socialist schoolmaster, Benito Mussolini, posted to the Trentino, was studying the linguistic struggle there,* and was, as well, reading the same authors as the violent nationalists, his opponents. He contributed articles on Nietzsche and Sorel to the advanced periodicals. 'To understand Nietzsche,' he wrote, 'we must envisage a new race of "free spirits", strengthened in war, in solitude, in great danger . . . spirits endowed with a kind of sublime perversity, spirits which will liberate us from the love of our neighbour.'[6]

Marinetti was as much impressed by these Nietzschean ideas as Mussolini, and he was as ready as his Milanese friends to get excited about the question of Trieste and the fate of Oberdan. He went to Trieste in 1908 to carry a wreath at the funeral of Oberdan's mother, and was arrested by the Austrian authorities for a speech against Austria. Marinetti had many qualities that fitted him to be a leader of a new movement—a quick, eclectic, superficial intelligence, leisure, money, considerable personal charm, optimism and, above all, boundless energy. 'His arrival in the peaceful Florence of those days was like a meteorite landing in an old palace garden,' Papini was later to recall. 'Telegrams, telephone calls, rides in motor cars, appointments made and put off, tumultuous dinner parties, mass invasions of respectable cafés. . . .'[7] And one of his disciples remembers his first introduction to Marinetti as he was sitting in a bath, conducting a conversation at the top of his voice above the sound of the running water.[8] He was always rushing

*His study was published by *La Voce* in 1911.

from one place to another, writing, orating, organising. The Futurist Manifesto was a typical product both of his fantasy and of his powers as an impresario.

It was produced by Marinetti and a group of his younger Milanese friends in two days of intense excitement in February 1909. After spending an evening sitting and discussing their plans, surrounded by the Persian carpets and oriental hangings with which Marinetti's house was decorated, on the next day, first in a café and then back in Marinetti's house, they drafted the Manifesto.

The Futurist Manifesto starts with a statement of aims which were to recur in one form or another in all subsequent Futurist pronouncements:

'We want to sing the love of danger, the habit of energy and rashness.

'The essential elements of our poetry will be courage, audacity and revolt.

'Literature has up to now magnified pensive immobility, ecstasy and sleep. We want to exalt movements of aggression, feverish sleeplessness, the double march, the perilous leap, the slap and the blow with the fist.

'We declare that the splendour of the world has been enriched by a new beauty. the beauty of speed. A racing automobile . . . is more beautiful than the Victory of Samothrace. . .

'Beauty exists only in struggle. There is no masterpiece that has not an aggressive character. . . .

'We are on the extreme promontory of the centuries! What is the use of looking behind. . . . We are already living in the absolute, since we have already created eternal, omnipresent speed.

'We want to glorify war—the only cure for the world—militarism, patriotism, the destructive gesture of the anarchists . . . and contempt for woman.

'We want to demolish museums, libraries, fight morality, feminism and all opportunism and utilitarian cowardice.

'We will sing of great crowds agitated by work, pleasure and revolt; the multicoloured and polyphonic surf of revolutions in modern capitals: the nocturnal vibration of the arsenals and the workshops beneath their violent electric moons: the gluttonous railway stations devouring smoking serpents; factories suspended from the clouds by the thread of their smoke; . . . and the gliding flight of aeroplanes whose propeller sounds like the flapping of a flag and the applause of enthusiastic crowds.'*

With the publication of this Manifesto, the Futurist movement was launched; it remained to put these general, and not always consistent ideas into practice. The Manifesto created something of a stir in the Italian intellectual circles at which it was primarily directed. Papini showed it to Ardengo Soffici, and they both realised that here was something new and exciting, though they were shocked by the brashness and violence of Marinetti's style. Their first reaction—perhaps, as has been suggested,[9] in a moment of jealousy that Milan seemed to be getting a step ahead of Florence—was, however, to point out that there was nothing very original in all this. This was, as we have seen, partly true, and Papini suggested that others had praised modern life, that the desire to destroy museums and libraries was simply a belated manifestation of Rousseau's influence, while the contempt for women had, he said, already been preached by Strindberg. In fact, however, both Papini and Soffici were, before long, to join the Futurists, and Papini's collection of essays from this period[10] remains one of the best assessments of the movement's importance. After all, as Papini saw, even if the ideas of the Manifesto were not very original, they were new to Italy. 'In Russia or America, Futurism would be ridiculous: it is necessarily a product of Italy.'[11] (He was wrong about Russia, where, as will be seen, Futurism was to produce an important literary and artistic movement.) The praise of war and patriotism was just what young Italians wanted to hear, and the Futurist Manifesto enabled them to gratify these passions while taking the lead in a new artistic movement, and thus simultaneously to overcome

---

*A translation of the full text of the Futurist Manifesto is printed as an Appendix. The main documents of the Futurist Movement have been reprinted in *Archivi del Futurismo* collected and edited by Maria Drudi Gambillo and Teresa Fiori (Rome 1958).

their feelings of political and cultural inferiority. 'I am a Futurist,' Papini wrote after joining the movement, 'because Futurism means Italy, an Italy greater than the Italy of the past, more modern, more courageous, more advanced than other nations. The most lively flame of this Italy burns brightest among the Futurists, and I am proud of being one of them.'[12]

Immediately after the publication of the Manifesto, Marinetti started to organise the Futurists into a movement that should embody both his ideas of a new twentieth century aesthetic and the desire for a new, up-to-date, modern Italy. Futurism was to leave no aspect of life untouched; and the battle between Futurists and *Passéistes* or *Passatisti* was to be engaged on all fronts. This, in fact, at once involved the practical problem of what the Futurists' political attitude was to be, especially in view of the forthcoming Italian elections. Accordingly, Marinetti produced his first public political statement. 'We Futurists have as our sole political programme the pride, the energy, and the expansion of the nation. We denounce to the country the inextinguishable shame that would result from the possibility of a clerical victory. . . . We want a national representative body, which, freed from mummies, released from all pacifist cowardice, will be ready to thwart any affront, to answer any insult.'[13] And, in March, 1909, Marinetti was proclaiming in a speech at Trieste: 'In politics we are as far removed from international and antipatriotic socialism—that ignoble exaltation of the rights of the belly—as we are from timid clerical conservatism symbolised by the bedroom slippers and the hot water bottle. . . . We sing of war, the only cure for the world, a superb blaze of enthusiasm and generosity, a noble bath of heroism without which races fall asleep in slothful egoism, in economic opportunism, in a miserly hoarding of the mind and will'.[14]

However, Marinetti was equally interested in the artistic aims of the movement, and, immediately after the publication of the Manifesto, he started a campaign to bring them before the public. He began to organise a series of '*soirées futuristes*', which were to cause a scandal in Italy and elsewhere over the next five years. A theatre would be hired; there would be a lecture by Marinetti or a recitation of his works or of those of other Futurists; later the programmes were extended to include other kinds of Futurist entertainment. What was novel about them was that their aim was deliberately to outrage and shock the public. And the more opposition and uproar that resulted, the better pleased Marinetti and his supporters were. Marinetti would delight the audience by calmly peeling, quartering and eating the oranges that were thrown at him. The meeting would break up in confusion and end in a free fight between the Futurists and their opponents. The police would have to be summoned, and, when the members of the group finally retired to a nearby café, one or other of them would be without shoes, having hurled them at a fugitive *Passatista*. Marinetti describes one of the most famous of these evenings at the *Teatro Lirico*, Milan, as follows: 'In spite of the storms of interruptions and cat-calls, I declaimed from the beginning to end an ode to General Asinari de Bernezzo, who was unjustly placed on the retired list for having pronounced before his troops too Futurist a speech against Austria. . . . [One of the audience cried] Down with the Fatherland; it was then that I shouted these words at the top of my voice: Here is our first Futurist conclusion! Long live war! Down with Austria!'[15]

Marinetti's 'Futurist novel', *Mafarka le Futuriste*, published in 1909, was the subject of a prosecution for obscenity, and Marinetti was condemned to two months in prison (which he does not seemed to have served), all of which added to the notoriety and scandal that surrounded him, and gave this tedious, rhetorical tale of rape and battle in a mythical Africa more fame than it deserved. The constant attack on the prejudices and susceptibilities of the Italian bourgeoisie was kept up by a series of demonstrations 'against' the most famous cities of Italy. In July 1910, for instance, the Futurists scattered thousands of leaflets '*Contra Venezia Passatista*' from the Campanile in Venice. Marinetti pronounced a discourse against Florence, and Papini, after his adherence to the movement, one against Rome. 'For many years I have felt for Rome a repulsion that at certain moments almost becomes hatred. Not for the city of Rome, understand, which has beautiful squares and factories, but for what Rome represents in the art and history of Italy.'[16] It was perhaps this throwing overboard of the whole of Italian art that was the most exciting and at the same time the most shocking aspect of the Futurist agitation. No one was spared. 'Beethoven, Michelangelo, Dante make us sick,' said the painter Boccioni.[17] Nor were contemporary idols any better treated. D'Annunzio was *'il bidet delle Muse'* and Croce *'le mal de Naples'*.[18] There were more logical reasons for attacking D'Annunzio, too: 'He has refined from all his talent the four intellectual poisons that we must destroy at all costs: (i) The sickly, nostalgic poetry of distance and memory. (ii) Romantic sentimentalism streaming with moonlight, rising towards the Woman-Beauty, ideal and fatal. (iii) Obsession with lust and its eternal triangle of adultery seasoned with the pepper of incest and the stimulating spice of Christian sin. (iv) The profound passion for the past. . . .'[19]

Once the main lines of Futurist propaganda have been understood, what is interesting about Marinetti's activities in these years is the way in which he conducted his campaign to stir up public opinion. By stopping at nothing, by using all the devices of publicity he could think of, by revelling in noise, fights and opposition, he forced the public to listen to his slogans, and a good many of them stuck in their minds. As Benedetto Croce wrote in 1924: 'For anyone who has a sense of historical connections, the ideological origins of Fascism can be found in Futurism, in the determination to go down into the streets, to impose their own opinions, to stop the mouths of those who disagree, not to fear riots or fights, in this eagerness to break with all traditions, in this exaltation of youth which was characteristic of Futurism. . . .'[20]

2

THE CONNECTION BETWEEN Futurist ideas and methods and those of Fascism, and the later association of Marinetti with Mussolini, are not the main reason why the Futurist movement is of historical interest. The development of Futurist artistic ideas was to influence much subsequent twentieth century art, often in directions very different from those in which its original connection with extreme Italian nationalism might seem to point. Marinetti's own gifts were those of a propagandist and pamphleteer, and it is in these fields, rather than in his more extended literary works, that his undeniable talents reveal themselves. He conceived of Futurism as transforming all the arts, and, although his own interests were mainly literary and theatrical, and his eye for the visual arts not very acute, his friendship with young painters like Umberto Boccioni, Carlo Carrà and Luigi Russolo led Futurist doctrines to be applied immediately to painting and to produce their first notable results in this field. While Marinetti was repeating his ideas for Futurist literature in documents like *Tuons le Clair de Lune* (written in the summer of 1910 in a style that looks forward to surrealism),* his associates were elaborating the idea of a series of Manifestos devoted to the individual arts which would restate Futurist principles in technical terms appropriate to each particular field.

The first of these technical manifestos to appear was that of the Futurist painters, in April 1910, after a meeting in Turin to demonstrate the adherence of the artists to the movement. It was the work of the young painters who had been associated with Marinetti in the drafting of the original Futurist Manifesto, and it was also signed by another painter, Gino Severini, who was living in Paris and in touch with the most

*e.g. '*Deux aliénistes apparurent sur le seuil, catégoriques; mais comme je n'avais entre les mains qu'un éclatant fanal d'automobile, c'est avec son manche de cuivre poli que je leur inculquai la mort.*'[21]

advanced art there. The painters were excited by the idea of
a new aesthetic propounded by Marinetti. Except for Severini,
they were not in touch with advanced Parisian ideas and art,
and were delighted by something which they felt would give
a sense of direction to their work and place them in the fore-
front of the modern movement. The aim of Futurist painting
was not only to get rid of the traditional forms and objects of
art ('We demand the total suppression of the nude in painting
for ten years')[22] but also to convey a sense of the speed and
dynamism of modern life. A moving object is something different in kind from a static one. As Boccioni was to put it a few
years later: 'A horse in movement is not a stationary horse
which moves, it is a horse in movement, that is something else
which must be conceived and expressed completely differ-
ently'.[23] Thus the old conception of objects as self-contained
entities would have to be abandoned; surfaces penetrated each
other and the space around them. 'Our bodies sink into the
sofa upon which we are seated and the sofa penetrates our
bodies. The passing bus leaps into the houses which in turn
hurl themselves upon the bus and absorb it.'[24] Just as the
Impressionists had seen that light could completely change the
appearance of objects, so now movement too would make them
look different. 'Movement and light destroy the materiality of
objects.'[25] The result of this would, it was hoped, be to destroy
the conception of the spectator confronted by a picture which
was a separate, static object. 'We will henceforth place the
spectator in the centre of the picture.'[26]

A new choice of subject-matter, the depiction of speed and
motion, the destruction of the artist's and spectator's traditional viewpoint, all these were aims that it was easier to
formulate in a Manifesto than to work out in terms of actual
painting, and the immediate result of the Manifesto was simply
to produce large pretentious paintings with elaborate quasi-
modern subject matter.* In the autumn of 1911, however,

---

*Most of these have since been destroyed, but a good example of this
painting at its worst is Russolo's *Musica* (Estorick Collection), which shows
a small purple pianist, presumably in a night club, crouched over a keyboard
at the bottom of the painting. From his hands issue coils depicting the
music, terminating in seven masks symbolising the notes of the scale.

Marinetti paid for Boccioni, Carrà and Russolo to visit Paris at the suggestion of Severini, after they had been attacked by Soffici for their inept, provincial banality and had responded by beating Soffici up as he sat in a café. In Paris they were able to see the work of the Cubists, friends of Severini, who were preoccupied with somewhat similar problems of destroying traditional perspective and producing a new concept of form and space. In the process, they had developed certain technical devices which the Futurists were able to borrow and put to their own ends. But any superficial similarity between the styles marks a profound difference of aim, for the Futurists lacked the calm objectivity of the Cubists, and were, in fact, much more emotive and literary in their approach.[27] The fusion and interpenetration of an object and its surroundings, characteristic of contemporary Cubist painting, were taken over by the Futurists and used, as they thought, to depict motion, with the lines traversing the picture determining the composition and representing the 'lines of force' along which the objects move; the linear geometric structure of the Cubists became lines 'representative of the movement of matter along the trajectory determined by the structure of the object and its action'.[28] Some of the Futurist painters were less sophisticated, and represented motion by a succession of images in different positions as in a film strip,* a technique which, they were quick to see, could be better replaced by the cinema itself.

It was these new developments in Futurist painting, in addition to the general success of the movement, that persuaded Ardengo Soffici who, with Papini, was the animating spirit of *La Voce*, and who was a painter as well as a writer, to give his support to the Futurists; and, for the next two or three years, he was to join Boccioni as the great exponent of Futurist aesthetics. Soffici, indeed, was able to give a more philosophical flavour to the movement. Boccioni was excellent at conveying a sense of excitement and pride at being in the artistic vanguard that would spread the idea of a '*grande Italia futurista*', and reflect 'the marvellous youthful atmosphere that we are

---

*cf., e.g., Balla's *A Woman and Her Dog*, (Museum of Modern Art, New York) where the dog is made to look almost like a centipede to convey the motion of the legs.

creating, in which Italy is becoming a great industrial and military power, this atmosphere [which] is little suited to lungs which are corrupted by the dust of libraries and museums and the centuries-old stink of excavations'.[29] Soffici, however, could use the Hegelian dialectic to show that Impressionism was the thesis, Cubism the antithesis and Futurism the synthesis of modern painting.[30]

Indeed, it was hoped by the Futurists that their new art would express more than any previous painting. 'It is a question of uniting to the concept of space, to which Cubism is limited, the concept of time. . . . We synthesize all the properties (time, place, form, colour) and make the picture out of them.'[31] Boccioni called some of his paintings *States of Mind*; and, in the preface to the catalogue of the exhibition in which they were shown, he wrote 'The picture must be the synthesis of what is remembered and what is seen'.[32] His friend Carrà developed these ideas further and more fancifully, and wanted to paint 'sounds, noises and smells'. 'In railway stations, workshops, in the world of machinery and sport, the sounds, noises and smells are predominantly red.' (Elsewhere he writes, in typical Futurist language, of '*I rossi, rooooooosssissimi che griiiiidono*'.) 'In restaurants and cafés they are silver, yellow and violet. While the sounds, noises and smells of animals are yellow and blue, those of women are green, blue and violet.'[33]

Futurism was to be less important in its impact on arts other than literature and painting. It failed to secure the adherence of any first-class musicians. The author of the *Manifesto of Futurist Musicians* was Balilla Pratella, a serious and painstaking composer, whose *Musica Futurista*, written in 1912, is a monotonous repetition of rhythms in a steady crescendo, that reminds one somewhat of the later German composer Carl Orff. And, indeed, the musicians' Manifesto itself was less revolutionary than the others, as, even if Futurist music was 'to express the musical soul of crowds, of great industrial workshops, of trains, liners, warships, automobiles and aeroplanes',[34] the new forms of Futurist music were to be nothing more original than the symphonic poem and the opera. Under the circumstances, it is not surprising that attempts were made to claim Stravinsky and even Richard Strauss as the true Futurist musicians. A more interesting attempt to develop a new Futurist 'art of noises' was made in 1913 by Luigi Russolo, the painter who had been one of the original Futurist group, and who now described himself as *'pittore e rumorista'*. As the world grew more and more noisy, he considered, so music would become more and more complicated; but the new music must result from the sort of noises that were already being made outside the concert hall in any industrial city. Thus the instruments would be, or at least would imitate, the machines and engines of an industrial civilisation. The orchestra at one of Russolo's concerts, accordingly consisted of *'gorgogliatori, crepitatori, stropicciatori, scrosciatori, ululatori, rombatori, scoppiatori, sibilatori e ronzatori'*.*[35]

Russolo, indeed, assembled an orchestra of this kind and gave concerts in Italy and abroad—including an appearance as a turn in the bill at the Coliseum in London. And although he claimed that 'the Russian Futurist musician Stravinsky was studying' his new art with great interest,† and although the musicologist of the future may trace links between the *'Arte dei Rumori'* and the *'Musique concrète'* of the mid-twentieth century, it is hard to believe that Russolo always took himself quite seriously. 'At Milan' he wrote 'towards the end of the concert, while Russolo continued imperturbably to conduct his latest spiral of sounds, *Concourse of Aeroplanes and Automobiles*, Marinetti, Carrà, Boccioni, Mazza and Piatti quickly got down from the stage into the auditorium and confronted, with fists, sticks and chairs, more than five-hundred Philistines, many of whose faces they succeeded in dynamically deforming. The police intervened. The battle lasted half an hour. . . .'[36]

Futurist architecture was more serious, if only because Antonio Sant' Elia, the leading Futurist architect, was himself someone whose ideas were to be taken seriously by other members of his profession even though he died too young to carry out his daring designs. And the doctrines he preached—

---

*'Gurglers, cracklers, rubbers, crashers, screamers, roarers, exploders, whistles and buzzers'.

†In March 1915 Diaghilev proposed to Stravinsky a meeting with Russolo and Pratella to study the latter's latest works under the auspices of Marinetti.

apart from such eccentricities as laying down that Futurist buildings must have no stairs, only lifts—were those which were soon to be common to advanced architects everywhere, and which were taken up by Le Corbusier and his contemporaries: the use of steel and concrete and the absence of decoration would make 'the Futurist house like a giant machine'.[37] There is no need to follow some of the later developments of the movement as the Futurists sought further fields in which to apply their ideas—Futurist science, for instance, 'exploratory, highly sensitive, vibratory, influenced by the most remote intuitions, fragmentary, contradictory, happy to discover every day a new truth that destroys yesterday's truth, steeped in the unknown'.[38]

Marinetti's own contribution, apart from his supply of money and inexhaustible energy, was in the field of literature and the theatre. Here it was perhaps easier than elsewhere to put some at least of the Futurist principles into practice. In the theatre it should be possible both to bring art into touch with modern life by choosing modern subjects and by using already existing forms of entertainment—the variety theatre and the *café-chantant*. The theatre would be a final synthesis of all the arts; it would use the new twentieth century devices of electricity and the cinema; and this would enable plays to be extremely short, since all these technical means would enable the theatrical synthesis to be achieved in the shortest possible space of time, as all the elements could be presented simultaneously. This concept of 'simultaneity' was of the greatest importance in all Futurist art. Just as the paintings were to combine past, present and future, and convey motion, sound and smell as well as space, so Futurist literature, by abandoning conventional syntax and enjoying a complete freedom of imagery and analogy, would convey a sense of speed, noise and immediacy. 'The only preoccupation of the narrator: to convey all the vibrations of his ego. . . . The imagination of the poet should provide a link between distant objects and the writer and public without any conducting wires, by means of essential words in liberty.'[39] '*Paroles en liberté*' like 'simultaneity' was to be one of the great slogans of Futurist writing. The crudity and violence with which Marinetti declared his abandonment of syntax and traditional forms of language had its effect on one or two much better writers than he was. In Paris, Guillaume Apollinaire, who had already made himself the literary champion of the Cubist painters, became very excited by Futurism and wrote a pamphlet, *L'Antitradition Futuriste*, in which he shouted '*Merde à Versailles Pompei Bruges Oxford Nuremberg Toledo Benares etc!*'. But the study of Futurist literary techniques was not just to lead him to champion a wholesale destruction of past art, and he adopted some of Marinetti's suggestions about freedom from syntax and punctuation for his own ends, to produce some of the best lyrical poems of the century.

Marinetti's own use of '*paroles en liberté*' is without any subtlety or psychological interest. Onomatopoeic imitation and typographical tricks give a certain sense of speed and noise; and contemporaries were enthusiastic about Marinetti's own recital of his works (one wonders how he managed lines like that in his record of the siege of Adrianople, *Zang Tumb Tuum*: '20 *kmq di corvi volanti* 200000 *AMI* 100000 *carrrrrrruole Arruginite*').[40] Yet, once more, as one reads Marinetti's own work of the Futurist period (to say nothing of his later *aeropoesia* or his *Canto eroi e macchine della guerra mussoliniana*), one is forced back to the conclusion that his talent was that of a propagandist, pamphleteer and impresario. His theatrical ideas were taken up by writers and producers in the 1920s—he interrupted a performance of Pirandello's *Piccola Citta*, shouting 'This is plagiarism. I invented this synthetism'[41]—and his Futurist Variety Theatre foreshadows other types of 'crazy' humour of the twentieth century. Everything must be absurd: the actresses would have green hair, violet arms, blue bosoms and orange chignons: glue would be placed on the seats of the theatre and the same seat sold to two people: itching and sneezing powder would be scattered among the audience: free seats would be offered to notorious eccentrics, and so on.

It was clear that no one with Marinetti's restless nervous energy, propagandist zeal and ambition to lead a movement was going to be content with his scandals and triumphs in Italy; and, during the years 1910 to 1914, he was travelling constantly, lecturing, reciting, organising demonstrations, shocking his hosts and provoking violent reactions everywhere. He was, moreover, true to his own beliefs about the positive values of war, and he went to the front, both in Italy's war with the Turks in Tripoli, and to the siege of Adrianople in 1912 during the Balkan wars. The latter expedition, indeed, annoyed some of his friends, who thought he would do better to stay at home and look after the business interests of the Futurist movement. 'War is beautiful,' Boccioni wrote to Carrà, 'to see it is better, but ours and my future concerns me more.'[42] When the Italians invaded Tripoli in 1911 and won it from the Turks, Marinetti was an enthusiastic supporter of the new Italian Empire: 'We are proud to feel that the warlike fervour which inspires the whole country equals our own, and we invite the Italian Government, which has finally become Futurist, to magnify all the nation's ambitions, to despise the stupid accusations of piracy, and to proclaim the birth of Panitalianism'.[43]

One of the people who had been accusing the Italians of piracy, and criticising their methods in fighting the war was an English journalist, Francis McCullagh. 'While writing the present book [*Italy's War for a Desert*, 1912] in an isolated house on the Surrey Downs,' he recalled, 'I was interrupted one day by the arrival of three gentlemen who had come from London in a motor car and wanted to speak to me. They were Signor F. T. Marinetti who calls himself a "poet" and who said that he had just come from Tripoli and was staying at the Savoy Hotel; Signor Boccioni, who is, I believe, a "futurist" painter, and another gentleman. . . . The object of these gentlemen was to fight a duel with me, and they managed to find me at home when there was nobody in the house, save a maid servant. . . . I told them I would communicate with them in due course; whereupon one of them threatened to attack me then and there. . . . I promised to communicate with my challenger at the Savoy Hotel, in case I ever felt anxious to fight a duel with him. Then the "poet" got on his legs and began an oration which lasted a quarter of an hour and afforded me a good deal of amusement. He told me that I had never visited the trenches at Tripoli, having probably remained concealed in some *cantina* inside the town. . . . All this was very amusing, and the manner in which my visitor strutted about the room like a hero in melodrama was more amusing still. But there is a

serious side to this question. Is it not rather impudent of
foreigners enjoying the hospitality of this country to thus burst,
armed, and presume into the houses of men who criticise the
conduct of their troops in Tripoli?'[44]

It was not the only 'impudence' for which Marinetti was
responsible during his visits to England in 1911 and 1914. His
attitude to the English was mixed: 'What we like in you is your
indomitable and bellicose patriotism; we like your intelligent
and generous individualism which allows you to open your
arms to the individualists of all countries, libertarians and
anarchists. . . . You have kept an unbridled passion for fighting
in all its forms, from boxing—simple, brutal and swift—to the
roar from the monstrous throats of the guns crouched in their
revolving caves of steel on the decks of your Dreadnoughts,
when they smell in the distance appetising squadrons'.[45] Yet
the English had a lamentable love of tradition and a cult of
aristocracy, as well as a deplorable prudery. 'Remember the
dreary and ridiculous condemnation of Oscar Wilde which
Europe has not yet forgiven you.'[46] And English taste had been
corrupted by the love of the past—especially through the
influence of Ruskin, which 'has developed among you the
obsessional cult of our past and entirely perverted your judgement of contemporary Italy. You love above all the three
towns that we regard as the three festering sores of our
peninsula: Florence, Rome and Venice.'[47]

During his visit to the front during the Balkan Wars,
Marinetti had met the English journalist, Henry Nevinson, and
through him he met his son C. R. W. Nevinson, who was a
painter, and who had also heard of Marinetti through their
mutual friend Gino Severini. In the early summer of 1914,
Marinetti paid a second visit to England, complete with a suit of
Futurist clothing fastened by one dynamic button. There was
a dinner in a London restaurant organised by Nevinson and
Wyndham Lewis, and attended by about sixty guests, including
Harold Monro, Laurence Housman and R. Wilenski. 'It was an
extraordinary affair,' Nevinson wrote later. 'Marinetti recited
a poem about the siege of Adrianople with various kinds of
onomatopoeic noises and crashes in free verse, while all the
time the band downstairs played "You made me love you. I

didn't want to do it". It was grand if incoherent. . . . His French was good, having nothing of the Italian accent and phraseology I associated with Severini or Boccioni. It certainly was a funny meal. Most people had come to laugh, but there were few who were not overwhelmed by the dynamic personality and declamatory gifts of the Italian propagandist. . . .'[48] The performance was repeated at Cambridge, and there was a further meeting in London, at which Nevinson banged a drum. It was also during this visit that Marinetti persuaded Sir Oswald Stoll to let Russolo do his turn at the Coliseum.

Nevinson's friendship with Marinetti was symbolised by the publication of a *Manifesto against English Art*. In fact, this bears the mark of being largely Nevinson's work, for it has an inside knowledge of the English scene that Marinetti never had; and many of its criticisms are shrewd and to the point. The objects of the attack were 'the worship of tradition and the conservatism of Academies, the commercial acquiescence of English artists, the effeminacy of their art . . . the pessimistic sceptical and narrow views of the English public, who stupidly prefer the pretty-pretty, the commonplace, the soft, sweet and mediocre. The sickly revivals of mediaevalism, the Garden Cities with their curfews and artificial battlements, the Maypole Morris dances, Aestheticism, Oscar Wilde, the pre-Raphaelites, neo-Primitives, and Paris. The perverted snob who ignores and despises all English originality and daring but welcomes eagerly all foreign originality and daring. . . . The indifference of the King, the State and the politicians towards all arts. The English notion that Art is a useless pastime, only fit for women and schoolgirls, that artists are poor deluded fools to be pitied and protected, and Art a ridiculous complaint, a mere topic for table-talk. . . . The mania for immortality. A masterpiece must disappear with its author'. The proclamation ends with a typical Futurist exclamation—'Forward! Hurrah for motors! Hurrah for speed! Hurrah for draughts! Hurrah for lightning!' —and a demand for a strong, virile, anti-sentimental art, a fearless desire for adventure, a heroic instinct of discovery, a worship of strength and a physical and moral courage, all sturdy virtues of the English race.[49]

The manifesto was published in *The Times*, *Observer* and

Daily Mail, and Nevinson used to scatter copies from the galleries of London theatres. It was typical of the atmosphere of excitement, confusion and recrimination which Marinetti left behind him everywhere that Wyndham Lewis, who had been one of the original organisers of his reception in London, should at once have written to the papers that published the manifesto dissociating himself from Marinetti, and he led the hecklers at one of Marinetti's subsequent lectures.[50] But Wyndham Lewis, nevertheless, had been irrevocably influenced by Futurist ideas; and the periodical *Blast*, which he founded in 1914, was the nearest the British got to Futurist writing, just as the Vorticist movement in painting, which Nevinson and Wyndham Lewis developed during the war, was nearer to Futurism than to any other contemporary style.

Marinetti's two visits to Russia were to leave the same sort of dissensions as his visits to England, and were to have even more effect. He came to Russia at a moment when many of the younger writers were reacting against the vagueness and mysticism into which the Symbolist movement had drifted. Some of them (the 'Acmeists') were talking about the need for literature to interest itself in the sensory texture of objects, in the 'density' of things. And, with the sensibility to the newest ideas from Europe that the Russians always showed in the hundred years before the Revolution, they had read and discussed the Futurist Manifesto as soon as it appeared, and found that it fitted in very well with ideas that some of the Russian poets were already developing. Immediately after Marinetti's first visit, Futurist groups began to be formed (in Moscow they later called themselves Cubo-Futurists, and in Petrograd Ego-Futurists) and to announce their break with the 'stifling past' and the opening of an attack on 'common sense and good taste'. In December 1912, a pamphlet called *A Slap in the Face of Public Taste* was published by the poet Mayakovsky and others, and called, in good Futurist terms, for 'throwing Pushkin, Dostoevsky and Tolstoy overboard from the steamer of modern times', while proclaiming their 'uncompromising hatred for the language used hitherto'.[51] This suggests what, in fact, was to be the difference between Russian Futurism and the much more superficial Futurism of Marinetti. The Russian writers were genuinely concerned with inventing a new mode of expression and not just finding 'modern' subject matter and recording it in a startling or shocking way. 'Genuine novelty in literature does not depend on content,' one of them wrote. 'A new light thrown on the old world may produce a very interesting interplay. . . . If there is a new form, there must also exist a new content. . . . It is form that determines content.'[52]

It was inevitable that, once Russian Futurism was developing along lines of its own, the Russians should resent Marinetti's claim to dominate the movement; and his second visit, in 1914, was not the success of his first one. His arrival was greeted by a letter in the newspaper *Nov* from Mayakovsky and others, in which they denied 'any debt to the Italian Futurists'.[53] Mayakovsky interrupted a lecture on the theatre by Marinetti, and soon afterwards broke with him completely, as did the painter Larionov, who had been largely responsible for making Russian painters aware of advanced French art. Russian Futurism became one of the artistic movements that supported —and was recognised by—the Revolution in its early stages; and, while the painters who had been influenced by Futurism were soon absorbed into various plastic and pictorial movements with names like Rayonnism, Constructivism and Suprematism, Mayakovsky was to become one of the best poets of his generation.

Marinetti never gave up his pretensions to have originated these Russian movements, and was writing in 1919: 'I am happy to learn that the Russian Futurists are Bolshevists, and that Futurist art has been for a certain time a state art in Russia. . . . That does credit to Lenin and gives us pleasure as a victory for us. All the Futurists in the world are children of Italian Futurism created by us in Milan twelve years ago. But all the Futurist movements are autonomous. Each people had, or still has, its own traditionalism to overthrow. We are not Bolsheviks because we have to make our own revolution'.[54] Mayakovsky's comment was perhaps more apt. When he met Marinetti in Paris in 1925, he noted 'We didn't know what to talk about. I was a Bolshevik: he a Fascist'.[55]

Marinetti was called by a Parisian journalist 'the caffeine of Europe'; and it is as a stimulant to others rather than for its own achievements that Futurism has its greatest importance in the artistic history of the twentieth century. Boccioni, it is true, and to a lesser extent the other painters, produced painting and sculpture of great vitality and originality which remain of artistic value. Yet their work reflects the excitement produced by a few stimulating ideas and a new sense of the aesthetic potentialities of the modern world rather than any coherent doctrine or the particular teachings of the Futurist aesthetic. It was the Cubists and the Russian Constructivists who carried out the daring experiments with new materials. It was the Dadaists who carried the Futurist ideas about the anti-artistic and destructive purpose of art to their logical conclusion. And it was Fernand Léger who quickly saw that some of the intellectual and social implications of Futurism could be absorbed into a sounder and more purely pictorial art, so that it was he, rather than the Futurist painters, who was perhaps the first to be completely successful in assimilating machines and machine-made forms into twentieth century art. It was, too, Apollinaire and Mayakovsky, rather than Marinetti or any of his Italian followers, who were able to use the idea of *'paroles en liberté'*, and convey in literary terms a sense of the 'simultaneity' of experiences.

The Futurist movement left its mark on the art and literature of France, Russia and England. In Germany Futurist painting was received with excitement. The Futurists showed their work in Berlin shortly after their Paris exhibition, and a translation of the Futurist Manifesto was immediately published by Herwarth Walden in *Der Sturm*. This was a periodical which appeared from 1910 to 1929 and which set out to fuse the most modern artistic movements—expressionism, Futurism, abstract art—with the idea of art for the people, and to associate advanced artistic ideas with advanced political beliefs. It is obvious that *Der Sturm* would find much that was sympathetic in Futurism, and Futurist ideas thus became disseminated in German intellectual and artistic circles. Their influence was also felt in the smaller countries of Europe, for example, by the Dutch writers of the *Nieuwe Beweging*.

Freedom from the restraints of traditional language, technique and subject matter, the desire to shock, the belief that the civilisation of the twentieth century, urban and mechanical, could contribute something new and important to European art, a passion for speed and for the bombardment of the senses by the innumerable new simultaneous impressions of the modern world—all these were things with which the artists and writers of the new century were bound to be preoccupied; and the Futurist movement sharply and imperiously called their attention to some of them. But whereas many of the writers and artists who were affected by Futurist ideas—Mayakovsky and Léger, for example—were to be led by them towards the political beliefs of the internationalist Left, in Italy, on the other hand, where violent patriotism had always been an essential part of the movement, Futurism was to be one of the components of Fascism; and, if its artistic influence had been stimulating and liberating, its political results were to be deadening and oppressive.

3

THE SUCCESS—WHETHER of esteem or of scandal—of Marinetti's many trips abroad only served to increase his ambition to dominate and expand the Futurist movement at home in Italy. He had from the start envisaged the Futurist programme as being political as well as artistic, and he believed that the new twentieth century art he was preaching would only flourish in a revolutionary and rejuvenated Italian state. The conquest of Tripoli had given him a chance of reaffirming his political beliefs, and of repeating and elaborating the ideas he had thrown out before the elections of 1909. When the war in Tripoli broke out, Marinetti issued the second Futurist political manifesto: 'We can admire nothing else today except the formidable symphony of the shrapnel and the wild bursts of our inspired artillery,' and, in the same mood, 'Let all freedom be granted to the individual and to the people except the freedom to be cowardly'. And (this was to become one of the most used of all the Futurist slogans), 'Let it be proclaimed that the word Italy must overrule the word Freedom (*La parola Italia deve dominare sulla parola Liberta*).'[56]

Two years later, at the time of the parliamentary elections of 1913, the same ideas were expanded, though without becoming very much more precise. The Italian fleet and army were to be increased, so that the Italian people would be proud to be Italian through participating in war—'*sola igiene del mondo*'. The economic interests of the proletariat were to be protected, and the working class was to be given education in patriotism. But, while Futurist policy was to be anti-clerical, it was also anti-socialist. There should be a cult of progress, speed, sport, physical force and reckless courage—a 'predominance of gymnastics over books'—and, accordingly, 'a minimum of professors, very few lawyers, very many farmers, engineers, chemists, mechanics and active business men'. The 'Passatist' cities, Rome, Venice and Florence, were to be violently modernised, and the humiliating tourist industry was to be abolished.[57]

Some of the practical suggestions in the Futurist political programmes show how, in so far as they deal with actual political institutions at all, the Futurists were reacting against accepted liberal and parliamentary ideas and moving in the direction of the corporate state. Parliament was to be transformed into an 'assembly of industrialists, agriculturalists, engineers and tradesmen'. And, if it did not function properly, it was to be abolished altogether and replaced by a technical committee composed of twenty specialists not over thirty years old. 'Instead of a lower house composed of incompetent talkers and feeble-minded scholars held in check by a senate of octogenarians, Italy shall be governed by a government of twenty experts, vitalised by an assembly of young men.'[58] None of this was perhaps very serious, yet the slogans had a ring to them that made them linger in the mind.

The Futurists had noted with approval the revolutionary intransigence of the young Socialist agitator, Benito Mussolini, who had been reading and reviewing Sorel's *Reflexions on Violence* and—a work much admired by the Futurists—Verhaeren's poems *Les Villes Tentaculaires*, published a dozen years earlier. And, indeed, many of Mussolini's beliefs at this period were the product of the same frustrations, growths of the same climate, as those of the Futurists, so that his language often came very close to theirs: 'Socialism, if it is not to die, must have the courage to be barbarous'.[59] 'Revolutions must be considered as the revenge of madness on good sense.'[60] However, during the Tripoli war, Mussolini, a rising star on the left of the Socialist Party, at a moment when it was torn by internal conflicts, was a firm opponent of the war, and, indeed, was arrested for his part in the anti-war demonstrations organised by the Socialists. It was this attitude of hostility towards the Italian imperialist venture that made the Socialists the main object of Futurist hatred and scorn at this period. It took Mussolini some time to get over this antagonism, and he welcomed any attacks on Marinetti. 'Have you read the last number of *La Voce*?' he wrote to a friend in April, 1913. 'Futurism is down and out. It's finished. Marinetti has killed it. The moonlight is coming back.'[61]*

*The reference is, of course, to Marinetti's pamphlet *Tuons le Clair de Lune.*

The judgement was premature. Marinetti's influence was still spreading. By 1913, Papini and Soffici had become whole-hearted adherents of the Futurist movement—'the sole group of people with the guts to stand up, mockingly and assertively, in the name of free lyricism,' Papini called them,[62] and Soffici wrote 'The more I think about Futurism, the more clearly I see how many providential actions—even in the practical field —it might begin to champion. To demand—to mention only one—the immediate suppression of all the Academies of Fine Arts—to demand that the state should not interfere in any way whatsoever with anything that has anything to do with art. Abolition of national exhibitions, pensions for artists, prizes, etc. Provocation of armed conflicts if necessary'.[63] Papini and Soffici marked their new departure by the foundation of a new review, *Lacerba*, in succession to *La Voce*. 'The birth of *Lacerba* was an act of liberation;' they announced; 'some of us had been feeling hampered for too long in *La Voce*. . . . Art was always tolerated but without enthusiasm and no other theories were admitted except those which had received an idealist stamp or tinge.'[64]

Once the Futurists had gained the adherence of such established writers as Papini and Soffici, and were able to use *Lacerba* as a means of spreading their ideas, the movement inevitably changed somewhat in character. Up to now, Marinetti had been the patron, impresario and director of a group of little-known young men. But, from 1913 on, he was dealing with men who were quick to resent his attempts at dominating them, and their cooperation was not always harmonious. Within a few months of the start of his association with the Futurists, Soffici was being attacked by them—though in a friendly way—and receiving registered letters accusing him of 'appalling sentimentality' and of giving exaggerated importance in his writings to love, sex and women.[65] The Futurists' avowed disdain for women, whom they liked to regard as objects of sexual passion devoid of all romantic, sentimental feeling, was always causing trouble, although they had found a lady, Valentine de Saint-Point, to draft a Manifesto of Futurist Women for them. ('Women, too long perverted by morality and prejudice, return to your sublime instinct, to violence and cruelty. . . . You owe heroes to humanity. Give them.')[66] There were few fields of Futurist activity where precept and practice were further apart. It was typical, for instance, of Marinetti's warm-hearted generosity that he should have lent Severini the money on which to get married; and yet it was equally typical that, when the young couple arrived back in Milan, the speeches against marriage at the party held by the Futurists to celebrate their return were so violent that, according to Soffici, the bride, who was only sixteen, burst into tears.[67]

Marinetti had, in fact, very few new ideas beyond those he had already launched, and a work like *Down with the Tango and Parsifal*, published in January 1914, adds little except a resounding title to the attacks he had previously made on sickly sensuality and romantic obfuscation. Marinetti was, indeed, moving away from purely literary and artistic activities towards something more violent and dramatic. 'Marinetti's activity is going to take on more and more of a social character,' Carrà complained to Severini in June 1914.[68] The difference between Marinetti and his associates, such as Papini, for example, was well expressed by Papini himself a few years later, after his breach with the Futurists at the end of 1914. 'Marinetti was in his early years an artist, and had, as an author of manifestos, moments of true and great genius. But the passion to dominate and the need for action have removed him, perhaps for ever, from art and have made him neglect his mission as an animator.'[69] Just where Marinetti's dynamic energy and desire for action were to lead him became clear at the end of July 1914, when the war broke out in Europe.

From the start of the war Italy's position was equivocal. She was bound by an alliance with Germany and Austria-Hungary to enter the war if either of them was attacked. But, although the Triple Alliance had been renewed as recently as 1912, in fact Italian policy had also been aimed at retaining good relations with England and improving relations with France. For most Italians, too, the Austrians seemed a natural enemy, and a campaign to win Trieste and the South Tyrol seemed to be an obvious war aim. When, therefore, Germany and Austria went to war in 1914 against France, Russia and

England, the Italian government used the fact that it was Germany and Austria who had been the first to issue actual declarations of war, as a technical excuse to avoid acting on their obligations under the Triple Alliance, and waited to see which side would offer the higher price for Italian support. Inevitably, of course, the whole question of intervention and neutrality became at once the centre of acute and violent public controversy. There was no doubt about where the Futurists stood. Here was a war of a far more exciting and dramatic kind than the affairs in Tripoli or the Balkans which Marinetti had hurried to witness. Marinetti and his friends had long been consistently hostile to German influence, and violent in their enthusiasm for the cause of *Italia Irredenta*, while they were bound to France by many emotional and intellectual ties. Consequently, they immediately threw themselves into a passionate campaign for intervention in the war on the side of France and Britain.

Marinetti's first practical step to prepare for war was to join the Lombard Cyclist Volunteers along with Russolo. And he at once turned all his experience of propaganda and public agitation to serve the campaign against neutrality and in favour of intervention. *Lacerba* was quickly turned into a political review. 'I returned to Florence,' Marinetti wrote on 12 August, 'to transform, together with Soffici, *Lacerba* into a political journal with the intention of preparing the atmosphere in Italy for war.'[70] And on 15 August the leading article asserted 'If the present war were only a political and economic one, though not remaining indifferent, we would be involved somewhat at a distance. But as this is a war not only of guns and ships, but also of culture and civilisation, we insist on making our position clear at once and following events with our whole hearts. . . . Perhaps this is the most decisive hour of European history since the end of the Roman Empire. Starting with this number, *Lacerba* will be purely political, and to gain a wider circulation will be sold for two *soldi*'.[71]

This was followed by a series of public demonstrations, and the 'Futurist evenings' became frankly political. 'I have proposed a Futurist evening at Montecatini [a well-known spa and summer resort near Florence],' Marinetti was writing on

14 September. 'The evening would have an artistic and literary programme but would be transformed by us into a violent anti-neutral demonstration before the important audience of politicians present.'[72] There were more public demonstrations too. On 15 and 16 September Marinetti was in Milan, where he organised the waving of the tricolour and the burning of the German flag. For these activities he and Boccioni were arrested by the police and spent five days in prison,* to emerge with increased prestige and proclaim to the students of Italy 'War on the Germanic culture of the professors headed by Croce. . . .'[74] The other Futurists were adding their own ingenious touches to the campaign. The painter Balla, for example, advocated the wearing of 'anti-neutral clothing' that should include no neutral colours and possess the Futurist characteristics of flexibility and lack of symmetry, as well as being phosphorescent and not durable.

All this violent action worried some of the more literary and intellectual sponsors of *Lacerba*. Soffici had already had doubts about some of Marinetti's political beliefs (though this did not prevent him from ending up as enthusiastic a Fascist as Marinetti himself) and had objected to the slogan 'The word Italy must predominate over the word Liberty'. 'But the word Liberty—and also the thing, indeed especially the thing,' he protested, 'let us place it in front of everything else. Let us adore it as the only divinity worthy of being adored in art and in life. Liberty: the beginning of all greatness and happiness. . . .'[75] During the winter of 1914-15, Papini, too, was more and more uneasy about Marinetti's energy and ambition, and more and more scathing about his activities. 'The Futurist manifestations in favour of Italian intervention,' he wrote, 'which we demanded, and which we expected to be numerous and vigorous, have been crude and insignificant and have culminated in the trivial demonstration in Milan and the unsuitable and futile manifesto of Balla about neutral clothing.'[76] By February of 1915 Papini was drawing up an elaborate table of the differences between 'Futurism' and 'Marinettism', in which he contrasts Futurist sensibility and

*Boccioni reassured his mother that he was lodged in a 'paying cell with an excellent dinner sent in from outside'.[73]

Marinettist technocracy, Futurist passion for liberty and Marinettist solidarity and discipline, Futurist patriotism and Marinettist chauvinism, Futurist sexual liberty and Marinettist contempt for women, and so on. It was not surprising that with all these tensions, personal and ideological, *Lacerba's* life was not very long; and it ceased publication in May 1915, on Italy's entry into the war.

Marinetti, however, whatever difficulties he might be having with his associates, was in full sympathy with a growing movement of public opinion; and the way in which things were going is nowhere more clearly shown than by developments inside the Italian Socialist Party. The Socialists, like their comrades abroad, had been divided by a series of questions over the past few years; and at the party congress of 1912 they had split irrevocably on the issue of revolution versus reform. In the course of this controversy Mussolini had emerged as one of the leading figures of the uncompromising revolutionary Left. His violent temperament and his impulse to dominate, together with a certain ability to assimilate—if not always to understand—the most up-to-date ideas, were turning him into a successful political leader and an effective journalist; and in December 1912 he became editor of the leading Socialist daily, *Avanti*. When the war broke out, and the hopes which the Socialist parties of Europe had placed in the Second International were shattered and the promises they had made of action against war broken, the Italian Socialist Party was in a particularly difficult position. Their sympathies lay, for the most part, with Belgium, and they also mostly shared with other ordinary Italians a feeling of dislike for the Austrians. But they were proud of being almost the only Socialist party in Europe that had remained true to their repeated undertakings to oppose the war, and were prepared to accept the orthodox Marxist view that the war was one between capitalist powers and was no concern of the working class.

Mussolini's own attitude was a little ambiguous. His turbulent nature and his ambitious temperament were driving him to some sort of action, and he was soon trying to distinguish between 'active' and 'passive' neutrality. He had already, even before the war, had some doubts about what seemed the pallid internationalism of the orthodox socialists; and his personal experiences in the Trentino had made him fervently anti-Austrian. 'It is time to face another problem,' he had said in a speech in January 1914, 'to see whether socialism is anti-national, or whether it may not be on the contrary an integrating force for the nation. . . . We venture to say . . . that a national rebirth cannot be explained without the action of socialism.'[77] When the war actually started Mussolini was clearly fascinated by its possibilities, and expressed his feelings in language explicitly borrowed from the Futurists: 'The Europe of 1914 that danced the Argentinian "tango" and prostrated itself before the mystic Parsifal (the tango and Parsifal are not so distant from each other as it may seem to some people; it is a question of more or less transcendental "sexuality"), this "civilian" Europe found itself after 3 August stained with the blood of the greatest war our history records'.[78] And again, on 6 August: 'Perhaps this war will, with its blood, set the wheels in motion'.[79] It was a phrase to which he became attached and which he was to use again in the form 'It is blood that sets in motion the resounding wheels of history,'[80] later in the year, after he had come out openly in support of the war.

The situation was an embarrassing one for Mussolini. He had the sense that an opportunity was being lost, and, at the same time, he could not risk an immediate breach with the Socialists by throwing in his lot with those who, like the Futurists, were demanding Italy's immediate entry into the war. 'You too are a victim of the sentimental ingenuousness,' he wrote to a friend soon after the outbreak of the war, 'which now unites the Right, nationalists, Futurists, republicans, Mazzinians, democrats and Freemasons. In fact there soon won't be any parties in Italy any more. Poor Socialism!'[81] During the next months, as this stream of opinion grew in volume and Mussolini was preparing to join it, he was careful to disassociate himself from the Futurist campaign: 'For the moment,' he told a group of Socialists on 9 September, 'we can say nothing definite. We will evaluate our attitude according to circumstances. . . . We might accept the war, but to defend it would signify crossing the barricades and becoming involved with those others who see in war the only cure for the world (*sola igiene del mondo*)'.[82] Within two months these barricades were crossed. By the middle of October, Mussolini was openly in favour of intervention and receiving the congratulations of all those intellectual socialists whose convictions were on the side of the *Entente*—and who were later to become his bitterest opponents. ('Your strong and sound instincts have led you once again to take the right line of action,' the historian Gaetano Salvemini wrote. 'Yours is no small act of courage, to break the letter and save the spirit of internationalism.'[83]) On 20 October Mussolini failed to carry the executive of the Socialist Party with him in his policy and promptly resigned. On 27 October he wrote his last leading article as editor of *Avanti*; and on 15 November there appeared the first number of a new newspaper, the *Popolo d'Italia*, with Mussolini as editor, and a leading article headed '*Audacia*'. On 26 November, Mussolini was formally expelled from the Socialist Party. His career as a Socialist was at an end. Henceforth it was from the ranks of the interventionists that he was to draw his support, and eventually to find among them the elements of a new party and a new régime in Italy.

For Marinetti, too, the fact that intervention was becoming an increasingly popular cause meant a change in his position. He was no longer in the *avant-garde*, and was now ranged alongside a large part of the respectable Italian public he had so often challenged and insulted. But his agitation continued with undiminished energy. In December 1914, for example, he was in Rome and, with a band of Futurist followers, broke into the University and stopped a lecture by the 'neutralist' Professor de Lollis. He became more and more ambitious and prophetic: 'Let us make continual anti-Austrian demonstrations,' he wrote to Severini, 'but that is not enough. Inaction would kill me. . . . Meanwhile we have reached these conclusions: (1) This war will bit by bit envelop the whole world; (2) The world will remain at war (even if there are pauses, armistices, treaties, diplomatic congresses), that is in a state of aggression, dynamic and *futurist*, for at least ten years'.[84] Soon he joined forces with Mussolini. They were not dissimilar in character; and the violence of Mussolini's language, his duels, his love of brawls and public agitation, were all things that Marinetti found

sympathetic. He described him a year or two later as follows:
'Square, champing jaws; prominent, scornful lips, which spit
arrogantly and aggressively on everything that is slow, pedantic,
analytical, whimpering. . . . His eyes move ultradynamically,
race as fast as automobiles on the plain of Lombardy or Italian
seaplanes in the skies over the ocean; their whites flash from
right to left like those of a wolf. . . . The collar of his coat is
always raised through an instinctive need to mask the harsh
words which stream from his mouth, in the accent of the
Romagna. His right hand, in his pocket, grasps a stick, like a
sabre straight along the line of the muscles of his arm'.[85] It
might be Mafarka the Futurist himself.

Soon the two men were speaking at the same meetings.
Mussolini was rapidly moving away from any pretence that
he was still a Socialist; and, although he still claimed that he
was pressing for intervention in the war on humanitarian
grounds, in fact his language often approached the position
that Marinetti had expressed in the early days of the Futurist
movement when he wrote 'Patriotism and love of war have
nothing to do with ideology: they are principles of hygiene
without which there is nothing but decadence and death. . . .
We cannot advance resolutely towards the future without our
personal hygiene of daily struggle and our collective hygiene
of a bloody clash every ten years'.[86] Even if, in the spring of
1915, Mussolini was not going as far as this, phrases like 'It is
time for the diplomats to stop their intrigues and let the bayonets
speak, with which we want to affirm our ideals of patriotism
and humanity,'[87] or 'Peace today would be a crime of lèse-
humanité,' show how far he had moved away from the international socialist language of a year earlier. And on occasions
he echoed the phrases of Futurist invective: 'If neutrality
continues any longer, the Italy of tomorrow will be an abject
and accursed nation; a condemned nation without autonomy
and without a future; mountebanks, beggars, lodging-house
keepers, bootblacks and organ-grinders will continue to
represent the Italian character throughout the world'.[88]

At the end of 1914 a group of Mussolini's friends had founded
a group called 'Fascio d'Azione Rivoluzionare'. In January 1915
they held their first national congress, and Mussolini was their

hero. They began organising meetings and demonstrations in favour of intervention, and it was at one of these, in Milan on 31 March 1915, that Marinetti and Mussolini first appeared together, all earlier differences forgotten in a common desire to get Italy into the war. During the spring of 1915, the volume of agitation in favour of intervention was growing, and the political crisis caused by the government's hesitations, temporising and negotiations with both sides, was increasing in intensity. As the interventionist demonstrations became more frequent and more violent, the government's counter-measures became stricter. On 11 April, an attempt was made to hold a large-scale meeting in Rome, at which both Mussolini and Marinetti were to speak; but the police and troops filled the streets in order to stop it. In fact Marinetti, Mussolini and a couple of hundred of their supporters did succeed in gathering in the Piazza di Trevi, and Mussolini tried to speak. The police at once intervened and Marinetti was arrested, while Mussolini got away, only to be picked up shortly afterwards when trying to renew the demonstration in the Piazza Barberini. Both men were released very soon after; but the episode strengthened the ties of political comradeship between them.

During April and early May, in an atmosphere of growing tension and political crisis, the government gradually moved towards war. The secret treaty of London, which bound Italy to the Allies in return for lavish promises of territorial gains at the end of the war, was signed on 26 April, and the Triple Alliance with Germany and Austria was formally denounced on 3 May. Finally, after a final period of public confusion and political uncertainty, war was declared on 23 May. The aims of the interventionists had been achieved, and Mussolini declared in the *Popolo d'Italia*: 'And now that steel stands ready to meet the enemy steel, one cry alone bursts from our hearts: Long live Italy! We have never felt more than at this moment that our own country exists, that it is a datum of human consciousness which cannot be suppressed; never before the beginning of this war have we felt that Italy is a historic personality, living, corporeal, immortal'.[89]

The war meant the end of Futurism as a coherent movement. While its influence artistically was to continue outside

Italy, and while efforts were made to revive it in the 1920s, its impetus had gone, and Marinetti, its leader and founder, was to become just a minor figure in the new political movement of which Mussolini was the leader. Some of the leading members of the Futurist movement lost their lives in the war, including two of the most gifted among them: the architect Sant' Elia was killed on the Carso, and the painter Boccioni died after an accident, while Russolo was severely wounded. And, while Marinetti himself continued to sponsor a Futurist theatre throughout the war, he joined the Alpini soon after Italy's declaration of war, and was at the front much of the time. He remained as self-dramatising as ever: on the night before he first went into action he proclaimed, in a letter to two friends: 'I am happy to give my life to our great, strong and glorious Italy, my life as an Italian Futurist, my life which I consider *of the utmost importance*'.[90] He was a good officer and was decorated for gallantry: 'In command of a machine gun squad, with exemplary courage, impetuous patriotism and inspiring enthusiasm, he was the first to enter Tolmezzo. He captured the town's entire command, overcame all attempts to counterattack and subsequently destroyed all the enemy's communication lines'.[91]

Like Mussolini, Marinetti was wounded. (Mussolini was in fact invalided out of the army in 1917, and returned to the editorship of the *Popolo d'Italia*.) What is surprising is that neither of them seemed to have lost their taste for war or violent action. Marinetti remained as impressed as ever by the mechanical aspects of war, which seemed to justify his old enthusiasm for the aeroplane. (His play *Poupées Electriques*, written in 1909, and in which it is hard to find any specifically Futurist elements beyond the fact that one of the two heroes is a cynical maker of electric puppets who treats his wife badly, was dedicated 'To Wilbur Wright who knew how to raise our migrant hearts higher than the captivating mouth of a woman'.) And in 1918 Mussolini made his first flight, and was as rhapsodical about it as the Futurist practitioners of *aeropoesia*: 'I feel in all my veins the truly Dionysiac intoxication of the conquest of the azure.'[92] Moreover, he grew to share the Futurists' faith in technicians—the aviators and engineers: 'All people who belong to the new Italian race of producers, constructors, and creators. One of them told me about the Ansaldo steel foundry and a gigantic hammer that weighs fifteen thousand tons—a million five hundred kilograms!!! Astounding figures!'[93] Indeed he was later to acknowledge his debt to Marinetti, 'The innovator poet who gave me the feeling for the ocean and the machine'.[94]

As soon as the war ended, Marinetti was back in Milan, where Mussolini had returned in 1917, and both men soon plunged into political agitation with all their energy. The year 1919, indeed, was the year of Marinetti's greatest political notoriety, and he was not yet wholly eclipsed by Mussolini or submerged by the routine—and the compromises—of a practical political party. The atmosphere of 1919 in Italy was even more agitated and tense than that of the spring of 1915. Demobilised soldiers were expecting and demanding a better life than the Italy of before the war had offered them; and at the same time the economic conditions of the country were growing steadily worse. In these circumstances both the public and the politicians seized on Italy's claims to territory that had originally belonged to Austria-Hungary, as a symbol of Italy's rights and hopes. And so the insistence that Italy should get at least the areas promised her in the secret treaty made with the allies in 1915 became the central point for all the dissatisfaction of the nationalists, and united people of very different political origins, just as the cause of intervention had done four years earlier. At the same time the social and economic discontent of the Italian working class—a discontent with which the liberal politicians of the older generation who were still in power were quite unable to deal—was finding expression in a series of strikes and in an increase of strength for the Socialist Party. Mussolini quickly saw that any party which could combine the nationalist dissatisfaction at the terms of peace with the working class desire for a new social order would have a wider appeal than any existing party; and it was on this basis that he was, from the beginning of 1919, to build up the Fascist movement.

Marinetti, with his warlike tastes and his military record, was already actively involved in the various ex-service organisations that were springing up to protect the interests of the demobilised officers and soldiers. His house in Milan was the headquarters of the *Arditi*, the association that brought together the members of the *élite* shock troops, the commandos of the Italian army, to which Marinetti himself had belonged. Thus, in addition to his association with Mussolini in 1915, Marinetti was in natural sympathy with Mussolini's political aims, and he was immediately involved in Mussolini's plans for the foundation of the *Fasci Italiani di Combattimento* which took their name from the interventionist groups of 1915 and used, like them, the symbol of a bundle of rods (*fasci*), a Roman emblem of authority and discipline. At the first national congress of the Fascists, held at Milan in March 1919, Marinetti was elected to the central committee of the new movement. Mussolini still regarded him as an ally worth having: the *Popolo d'Italia* gave a lot of space to the Futurist exhibition that was being held in Milan at the same time as the Fascist congress (though it in fact contained little work that was of fresh interest). And, in July, Mussolini was writing: 'Fascism is an unprejudiced movement. It has not disdained to make contact with groups which have been ignored or condemned by the Philistine stupidity of the *bien-pensants*. Mediocrities have always pretended not to take Futurism seriously; and now, in spite of such people, the head of the Futurists, Marinetti, is a member of the central committee of the *Fasci di Combattimento*'.[95] Marinetti, indeed, had gifts as an agitator, orator and propagandist as well as his reputation with the artistic *avant-garde*, to contribute to the Fascist movement. His experience of demonstrations and of street brawls was useful too. On 15 April, for example, the Socialists had organised a twenty-four hour general strike and had planned a big procession in Milan in connection with it. Marinetti and Mussolini determined to use the occasion for a spectacular counter-demonstration. Accordingly, they prepared to waylay the demonstrators as they came back from their mass meeting. Marinetti and some of his *Arditi* friends took up their position in the Galleria, the big arcades that run off the Piazza del Duomo in the centre of Milan, and soon became involved in heavy fighting. (The whole affair was to pass into Fascist legend as 'the Battle of Piazza Mercanti'.) The battle

culminated in the sacking of the offices of the Socialist paper
Avanti by Marinetti and his followers.

Marinetti had other uses too, besides his experience of
organising street demonstrations and taking part in riots.
When the Fascists were preparing a list of candidates for the
elections in the autumn of 1919, it was Marinetti, himself the
second man on the list after Mussolini, who, with two of his
friends, was sent to try and persuade Arturo Toscanini to agree
to stand. The great conductor was known for his intense
patriotism and for the interest with which he had been following the activities of the Fascists, but he had never had any
desire to enter politics, and it was only the torrential eloquence
of Marinetti that swept aside his doubts and hesitations and
made him agree to let his name go forward. Toscanini's brief
association with Mussolini shows how wide an attraction a
movement based on an appeal both to nationalism and to
social justice had in the Italy of 1919, and how even the most
liberal-minded men could be deceived by Mussolini. In fact,
apart from Mussolini and Marinetti, only one of the twenty
candidates at the 1919 elections went on subsequently to be a
prominent Fascist. Toscanini himself was later to be beaten
up by Fascist thugs for refusing to conduct the Fascist hymn
at a concert, and was to remain an open and bitter critic of the
Fascists; and one of the other candidates later fought a duel
with Mussolini. In any case, the 1919 elections were a failure
from the point of view of Mussolini's party, and none of their
candidates were elected. Their Socialist opponents triumphantly
burnt effigies of Mussolini and Marinetti; and although the
two leaders were soon afterwards once again arrested for
breaches of the peace, even this martyrdom could not make up
for their lack of orthodox political success. The elections of
1919 were an experience that led Mussolini to revise his tactics
and methods.

During 1919 and 1920, however, it was Gabriele D'Annunzio,
rather than Mussolini or Marinetti, who was the romantic hero
of the nationalist movement in Italy. D'Annunzio, who saw himself as a sort of twentieth century Byron, had had a glamorous
and unorthodox career during the war. He had persuaded the
Italian government to let him serve as an aviator, and had

carried out a number of flights over Austrian territory dropping leaflets. He regarded himself as the spokesman of those Italians not yet reunited with the motherland, and as the embodiment of the Italian will to win the territories that they asserted to be rightly theirs. The Italians at the Peace Conference had been pressing their claims to the port of Fiume—which had been in the Hungarian part of the Austro-Hungarian monarchy, and which was now claimed by the new state of Yugo-Slavia. But the Italian representatives had met with a firm refusal from their allies, on the grounds, among others, that no mention had been made of Fiume in the Treaty of London. In September 1919, therefore, D'Annunzio, with a group of just under three-hundred volunteers marched to Fiume, evicted the Allied control commission there, which was not difficult as it was under Italian command, and took over the administration of the city, ostensibly in the name of the Italian government, which was extremely embarrassed by the whole affair. D'Annunzio succeeded in maintaining himself in Fiume for over a year, in spite of being blockaded rather half-heartedly by the Italian authorities. Mussolini had had his first exchange of letters with D'Annunzio in December 1918, and each was, perhaps, a little jealous of the other; and, while Marinetti had welcomed the March to Fiume, his previous relations with D'Annunzio had been far from good. (In the early days he had accused the poet of 'following us from a distance, like a con-verted *Passéiste*, without, of course, having the courage to give up his innumerable *clientèle* of unhealthy erotic maniacs and elegant archaeologists'.)[96] On arrival at Fiume, D'Annunzio sent Mussolini a rather angry letter, complaining of lack of support: 'Where are the ex-servicemen, the *Arditi*, the volunteers, the Futurists?'[97] Mussolini responded by flying into Fiume for a conversation with D'Annunzio, since their alliance seemed essential for his electoral prospects, and soon many members of the Fascist party made their way to Fiume. In September of the following year, Marinetti was copying D'Annunzio's own tech-nique and flying over Rome in an aeroplane, dropping copies of a message he had received from the besieged commander in Fiume. It was only after the Italian government, under pressure from their allies, in November 1920 had reached an agreement with the Yugoslavs for the establishment of Fiume as a free city, that D'Annunzio, whose administration of the city had become more and more unpopular and disorganized, was forced finally to withdraw.

The Fascist failure at the election of 1919 and the demonstration that romantic swashbuckling patriotism as practised by D'Annunzio could not succeed in the twentieth century each showed that, even in the explosive and confused political situation of post-war Italy, a higher degree of political organisation and greater tactical skill would be necessary if the Fascist movement were going to have any success. It was a lesson that Mussolini was slowly learning in 1920 and 1921; and his final success in the autumn of 1922 was due, in so far as it was not just the result of the mistakes of his liberal and socialist opponents, to the combination of violence and terrorism with political temporising and the exploitation of the parliamentary situation. Moreover, he saw that the Fascists would need a broader basis of popular support and a real political programme if they were to win power; and, by 1922, the Fascists were a properly organised political party. It was inevitable, in these developments, that Marinetti should be left behind, and, although he remained a loyal Fascist and was later rewarded with jobs, he was never again as important as he had been in 1919. Although Mussolini, just before the elections of 1919, had instructed one of his journalists to write a 'robust' profile of Marinetti 'to show these Italian parrots that Marinetti is one of our most powerful political brains,'[98] the statement was not true. Marinetti was out of place in any movement that became highly organised and pompous. By 1920 he was emphasizing his artistic interests again: 'All power to the artists! The vast proletariat of geniuses shall govern. . . . Thanks to us the time will come when life will not simply be a matter of bread and toil or a life of leisure but when life will be itself a work of art. . . . We shall not have heaven on earth, but our economic hell will be reanimated and soothed by innumerable festivals of art'.[99] Moreover, he had genuine differences of opinion with Mussolini. At the second national congress of the Fascists in May 1920, Mussolini was making overtures to the Catholics: 'No one in Italy who does not want to unleash a religious war can attack (the Pope's) spiritual sovereignty. Even Lenin has stopped short before the authority of the Holy Synod, and in Russia religion is respected'.[100] Mussolini was ill-informed about Russia, but in any case such statements were too much for Marinetti's anti-clericalism, and he burst out with a violent anti-clerical and republican tirade. This was the beginning of an estrangement between the two men; Mussolini is reported to have told his friends after this that he had no opinion of 'this extravagant buffoon who wants to play politics and whom nobody in Italy, least of all me, takes seriously'.[101]

After 1919 the Futurist phase of Fascism was over. Marinetti even resigned from the *Fasci di Combattimento*, though he later rejoined the Fascist party and was to remain loyal to it and to Mussolini personally right up to his death. He was to spend another quarter of a century writing *aeropoesia*; he was to publish poems in praise of the heroes of Mussolini's wars; true to his youthful enthusiasms at the age of sixty, he was to hurry off as a volunteer to Mussolini's Ethiopian campaign, and he accompanied the Italian armies on the Don in the Second World War. Yet this later phase of his career is neither interesting nor important; and there is something rather pathetic as well as incongruous in the spectacle of the man who had led the campaign for the abolition of academies and museums being appointed, in 1929, secretary of the Fascist writers' union and a member of the *Accademia d'Italia* by a man who had once boasted that 'he had never put his foot inside a museum more than twice in his life'.[102] Occasionally there are flashes of the old spirit—in the Futurist Cookery, for example, and its attack on the Italian diet of *pasta*—but most of Marinetti's writing was an empty repetition of his earlier ideas, now drained of the originality and freshness that had once given them their impact. Marinetti died in 1944, ill and sad. 'I saw him for the last time in 1942' his old comrade, rival and adversary Papini wrote, 'ill, ageing, irritable and worried. I know that the last period of his life, in the feverish solitude of Venetia, as defeat grew nearer and as he was unnerved and undermined by several different kinds of serious illness, were very sad, almost tragic. Up to the last days he was dictating a book that will perhaps never see the light.'[103] He was buried in Milan on a cold and foggy December day with such empty honours as the tottering Fascist Republic could still provide in the last months of the war. It was almost the last public Fascist occasion and was a sad and ironical end to Marinetti's life and achievements.

Marinetti's own view of his contribution to Fascism is best summed up in a passage he wrote in 1923, a few months after Mussolini's March on Rome and assumption of the premiership. 'The victory of Vittorio Veneto and the coming to power of Fascism constitute the realisation of the minimum Futurist programme launched (along with a maximum programme not yet achieved) fourteen years ago by a group of bold young men who opposed themselves with persuasive arguments against the whole nation which had been defiled by senility and a foreigner-fearing mediocrity. This minimum programme preached pride at being Italian, unlimited confidence in the future of Italy, the destruction of the Austro-Hungarian Empire, daily heroism, love of danger, the rehabilitation of violence as the decisive argument, the glorification of war, the only cure for the world, the religion of speed, of novelty, of optimism and of originality, the coming to power of the young in opposition to the parliamentary, bureaucratic, academic and pessimistic spirit. Our influence in Italy and in the world has been enormous. . . . Futurism is a movement that is strictly artistic and ideological. It intervenes in political struggles only in hours of grave danger for the nation. We were the first among the first interventionists, imprisoned for interventionism in Milan . . . in prison with Mussolini for interventionism in Rome on 12 April 1915; imprisoned with Mussolini in 1919 at Milan for a Fascist attack on the security of the state. . . . Prophets and forerunners of the great Italy of today, we Futurists are happy to salute in our not yet forty-year-old Prime Minister a marvellous Futurist temperament.'[104]

There is, unhappily for Marinetti's reputation, something in his claim; Futurism was only one of the paths that led to Fascism; and, if it had been the only one, Fascism would not have had to be taken so seriously. The Fascist movement was a success because it combined the systematic use of terrorism as a political weapon with an ability to appeal to the desperate and disillusioned elements of the organised working class, as

well as to the disappointed nationalism of middle class intellectuals and ex-officers. What Mussolini learnt from the
Futurists was a certain technique of invective, a means of
publicity and popular agitation, together with a set of phrases
that would give his supporters the sense of moving with, indeed
ahead of, the times. (Marinetti would have been right in
claiming Mussolini as a Futurist on the strength of his repeated
use of Futurist language alone.) As a destroyer of orderly,
'bourgeois' values Marinetti had been unequalled, and the
Fascists were the chief people to profit by it.

Yet the revolt against the past had an importance beyond
its immediate political effects and consequences. Although
there are moments when the whole Futurist movement seems
little more than an expression of misguided Italian youthful
exuberance—a sort of revving-up of intellectual and artistic
Vespas—its effects were widespread, and extended far beyond
Italy. Its effect in Italy is well expressed by Papini: 'Marinetti,
even if he did nothing else, obliged a large part of the somnolent
and rheumatic Italian *bourgeoisie* to interest itself in new
problems of art and literature, and to enter into violent contact
with the researches of the new European spirit'.[105] And, in fact,
the Futurists made their own contribution to this new European
spirit. If the art and literature of the twentieth century have
learnt to deal with the phenomena of a mechanised age, if
writers and artists have learnt to try the boldest technical
innovations and to use the most violent juxtaposition of images
and ideas to achieve their effects, then it is to the Futurists
that this is in part due. As the painter Severini put it—and he
himself was to give up the practice of strictly 'Futurist' art—
'We cannot deny that Futurism has infinitely enlarged the
horizon of the creative act and given a fine example of boldness
in its passionate search for what is authentically new—an
example of which all the art of our time, from Dadaism to
Surrealism and recent Abstract Art, shows traces'.[106] If, in
the second half of the twentieth century, these phases of our art
are taken for granted and have passed into our day-to-day
surroundings—the advertisements we see, the furniture we use,
or the films we look at—this is partly the achievement of the
Futurists. And, even if Europe and the United States have

perhaps outgrown the childish nationalism of Marinetti, we may yet, by studying his techniques and ideas, understand a little more clearly the pathology of extreme nationalist feeling with which we are faced in other parts of the world. Finally, on the threshold of the Space Age, perhaps we may grant a certain prophetic gift to those who, in 1909, 'standing aloft on the world's summit launched an insolent challenge to the stars'.

The Futurist Manifesto

WE HAVE BEEN up all night, my friends and I, beneath mosque lamps whose brass cupolas are bright as our souls, because like them they were illuminated by the internal glow of electric hearts. And trampling underfoot our native sloth on opulent Persian carpets, we have been discussing right up to the limits of logic and scrawling the paper with demented writing.

Our hearts were filled with an immense pride at feeling ourselves standing quite alone, like lighthouses or like the sentinels in an outpost, facing the army of enemy stars encamped in their celestial bivouacs. Alone with the engineers in the infernal stokeholes of great ships, alone with the black spirits which rage in the belly of rogue locomotives, alone with the drunkards beating their wings against the walls.

Then we were suddenly distracted by the rumbling of huge double decker trams that went leaping by, streaked with light like the villages celebrating their festivals, which the Po in flood suddenly knocks down and uproots, and, in the rapids and eddies of a deluge, drags down to the sea.

Then the silence increased. As we listened to the last faint prayer of the old canal and the crumbling of the bones of moribund palaces with their green growth of beard, suddenly the hungry automobiles roared beneath our windows.

'Come, my friends!' I said. 'Let us go! At last Mythology and the mystic cult of the ideal have been left behind. We are going to be present at the birth of the centaur and we shall soon see the first angels fly! We must break down the gates of life to test the bolts and the padlocks! Let us go! Here is the very first sunrise on earth! Nothing equals the splendour of its red sword which strikes for the first time in our millennial darkness.'

We went up to the three snorting machines to caress their

breasts. I lay along mine like a corpse on its bier, but I suddenly revived again beneath the steering wheel—a guillotine knife—which threatened my stomach. A great sweep of madness brought us sharply back to ourselves and drove us through the streets, steep and deep, like dried up torrents. Here and there unhappy lamps in the windows taught us to despise our mathematical eyes. 'Smell,' I exclaimed, 'smell is good enough for wild beasts!'

And we hunted, like young lions, death with its black fur dappled with pale crosses, who ran before us in the vast violet sky, palpable and living.

And yet we had no ideal Mistress stretching her form up to the clouds, nor yet a cruel Queen to whom to offer our corpses twisted into the shape of Byzantine rings! No reason to die unless it is the desire to be rid of the too great weight of our courage!

We drove on, crushing beneath our burning wheels, like shirt-collars under the iron, the watch dogs on the steps of the houses.

Death, tamed, went in front of me at each corner offering me his hand nicely, and sometimes lay on the ground with a noise of creaking jaws giving me velvet glances from the bottom of puddles.

'Let us leave good sense behind like a hideous husk and let us hurl ourselves, like fruit spiced with pride, into the immense mouth and breast of the wind! Let us feed the unknown, not from despair, but simply to enrich the unfathomable reservoirs of the Absurd!'

As soon as I had said these words, I turned sharply back on my tracks with the mad intoxication of puppies biting their tails, and suddenly there were two cyclists disapproving of me and tottering in front of me like two persuasive but contradictory reasons. Their stupid swaying got in my way. What a bore! Pouah! I stopped short, and in disgust I hurled myself —vlan!—head over heels in a ditch.

Oh, maternal ditch, half full of muddy water! A factory gutter! I savoured a mouthful of strengthening muck which recalled the black teat of my Sudanese nurse!

As I raised my body, mud-spattered and smelly, I felt

the red hot poker of joy deliciously pierce my heart. A crowd of fishermen and gouty naturalists crowded terrified around this marvel. With patient and tentative care they raised high enormous grappling irons to fish up my car, like a vast shark that had run aground. It rose slowly leaving in the ditch, like scales, its heavy coachwork of good sense and its upholstery of comfort.

We thought it was dead, my good shark, but I woke it with a single caress of its powerful back, and it was revived, running as fast as it could on its fins.

Then with my face covered in good factory mud, covered with metal scratches, useless sweat and celestial grime, amidst the complaint of the staid fishermen and the angry naturalists, we dictated our first will and testament to all the *living* men on earth.

MANIFESTO OF FUTURISM

1. We want to sing the love of danger, the habit of energy and rashness.

2. The essential elements of our poetry will be courage, audacity and revolt.

3. Literature has up to now magnified pensive immobility, ecstasy and slumber. We want to exalt movements of aggression, feverish sleeplessness, the double march, the perilous leap, the slap and the blow with the fist.

4. We declare that the splendour of the world has been enriched by a new beauty: the beauty of speed. A racing automobile with its bonnet adorned with great tubes like serpents with explosive breath . . . a roaring motor car which seems to run on machine-gun fire, is more beautiful than the Victory of Samothrace.

5. We want to sing the man at the wheel, the ideal axis of which crosses the earth, itself hurled along its orbit.

6. The poet must spend himself with warmth, glamour and prodigality to increase the enthusiastic fervour of the primordial elements.

7. Beauty exists only in struggle. There is no masterpiece that has not an aggressive character. Poetry must be a violent

assault on the forces of the unknown, to force them to bow before man.

8. We are on the extreme promontory of the centuries! What is the use of looking behind at the moment when we must open the mysterious shutters of the impossible? Time and Space died yesterday. We are already living in the absolute, since we have already created eternal, omnipresent speed.

9. We want to glorify war—the only cure for the world— militarism, patriotism, the destructive gesture of the anarchists, the beautiful ideas which kill, and contempt for woman.

10. We want to demolish museums and libraries, fight morality, feminism and all opportunist and utilitarian cowardice.

11. We will sing of great crowds agitated by work, pleasure and revolt; the multi-coloured and polyphonic surf of revolutions in modern capitals: the nocturnal vibration of the arsenals and the workshops beneath their violent electric moons: the gluttonous railway stations devouring smoking serpents; factories suspended from the clouds by the thread of their smoke; bridges with the leap of gymnasts flung across the diabolic cutlery of sunny rivers: adventurous steamers sniffing the horizon; great-breasted locomotives, puffing on the rails like enormous steel horses with long tubes for bridle, and the gliding flight of aeroplanes whose propeller sounds like the flapping of a flag and the applause of enthusiastic crowds.

It is in Italy that we are issuing this manifesto of ruinous and incendiary violence, by which we today are founding Futurism, because we want to deliver Italy from its gangrene of professors, archaeologists, tourist guides and antiquaries.

Italy has been too long the great second-hand market. We want to get rid of the innumerable museums which cover it with innumerable cemeteries.

Museums, cemeteries! Truly identical in their sinister juxtaposition of bodies that do not know each other. Public dormitories where you sleep side by side for ever with beings you hate or do not know. Reciprocal ferocity of the painters and sculptors who murder each other in the same museum with blows of line and colour. To make a visit once a year, as one goes to see the graves of our dead once a year, that we could allow! We can even imagine placing flowers once a year at the feet of the Gioconda! But to take our sadness, our fragile courage and our anxiety to the museum every day, that we cannot admit! Do you want to poison yourselves? Do you want to rot?

What can you find in an old picture except the painful contortions of the artist trying to break uncrossable barriers which obstruct the full expression of his dream?

To admire an old picture is to pour our sensibility into a funeral urn instead of casting it forward with violent spurts of creation and action. Do you want to waste the best part of your strength in a useless admiration of the past, from which you will emerge exhausted, diminished, trampled on?

Indeed daily visits to museums, libraries and academies (those cemeteries of wasted effort, calvaries of crucified dreams, registers of false starts!) is for artists what prolonged supervision by the parents is for intelligent young men, drunk with their own talent and ambition.

For the dying, for invalids and for prisoners it may be all right. It is, perhaps, some sort of balm for their wounds, the admirable past, at a moment when the future is denied them. But we will have none of it, we, the young, strong and living Futurists!

Let the good incendiaries with charred fingers come! Here they are! Heap up the fire to the shelves of the libraries! Divert the canals to flood the cellars of the museums! Let the glorious canvases swim ashore! Take the picks and hammers! Undermine the foundation of venerable towns!

The oldest among us are not yet thirty years old: we have therefore at least ten years to accomplish our task. When we are forty let younger and stronger men than we throw us in the waste paper basket like useless manuscripts! They will come against us from afar, leaping on the light cadence of their first poems, clutching the air with their predatory fingers and sniffing at the gates of the academies the good scent of our decaying spirits, already promised to the catacombs of the libraries.

But we shall not be there. They will find us at last one winter's night in the depths of the country in a sad hangar echoing with the notes of the monotonous rain, crouched near our trembling aeroplanes, warming our hands at the wretched fire which our books of today will make when they flame gaily beneath the glittering flight of their pictures.

They will crowd around us, panting with anguish and disappointment, and exasperated by our proud indefatigable courage, will hurl themselves forward to kill us, with all the more hatred as their hearts will be drunk with love and admiration for us. And strong healthy Injustice will shine radiantly from their eyes. For art can only be violence, cruelty and injustice.

The oldest among us are not yet thirty, and yet we have already wasted treasures, treasures of strength, love, courage and keen will, hastily, deliriously, without thinking, with all our might, till we are out of breath.

Look at us! We are not out of breath, our hearts are not in the least tired. For they are nourished by fire, hatred and speed! Does this surprise you? It is because you do not even remember having been alive! Standing on the world's summit, we launch once more our challenge to the stars!

Your objections? All right! I know them! Of course! We know just what our beautiful false intelligence affirms: 'We are only the sum and the prolongation of our ancestors,' it says. Perhaps! All right! What does it matter? But we will not listen! Take care not to repeat those infamous words! Instead, lift up your head!

Standing on the world's summit we launch once again our insolent challenge to the stars!

NOTES

INTRODUCTION

1. Léon Blum: *Nouvelles Conversations de Goethe avec Eckermann.
L'Oeuvre de Léon Blum 1891-1905* (Paris 1954) pp. 244-5.
2. Léon Blum: *Stendhal et le Beylisme* (Paris 1914, reprinted 1930)
p. 142.
3. Walther Rathenau: *Unser Nachwuchs.* (*Neue Freie Presse,* 23
December 1909).
4. Walther Rathenau: *Auf dem Fechtboden des Geistes. Aphorismen
aus seiner Notizbücher* (Wiesbaden 1953) p. 39.
5. Léon Blum: *A l'Echelle Humaine. L'Oeuvre de Léon Blum 1940-
1945* (Paris 1955) p. 472.
6. To Ernst Norlind, 1 April 1917. Walther Rathenau: *Briefe*
(Dresden 1926) Vol. I p. 250.
7. Filippo Masci: *La Vita e le Opere di Gabriele D'Annunzio* (Rome
1950) p. 265.

LÉON BLUM

1. *La Revue Blanche* 1 March 1899. Reprinted in *L'Oeuvre de Léon
Blum 1891-1905* p. 65.
2. *Nouvelles Conversations de Goethe avec Eckermann. Ibid.* p. 197.
3. *Ibid.* p. 305.
4. Léon Blum: *Commentaires sur le programme d'Action du Parti
Socialiste* (Speech at Extraordinary National Congress of
Socialist Party, April, 1919) (Paris 1925) p. 20.
5. Léon Blum: *Pour être Socialiste* (Paris 1930) p. 5.
6. *Nouvelles Conversations* p. 210 (23 August 1897).
7. *Le Temps* 7 June 1936 (based on an interview given to the
Revue de Paris in 1924). For Blum's early life see Geoffrey
Fraser and Thadée Natanson: *Léon Blum* (London 1936); also
Marc Vichniac *Léon Blum* (Paris 1937).
8. q. André Blumel: *Léon Blum, Juif et Zioniste* (Paris 1951) p. 5.
9. *Nouvelles Conversations* p. 262 (11 April 1899).
10. Léon Blum: *Souvenirs sur l'Affaire* (Paris 1935) p. 27.
11. To Guy de Rothschild. q. Blumel *op. cit.* p. 13.

12. André Gide: *Journal* (Paris 1939) p. 396 (24 January 1914).
13. *Nouvelles Conversations* p. 267 (11 April 1899).
14. *Sou 'enirs sur l'Affaire* p. 30.
15. *La Revue Blanche* 1 July 1896. *L'Oeuvre de Léon Blum 1891–1905* p. 27.
16. *La Revue Blanche* February 1896. *Ibid.* p. 15.
17. *Nouvelles Conversations* p. 216.
18. Léon Blum: *Stendhal et le Beylisme* (Paris 1914, reprinted 1930) p. 142.
19. *Stendhal et le Beylisme* p. 313.
20. André Gide: *Journal* p. 228 (5 January 1907).
21. Jules Renard: *Journal* (Paris 1935) p. 437 (14 March 1901).
22. *Nouvelles Conversations* pp. 244–5.
23. *Ibid* p. 252.
24. Léon Blum: *Souvenirs sur l'Affaire* p. 17.
25. Jules Renard: *Journal* p. 209 (31 January 1901).
26. *A l'Echelle Humaine. L'Oeuvre de Léon Blum 1940–1945* (Paris, 1955) pp. 465–6.
27. *La Revue Blanche* June 1896. *L'Oeuvre de Léon Blum 1891–1905* p. 21.
28. André Gide: *Journal* p. 209 (27 April 1906).
29. Jules Renard: *Journal* p. 547 (3 March 1903).
30. Léon Blum: *Du Mariage*, Introduction to Second Edition (Paris 1937).
31. *Stendhal et le Beylisme* p. 75.
32. *Revue de Paris*, December 1917, January 1918. Reprinted in book form in 1918 (anonymously) and under Blum's name in 1936.
33. Léon Blum: *Pour la Vieille Maison. Intervention au congrès de Tours (1920)* (Paris 1934) p. 7.
34. *Stendhal et le Beylisme* pp. 6–7.
35. See e.g. for these respective views: Milorad M. Drachkovitch: *De Karl Marx à Léon Blum* (Geneva 1954) and Colette Audry: *Léon Blum ou la Politique du Juste* (Paris 1955).
36. *Pour la Vieille Maison* p. 36.
37. Léon Blum: *Commentaires sur le Programme d'Action du Parti Socialiste* p. 22.
38. *Pour la Vieille Maison* pp. 13, 31–32.
39. *Commentaires sur le Programme d'Action* pp. 4, 20.
40. *Ibid.* p. 16.
41. *Pour la Vieille Maison* p. 37.
42. For a detailed discussion of this doctrine see Joel Colton: *Léon Blum and the French Socialists as a Government Party. (Journal*

of Politics Vol. XV, 1953). There is also much useful material in Mary Katherine Watson Downs: *Léon Blum: the Evolution of his Socialist Doctrine.* (Unpublished M.A. thesis, Stanford University 1956).

43. Léon Blum: Speech at Party Congress at Bellevilloise, 1926. *La Revue Socialiste* Nos. 38–39 (1950) p. 60.
44. *Ibid.*
45. *Lettres sur la Réforme Gouvernementale. Revue de Paris* January–February 1918 p. 142.
46. *Manchester Guardian* 16 July 1936.
47. *Le Populaire* 10 January 1934.
48. *Ibid.* 8 May 1928. Reprinted in *La Revue Socialiste* Nos. 38–39, 1950.
49. XIII Plenum EKKI: *Theses and Resolutions* (London 1934) p. 27.
50. See Max Beloff: *The Sixth of February. St Antony's Papers* No. V (London 1959.)
51. *Journal Officiel. Chambre des Députés. Débats* 6 February 1934 p. 413.
52. *Le Populaire* 9 February 1934. See also Blum's statement on 18 June 1946 to the Parliamentary Committee of Enquiry. *Les Evènements survenus en France 1933–1945* Vol. I p. 764.
53. *Le Populaire.* 13 February 1934.
54. For a detailed account of these negotiations see James Joll: *The Making of the Popular Front. St Antony's Papers* No V. See also John T. Marcus: *French Socialism in the Crisis Years* (New York 1958).
55. *Le Populaire* 20 July 1934.
56. *Ibid.*
57. *Ibid.* 9 July 1934.
58. Speech at Mulhouse Congress 10 June 1935. *Le Populaire* 11 June 1935.
59. *Le Populaire* 26 January 1936.
60. Geoffrey Fraser & Thadée Natanson: *Léon Blum* (London 1937) p. 250.
61. *Le Populaire* 1 June 1936.
62. The following account is based on Blum's statement to the Parliamentary Commission of Enquiry in 1947, and has been confirmed and amplified by M Oreste Rosenfeld, a close friend and associate of Blum's, and his assistant in the editing of *Le Populaire*. Blum's evidence was given to the Committee on 23 July 1947. *Les Evènements survenus en France 1933–1945. Témoignages* Vol. I, p. 215 ff.

63. Léon Blum: *Les Evènements d'Espagne*. Speech at Luna Park 6 September 1936 (Paris 1936) p. 19.

64. *Le Matin* 1 January 1937.

65. Speech at Saint Nazaire 21 February 1937. *Le Matin* 22 February 1937.

66. *Journal Officiel. Chambre des Députés. Débats* 7 May 1937, p. 1462.

67. *Le Matin* 30 May 1937.

68. Charles de Gaulle: *Mémoires de Guerre* Vol. I (Paris 1954) p. 21. De Gaulle says that this meeting took place in October 1936. Blum, in his evidence to the parliamentary commission in 1947, gave the date as September.

69. *A l'Echelle Humaine. L'Oeuvre de Léon Blum 1940–1945* pp. 440–1.

70. *Le Matin* 23 June 1937.

71. Zyromski at National Council 22 June 1937. *Le Matin* 23 June 1937.

72. *Le Populaire* 1 June 1936.

73. *Journal Officiel. Chambre des Députés. Débats* 26 February 1937, p. 787.

74. *Le Matin* 17 January 1937.

75. Speech at Socialist Party congress at Royan 7 June 1938. *Le Matin* 8 June 1938.

76. Léon Blum at Socialist Party congress at Nantes 30 May 1939. *Le Matin* 31 May 1939.

77. Sir Edward L. Spears: *The Fall of France* (London 1954) p. 31.

78. Léon Blum: *Mémoires. L'Oeuvre de Léon Blum 1940–1945* p. 55.

79. *A l'Echelle Humaine. Ibid.* p. 495.

80. *Ibid.* p. 472.

81. *Le Prison et Le Procès. Ibid.* p. 381.

82. *A l'Echelle Humaine. Ibid.* p. 415.

83. *Notes d'Allemagne. Ibid.* p. 513.

84. André Gide: *Journal* p. 250 (22 June 1907).

85. *Notes d'Allemagne* (21 February 1945). *Op. cit.* p. 514.

86. *Le Populaire* 17 May 1945.

87. *Le Socialisme Maître de l'Heure*. Speech at Party congress at Paris 13 August 1945. *L'Oeuvre de Léon Blum 1945–1947* (Paris 1958) pp. 69–70.

WALTHER RATHENAU

1. Walther Rathenau: *Apologie* printed in *Kritik der Dreifachen Revolution* (Berlin 1919) p. 80.

2. Count Harry Kessler: *Walther Rathenau: his life and work*, Tr. by W. D. Robson-Scott and Lawrence Hyde, (London 1929) p. 45. This excellent biography is an indispensable source for the study of Rathenau's life, character and thought. It has not been superseded by Hellmuth M. Böttcher: *Walther Rathenau* (Bonn 1958).

3. Kessler. *Op. cit.* p. 24.

4. W. Rathenau: *Stimme der Sehnsucht* in *Gesammelte Schriften* Vol. I (Berlin 1918) p. 293.

5. W. Rathenau: *Bildner der Jugend*, undated fragment in *Nachgelassene Schriften* Vol. II (Berlin 1928) p. 362.

6. Letter to Wilhelm Schwaner 30 June 1915. *Walther Rathenau— ein Preussischer Europäer. Briefe* cd. M. von Eyncrn (Berlin 1955) p. 137. This is a convenient and fairly full selection of Rathenau's letters, though it needs supplementing by the volumes of correspondence published in Dresden 1926–8. It is subsequently referred to as *P.E.*

7. Bernhard von Bülow: *Denkwürdigkeiten* Vol. III (Berlin 1931) p. 40.

8. Etta Federn-Kohlhaas: *Walther Rathenau* (Dresden 1927) p. 82.

9. Letter to Lore Karrenbrock 26 November 1919. *Briefe* II (Dresden 1926) p. 197.

10. To Emil Rathenau, 14 February 1892. *P.E.* p. 50.

11. To Frau Rathenau, 30 January 1887. *P.E.* p. 34.

12. To Emil Rathenau, 18 February 1892. *P.E.* p. 50.

13. To Frau Rathenau, 29 September 1892. *P.E.* p. 55.

14. W. Rathenau: *Staat und Judentum: eine Polemik*, in *Ges. Schriften* I pp. 188–9.

15. To Frau von Hindenburg, 12 December 1917. *P.E.* p. 243.

16. To Wilhelm Schwaner, 18 August 1916. *P.E.* p. 155.

17. To Leopold Sander, 25 February 1918. *Briefe* II p. 10.

18. To Dr Apfel, 16 November 1918. *Briefe* II p. 76.

19. q. Kessler p. 36.

20. W. Rathenau: *An Deutschlands Jugend* (Berlin 1918) p. 9.

21. Bülow: *Denkwürdigkeiten* III pp. 39–40.

22. *Apologie* pp. 97–98.

23. Bülow: *Denkwürdigkeiten* III p. 41.

24. To Wilhelm Schwaner 18 August 1916. *P.E.* p. 155.

25. To Wilhelm Schwaner 24 September 1918. *P.E.* p. 274.

26. Kessler p. 43.

27. Stefan Zweig: *Die Welt von Gestern* (Second Edition, Berlin 1955) p. 170.

28. *An Deutschlands Jugend* p. 83.

29. Johannes Ziekursch: *Das Zeitalter Wilhelms II* (Frankfurt-a-M 1930) p. 6.
30. W. Rathenau: *Der Kaiser: Eine Betrachtung* (Berlin 1919) p. 27.
31. To Dr Meissner, 26 November 1907. *Briefe* I p. 53.
32. Kessler p. 121.
33. *Neue Freie Presse* 23 December 1909.
34. *Apologie* p. 91.
35. 9 November 1916. *P.E.* p. 166.
36. To Professor G. Holzer, 29 April 1918. *Briefe* II p. 38.
37. W. Rathenau: *Auf dem Fechtboden des Geistes: Aphorismen aus seiner Notizbücher* (Wiesbaden 1953) p. 98.
38. To Herr E., 11 April 1918. *Briefe* II pp. 33–4.
39. To same, 10 May 1918. *Ibid.* p. 44.
40. W. Rathenau: *Wirtschaftliche Lehren 1902–1908. Ges. Schriften* IV (Berlin 1918) p. 87.
41. W. Rathenau: *Physiologie der Geschäften. Ges. Schriften* IV p. 262.
42. To War Minister von Wandel, 1 May 1917. *P.E.* p. 200.
43. To Herr L. (egst?), 2 September 1913. *Briefe* I p. 121.
44. W. Rathenau: *Englands Industrie*, 1906. *Ges. Schriften* IV p. 145.
45. To Hermann Kroepelin, 21 July 1909. *Briefe* I p. 66.
46. Gustav Hillard: *Herren und Narren der Welt* (Munich 1954) p. 240.
47. W. Rathenau: *Vom Werte und Unwerte des Kinos (Berliner Morgenpost* 17 December 1912). In *Nachgelassene Schriften* (Berlin 1927) Vol. II p. 327.
48. *Auf dem Fechtboden des Geistes* p. 100.
49. W. Rathenau: *Das Grundgesetz der Aesthetik* (1900–1908). *Ges. Schriften* IV p. 327.
50. André Gide: *Feuillets. Journal* (Paris 1939) p. 711.
51. André Gide: *Journal* p. 727 (3 January 1922.)
52. 23 October 1914. *P.E.* p. 123.
53. 21 July 1920. *Briefe* II pp. 246–7.
54. Kessler pp. 166–7.
55. Ernst Norlind: *Gespräche und Briefe Walther Rathenaus* (Dresden n.d.) p. 82.
56. W. Rathenau: *Nachgelassene Schriften* II p. 171. See also Kessler p. 75.
57. W. Rathenau: *Zur Mechanik des Geistes. Ges. Schriften* II p. 194.
58. *Ibid.* p. 48.
59. To Hermann Gottschalk, 7 December 1920. *Briefe* II p. 280.
60. To Dr P. A., 'Ascension Day' 1917. *Briefe* I p. 280.
61. *Auf dem Fechtboden des Geistes* p. 39.
62. To Dr Schottlaender, 31 August 1917. *P.E.* p. 231.

63. W. Rathenau: *Von Kommenden Dingen* (1916). *Ges. Schriften* III p. 73.

64. *Zur Kritik der Zeit. Ges. Schriften* I pp. 75–6.

65. W. Rathenau: *Politische Auslese* 1912. *Ges. Schriften* I p. 231.

66. *Zur Mechanik des Geistes. Ges. Schriften* II p. 340.

67. *Neue Rundschau* July 1914 pp. 556 ff.

68. To Franz Blei, 20 July 1914. *P.E.* p. 115.

69. Kurt Singer: *Staat und Wirtschaft seit dem Waffenstillstand* (Jena 1924) p. 145.

70. To Fanny Künstler, 19 August 1914. *P.E.* p. 117.

71. Freidrich Meinecke: *Strasburg–Freiburg–Berlin. Erinnerungen* (Stuttgart 1949) p. 137.

72. W. Rathenau: *Staat und Vaterland* (October 1918) p. 43.

73. To Bethmann-Hollweg, 7 September 1914. *P.E.* p. 120.

74. *Ibid.*

75. To Wilhelm Schwaner, 14 November 1914. *Briefe* I p. 173.

76. To Stefan Zweig, 24 October 1914. *P.E.* p. 130.

77. W. Rathenau: *Deutschlands Rohstoffversorgung.* Lecture to *Deutsche Gesellschaft 1914* 20 December 1915. *Ges Schriften* V (Berlin 1918) p. 41.

78. To Emil Ludwig, 17 May 1916. *P.E.* p. 151.

79. Kessler p. 235.

80. To Wilhelm Schwaner, 16 September 1915. *P.E.* pp. 141–2.

81. To Dr van Eeden, 24 October 1914. *P.E.* p. 130.

82. Charles Seymour: *The Intimate Papers of Colonel House* Vol. I (London 1926) p. 406.

83. *Von Kommenden Dingen* (1916). *Ges. Schriften* III p. 236.

84. To Lieut Col von Feldmann, 18 May 1916. *Briefe* I p. 213.

85. W. Rathenau: *Schicksalspiel, Berliner Tageblatt* 23 November 1919. q. Kessler p. 242.

86. To Herr L., 26 February 1917. *Briefe* I p. 239. See also W. Rathenau: *Zeitliches* (1918).

87. To Baroness von S., 28 April 1917. *Briefe* I p. 239.

88. To Fanny Künstler, 6 December 1914. *P.E.* p. 134.

89. *Von Kommenden Dingen* (1916). *Ges. Schriften* III p. 96.

90. W. Rathenau: *Die Neue Wirtschaft* (1917). *Ges. Schriften* V p. 261.

91. *Von kommenden Dingen. Ges. Schriften* III p. 154.

92. *Ibid.* p. 135.

93. *Ibid.* p. 286.

94. To Ernst Norlind, 1 April 1917. *Briefe* I p. 250.

95. *Von Kommenden Dingen. Ges. Schriften* III pp. 260–1.

96. *Ibid.* p. 263.

97. To Dr Schmitt, 14 October 1918. *Briefe* II p. 67.
98. *Von Kommenden Dingen. Ges. Schriften* III, p. 234.
99. To Fanny Künstler, 1 November 1914. *P.E.* p. 133.
100. *An Deutschlands Jugend* p. 14.
101. *Ibid.* p. 74.
102. *Ibid.* pp. 90–1.
103. *Ibid.* p. 87.
104. W. Rathenau: *Festigkeit.* (*Berliner Tageblatt* 30 September 1918). *Nachgelassene Schriften* I p. 67.
105. W. Rathenau: *Ein dunkler Tag. Vossische Zeitung* 7 October 1918.
106. To Maximilian Harden, 8 October 1918. *P.E.* p. 275.
107. To Curt Bran, 16 December 1918. *P.E.* p. 292.
108. To Dr Robert Bosch, 27 November 1918. *P.E.* p. 289.
109. *Apologie* p. 107; Kessler pp. 265–6.
110. To Friedrich Ebert, 16 December 1918. *P.E.* p. 293.
111. To Lore Karrenbrock, 3 November 1919. *Briefe* II p. 190.
112. W. Rathenau: *Kritik der dreifachen Revolution* (Berlin 1919) p. 9.
113. W. Rathenau: *Arbeit* (29 March 1919). In *Der Neue Staat* (Berlin 1919) p. 49.
114. To Wolfgang Kapp, 27 December 1909. *Briefe* I p. 71.
115. Kessler p. 279.
116. To E.M., 27 August 1920. *Briefe* II p. 254.
117. To Wilhelm Schwaner, 19 July 1920. *P.E.* p. 368.
118. To Frau Rathenau, July 1920. *P.E.* p. 367.
119. To Dr Pfannl, 1 July 1919. *Briefe* II p. 164.
120. W. Rathenau: *Unsere Kriegsgefangene* (30 January 1919). *Nachgelassene Schriften* I p. 96.
121. Kessler p. 291.
122. *Ibid.* p. 296.
123. To Professor Max Dessoir, 1 June 1921. *Briefe* II p. 314.
124. To Gerhart Hauptmann, 25 May 1921. *P.E.* p. 390.
125. To Wilhelm Schwaner, 26 May 1921. *P.E.* p. 390.
126. To Frau Rathenau, 1 June 1921. *P.E.* p. 392.
127. To Frau Rathenau, 8 June 1921. *P.E.* p. 394.
128. W. Rathenau: (27 November 1920). *Nachgelassene Schriften* I p. 261.
129. To Ernst Norlind, 31 January 1922. *P.E.* p. 415.
130. Kessler p. 316.
131. Federn-Kohlhaas. *Op. cit.* p. 276.
132. W. von Blücher: *Deutschlands Weg nach Rapallo* (Wiesbaden 1951) p. 156.
133. For a detailed discussion of Rathenau's period at the Foreign Ministry, see especially: Gerald Freund: *Unholy Alliance*

(London 1957); Wipert von Blücher: *Deutschlands Weg nach Rapallo* (Wiesbaden 1951); Eric Kollmann: *Walther Rathenau and German Foreign Policy* (*Journal of Modern History* XXIV 1952); Herbert Helbig: *Die Träger der Rapallo–Politik* (Göttingen 1958).

134. To Hermann Hesse, 29 January 1918. *P.E.* p. 252.
135. To Professor Hofmann, 10 March 1920. *P.E.* p. 368.
136. To Freiherr von Mumm, 6 April 1920. *P.E.* p. 364.
137. Viscount d'Abernon: *An Ambassador of Peace* Vol. I (London 1929) pp. 320–1.
138. To Frau Rathenau, 16 April 1922. *P.E.* p. 419. (The date is wrongly given as 19 April in both *Briefe* and *P.E.*)
139. d'Abernon. *Op. cit.* p. 310.
140. To Max Warburg, 3 June 1918. *P.E.* p. 392.
141. Kessler, p. 361.
142. *Ibid.* p. 362.
143. *An Deutschlands Jugend* p. 127.
144. *Verhandlungen des Reichstags. Stenographische Bericht.* (Berlin 1922) pp. 1988 ff. q. Kessler p. 374.
145. A slightly different translation is printed in Kessler p. 381. The original is in the German edition (Berlin 1928) p. 368.
146. Ernst-Werner Techow: *Gemeiner Mörder?! Das Rathenau-Attentat* (Leipzig 1933) p. 20.

F. T. MARINETTI

1. *Lacerba* 14 December 1913. See Aurelia Bobbio: *Le Riviste Fiorentine del Principio del Secolo* (Florence 1936).
2. *Invocation à la mer vengeresse pour qu'elle me délivre de l'infame réalité.* q. in Enrico Falqui: *Il Futurismo: Il Novecentismo* (Turin 1955) p. 16.
3. G. Severini: *Tutta la Vita di un Pittore* (Milan 1946) pp. 107, 110, note 1.
4. q. A. W. Salomone, *Italian Democracy in the Making* (Philadelphia 1945) p. 91.
5. q. G. Pini and D. Susmel: *Mussolini—L'Uomo e l'Opera* Vol. I (Florence 1950) p. 3.
6. Article in *Il Pensiero Romagnolo* November–December 1908. q. Pini and Susmel Vol. I p. 117.
7. G. Papini: *Passato Remoto* (Florence 1948) p. 262, describing Marinetti a few years later when the Futurist Movement was in full swing.

8. Auro d'Alba, q. Falqui. *Op. cit.* p. 22.

9. By Aurelia Bobbio in *Le Riviste Fiorentine del Principio del Secolo.*

10. G. Papini: *L'Esperienza Futurista* (Florence 1919).

11. G. Papini: *Aspettativa* (February 1913). *Op. cit.* p. 29.

12. G. Papini: *L'Esperienza Futurista* p. 62. (This passage was published in December 1913.)

13. Reprinted in *Noi Futuristi* (Milan 1917) p. 30.

14. *I Manifesti del Futurismo* (Milan 1920) Vol. I p. 36.

15. F. T. Marinetti: *Le Futurisme* (Paris 1911) pp. 6–7.

16. Falqui, pp. 39–40.

17. U. Boccioni: *Pittura Scultura Futurista* (Milan 1914) p. 55.

18. G. Papini: *Passato Remoto* p. 28.

19. F. T. Marinetti: *Le Futurisme* p. 88.

20. *La Stampa* 15 May 1924 q. Falqui p. 39.

21. F. T. Marinetti: *Tuons le Clair de Lune* (1910). *Le Futurisme* p. 164.

22. Manifesto of Futurist Painters. *Ibid.* p. 188.

23. U. Boccioni. *Op. cit.* p. 187.

24. Technical Manifesto of Futurist Painters. *Archivi del Futurismo* Vol. I (Rome 1958) p. 66.

25. *Ibid.* p. 67.

26. *Ibid.* p. 66.

27. See John Golding: *Cubism* (London 1959) pp. 40 ff.

28. Rosa Trillo-Clough: *Looking Back on Futurism* (New York 1942) p. 109.

29. U. Boccioni. *Op. cit.* p. 76.

30. Trillo-Clough. *Op. cit.* p. 81.

31. U. Boccioni: *Il Dinamismo Plastico.* In *Noi Futuristi* p. 45.

32. Introduction to Catalogue of Exhibition at Galerie Bernheim, Paris 1912.

33. C. Carrà: *La Pittura dei suoni rumori e odori* in *Noi Futuristi* p. 49.

34. Manifesto of Futurist Musicians in *Le Futurisme* p. 204.

35. L. Russolo: *L'Arte dei Rumori* in *Noi Futuristi* p. 69.

36. *Ibid.* p. 68.

37. A. Sant'Elia: *L'Architettura Futurista.* In *Noi Futuristi* p. 73.

38. *La Scienza Futurista.* In *Noi Futuristi* p. 111.

39. F. T. Marinetti: *Zang Tumb Tuum* (Milan 1914) pp. 11–12.

40. *Ibid.* p. 63.

41. Falqui p. 59.

42. *Archivi del Futurismo* Vol. I (1958) p. 247.

43. F. T. Marinetti: *Tripoli Italiana* 11 October 1911, in *I Manifesti del Futurismo* Vol. II pp. 10–11.

44. Francis McCullagh: *Italy's War for a Desert* (London 1912) pp. xxii–xxiv.
45. F. T. Marinetti: *Le Futurisme* pp. 22–23.
46. *Ibid.* p. 26.
47. *Ibid.* p. 37.
48. C. R. W. Nevinson: *Paint and Prejudice* (London 1937) p. 57.
49. *Ibid.* pp. 58–60.
50. Wyndham Lewis: *Rude Assignment* (London 1950) p. 164.
51. q. Victor Erlich: *Russian Formalism* (The Hague 1955) p. 24.
52. Kruchenykh q. *ibid.* pp. 26–7.
53. B. Katanyan: *Mayakovsky* (Second Edition, Moscow 1948) pp. 59–60.
54. F. T. Marinetti: *Au delà du Communismo*, written in December 1919. Published August 1920. q. *Archivi del Futurismo* pp. 38–40. See also Graziella Lehrmann: *De Marinetti à Mayakovsky* (Fribourg 1942) p. 8.
55. Katanyan. *Op. cit.* p. 226 (June 1925).
56. *Noi Futuristi* pp. 30–31.
57. *Ibid.* pp. 31–32.
58. F. T. Marinetti: *Futurismo e Fascismo* (Foligno 1924) pp. 145 ff q. Trillo-Clough p. 39.
59. *Il Popolo* 25 June 1909 q. Guido Dorso: *Benito Mussolini alla conquista della potere* (Turin 1949) p: 35.
60. q. Pini and Susmel Vol. I p. 200.
61. Mussolini to Leda Rafanelli, April 1913. q. Pini and Susmel, Vol I p. 201.
62. 10 February 1913. q. Bobbio: *Le Riviste Fiorentine* p. 190.
63. A. Soffici: *Giornale di Bordo* 25 March 1913 (3rd Ed. Florence 1921) pp. 61–2.
64. C. Martini: *La Voce* (Rome 1953) p. 25.
65. A. Soffici: *Giornale di Bordo* 8 August 1913.
66. *Les Manifestes du Futurisme* II p. 50.
67. A. Soffici: *Giornale di Bordo* 8 September 1913, but see G. Severini: *Tutta la Vita di un Poeta* pp. 193–4.
68. Carrà to Severini, 3 June 1914. *Archivi del Futurismo* p. 346.
69. G. Papini: *L'Esperienza Futurista* pp. 9–10.
70. Ballilla Pratella: *Il Futurismo e la Guerra. Cronica sintetica* in *Noi Futuristi* p. 128.
71. *Lacerba* 15 August 1914, q. Bobbio p. 285.
72. *Noi Futuristi* p. 128. The meeting was never held, see *Archivi del Futurismo* p. 345.
73. Boccioni to his mother, 19 September 1914 *Archivi del Futurismo* p. 346.

74. *Noi Futuristi* p. 128.
75. A. Soffici: *Giornale di Bordo* p. 221.
76. G. Papini: *L'Esperienza Futurista* p. 151.
77. Speech at Milan 14 January 1914 q. Pini and Susmel Vol I p. 216.
78. *Note di Guerra*, in *Utopia* 3 August 1914, reprinted B. Mussolini *Opera Omnia* Vol. VI (Florence 1953) p. 321.
79. Letter to Roberto Marvasi, 6 August 1914. q. B. Mussolini *La Mia Vita* (Rome 1947) p. 200.
80. Speech at Parma 13 December 1914. B. Mussolini: *Opera Omnia* Vol VII p. 81.
81. Letter to A. Marchetti, August 1914 q. Pini and Susmel Vol. I p. 242.
82. q. Pini and Susmel Vol. I p. 244.
83. *Avanti* 21 October 1914, reprinted in B. Mussolini *Opera Omnia* Vol. VI p. 416.
84. Marinetti to Severini, 20 November 1914. *Archivi del Futurismo* p. 349.
85. q. Pini and Susmel II p. 8. See also F. T. Marinetti: *Preface* to Ivon de Begnac: *Trent'Anni di Mussolini* (Rome 1934) p. v.
86. F. T. Marinetti: Speech at Trieste, March 1909. *I Manifesti del Futurismo* Vol. I pp. 39–40.
87. B. Mussolini: Speech from window of *Popolo d'Italia* offices 15 March 1915. *Opera Omnia* VII p. 256.
88. *Popolo d'Italia* 1 April 1915. *Ibid.* p. 298.
89. *Popolo d'Italia* 24 May 1915. *Ibid.* p. 419.
90. Marinetti to Pratella and Bazzi, 22 October 1915. *Archivi del Futurismo* p. 365.
91. Trillo-Clough p. 35.
92. Pini and Susmel I p. 359.
93. *Ibid.*
94. Ermanno Amicucci: *1600 Giorni di Mussolini* (Rome 1948) p. 196.
95. *Popolo d'Italia* 3 July 1919.
96. F. T. Marinetti: *Le Futurisme* p. 11.
97. Pini and Susmel II p. 30.
98. Pini and Susmel II p. 41.
99. F. T. Marinetti *Al di la del Comunismo* (1920) q. *Archivi del Futurismo* p. 38.
100. Pini and Susmel II p. 68.
101. Cesare Rossi. q. Pini and Susmel II p. 68.
102. F. T. Marinetti: *Preface* to I. de Begnac: *Trent'Anni di Mussolini* (Rome 1934) p. vii.

103. G. Papini: *Passato Remoto* p. 264.
104. F. T. Marinetti: Appendix to A. Beltramelli: *L'Uomo Nuovo* (Milan 1923).
105. G. Papini: *Passato Remoto* p. 263.
106. Falqui: p. 56.

INDEX

ABOUT THE AUTHOR

James Joll was born in 1918 in Bristol, England. He was educated at Winchester and New College, Oxford, and is now a fellow of St. Antony's College, Oxford, and university lecturer in history and politics. He has also been a member of the Institute for Advanced Study at Princeton University and a visiting professor of history at Stanford University. His previous publications in England include *The Second International* and part of *Documents on German Foreign Policy*, a series of which he was joint editor-in-chief for the Foreign Office–State Department project. His most recent book is *The Anarchists*.

HARPER COLOPHON BOOKS